Seven Steps To a Vital Faith

Seven Steps To a Vital Faith

With Special Introductions by
NORMAN VINCENT PEALE

GUIDEPOSTS ASSOCIATES, INC.   •   Carmel, New York

CREDITS

"Eight Ways God Can Guide Your Life" by Dr. E.
Stanley Jones, from a booklet, *How Does God Guide
Us?*, published by The Upper Room, Nashville, Tenn.
"Thank You, Dad" by James Stewart as told to Floyd
Miller, reprinted from *McCall's*, © 1964, McCall Corp.,
N.Y.C. "The Skeptical Mr. Worth" by Stella Terrill
Mann, adapted from *How To Analyze and Overcome
Your Fears,* © 1962, Stella Terrill Mann; Dodd, Mead
& Co., Inc., N.Y.C. "The Host of Heaven" by Dr. S.
Ralph Harlow, condensed from *A Life After Death,* ©
1961, Dr. S. Ralph Harlow and Evan Hill, Doubleday
& Co., Inc., N.Y.C.

How to use this book

Seven Steps to a Vital Faith has been carefully prepared to serve a variety of needs.

This book on your bedside table, or by your reading chair, can be like a personal companion, ready to offer inspiration and help whenever needed.

It can supplement Sunday School teaching, Bible study discussions, and serve as source material for spiritual fellowship groups; in its pages are countless illustrations for one who does public speaking.

It is an ideal gift for an individual who yearns for help in seeking a stronger faith, for a shut-in, or for a person who is lonely or bereaved.

Seven Steps to a Vital Faith includes 70 personal-experience stories selected from the pages of Guideposts, the magazine of inspiration for all faiths, now in its 20th year, which is read by more than five million people each month. The purpose of Guideposts is to serve God and help people.

If this book in any way contributes to your spiritual growth, our efforts will have been well worth while.

The Editors

Contents

1 Change

2 Prayer

3 Guidance

4 Bible

5 Love

6 Courage

7   Immortality

Change

STRANGE and often baffling is the word *change*. Webster's dictionary describes change as "to make different." Most of us resist change, but it is essential if we are to grow in faith, for the inability to change indicates selfcenteredness, rigidity of thought and belief.

Then comes the question, "How must I change?" There is no one answer. If your convictions are already strong, perhaps the change will come in your ability to love more fully. If your faith is weak, perhaps a change will take place in your willingness to discipline yourself to more prayer and Bible study.

In this section, you will read some dramatic stories about people who changed. Max Ellerbusch was obsessed with hatred. Jane Page was an alcoholic. Joe Csikos was arrogant. Rilla Scott was afraid. Arthur De Moss was hard-hearted. In every case, change came differently. But it came and was then followed by a surge of spiritual growth.

In each of the following 10 stories there is one common denominator in the "changing" process. Each person came to a dead-end and reached out for something higher and better, made a start, took a step. In long journeys, that first step is often the toughest.

NORMAN VINCENT PEALE

Max Ellerbusch felt he had good reason to hate a certain person, to hate violently and bitterly. This emotion was poisoning his mind and heart when suddenly he was free of it. Here's the story of a remarkable change and the dramatic event that followed.

In One Blinding Moment

by MAX ELLERBUSCH

IT was a busy Friday, six days before Christmas, 1958. I was in my instrument-repair shop, working feverishly so that I could have all of the Christmas holiday at home with my family. Then the phone rang and a voice was saying that our five-year-old Craig had been hit by a car.

There was a crowd standing around him by the time I got there, but they stepped back for me. Craig was lying in the middle of the road; his curly blond hair was not even rumpled.

He died at Children's Hospital that afternoon.

There were many witnesses. It had happened at the school-crossing. They told us that Craig had waited on the curb until the safety-patrol boy signaled him to cross. Craig, how well you remembered! How often your mother called after you as you started off for kindergarten, "Don't cross till you get the signal!" You didn't forget!

The signal came, Craig stepped into the street. The car came so fast no one had seen it. The patrol boy shouted, waved, had to jump for his own life. The car never stopped.

Grace and I drove home from the hospital through the Christmas-lighted streets, not believing what had happened to us. It wasn't until night, passing the unused bed, that I knew. Suddenly I was crying, not just for that empty bed but for the emptiness, the senselessness of life itself. All night long, with Grace awake beside me, I searched what I knew

2

of life for some hint of a loving God at work in it, and found none.

As a child I certainly had been led to expect none. My father used to say that in all his childhood he did not experience one act of charity or Christian kindness. Father was an orphan, growing up in 19th century Germany, a supposedly Christian land. Orphans were rented out to farmers as machines are rented today, and treated with far less consideration. He grew into a stern, brooding man who looked upon life as an unassisted journey to the grave.

He married another orphan and, as their own children started to come, they decided to emigrate to America. Father got a job aboard a ship; in New York harbor he went ashore and simply kept going. He stopped in Cincinnati where so many Germans were then settling. He took every job he could find, and in a year and a half had saved enough money to send for his family.

On the boat coming over, two of my sisters contracted scarlet fever; they died on Ellis Island. Something in Mother died with them, for from that day on she showed no affection for any living being. I grew up in a silent house, without laughter, without faith.

Later, in my own married life, I was determined not to allow these grim shadows to fall on our own children. Grace and I had four: Diane, Michael, Craig and Ruth Carol. It was Craig, even more than the others, who seemed to lay low my childhood pessimism, to tell me that the world was a wonderful and purposeful place. As a baby he would smile so delightedly at everyone he saw that there was always a little group around his carriage. When we went visiting it was Craig, three years old, who would run to the hostess to say, "You have a lovely house!" If he received a gift he was touched to tears, and then gave it away to the first child who envied it. Sunday morning when Grace dressed to sing in the choir, it was Craig who never forgot to say, "You're beautiful."

And if such a child can die, I thought as I fought my bed

that Friday night, if such a life can be snuffed out in a minute, then life is meaningless and faith in God is self-delusion. By morning my hopelessness and helplessness had found a target, a blinding hatred for the person who had done this to us. That morning police picked him up in Tennessee: George Williams.* Fifteen years old.

He came from a broken home, police learned. His mother worked a night shift and slept during the day. Friday he had cut school, taken her car keys while she was asleep, sped down a street . . . All my rage at a senseless universe seemed to focus on the name George Williams. I phoned our lawyer and begged him to prosecute Williams to the limit. "Get him tried as an adult, juvenile court's not tough enough."

So this was my frame of mind when the thing occurred which changed my life. I cannot explain it, I can only describe it.

It happened in the space of time that it takes to walk two steps. It was late Saturday night. I was pacing the hall outside our bedroom, my head in my hands. I felt sick and dizzy, and tired, so tired. "Oh God," I prayed, "show me why!"

Right then, between that step and the next, my life was changed. The breath went out of me in a great sigh—and with it all the sickness. In its place was a feeling of love and joy so strong it was almost pain.

Other men have called it "the presence of Christ." I'd known the phrase, of course, but I'd thought it was some abstract, theological idea. I never dreamed it was Someone, an actual Person, filling that narrow hall with love.

It was the suddenness of it that dazed me. It was like a lightning stroke that turned out to be the dawn. I stood blinking in an unfamiliar light. Vengefulness, grief, hate, anger—it was not that I struggled to be rid of them—like goblins imagined in the dark, in morning's light they simply were not there.

And all the while I had the extraordinary feeling that I was

---

* At the Ellerbusches' request George's real name is not used.

two people. I had another self, a self that was millions of miles from that hall, learning things men don't yet have words to express. I have tried so often to remember the things I knew then, but the learning seemed to take place in a mind apart from the one I ordinarily think with, as though the answer to my question was too vast for my small intellect. But, in that mind beyond logic, that question was answered. In that instant I *knew* why Craig had to leave us. Though I had no visual sensation, I knew afterward that I had met him, and he was wiser than I, so that I was the little boy and he the man. And he was so busy. Craig had so much to do, unimaginably important things into which I must not inquire. My concerns were still on earth.

In the clarity of that moment it came to me: this life is a simple thing! I remember the very words in which the thought came. "Life is a grade in school; in this grade we must learn only one lesson: we must establish relationships of love."

"Oh, Craig," I thought. "Little Craig, in your five short years how fast you learned, how quickly you progressed, how soon you graduated!"

I don't know how long I stood there in the hall. Perhaps it was no time at all as we ordinarily measure things. Grace was sitting up in bed when I reached the door of our room. Not reading, not doing anything, just looking straight ahead of her as she had much of the time since Friday afternoon.

Even my appearance must have changed because as she turned her eyes slowly to me she gave a little gasp and sat up straighter. I started to talk, words tumbling over each other, laughing, eager, trying to say that the world was not an accident, that life meant something, that earthly tragedy was not the end, that all around our incompleteness was a universe of purpose, that the purpose was good beyond our furthest hopes.

"Tonight," I told her, "Craig is beyond needing us. Someone else needs us. George Williams. It's almost Christmas. Maybe, at the Juvenile Detention Home, there'll be no Christmas gift for him unless we send it."

Grace listened, silent, unmoving, staring at me. Suddenly she burst into tears.

"Yes," she said. "That's right, that's right. It's the first thing that's been right since Craig died."

And it has been right. George turned out to be an intelligent, confused, desperately lonely boy, needing a father as much as I needed a son. He got his gift, Christmas Day, and his mother got a box of Grace's good Christmas cookies. We asked for and got his release, a few days later, and this house became his second home. He works with me in the shop after school, joins us for meals around the kitchen table, is a big brother for Diane and Michael and Ruth Carol.

But more was changed, in that moment when I met Christ than just my feeling about George. That meeting has affected every phase of my life, my approach to business, to friends, to strangers. I don't mean I've been able to sustain the ecstasy of that moment; I doubt that the human body could contain such joy for very many days.

But I now know with infinite sureness that no matter what life does to us in the future, I will never again touch the rock-bottom of despair. No matter how ultimate the blow seems, I glimpsed an even more ultimate joy that blinding moment when the door swung wide.

*"Jane! Don't forget me!" But Jane Page, a former al-
coholic, seemed hardly to listen to her friend as she
walked out the gates of the mental institution to freedom. The fact that Jane did not forget, however, resulted in a unique project that has helped thousands
change their way of life.*

The Women Who Came Back

by JANE PAGE

SHE was 50, I was 26, when I told her of my plan to escape.
I was confined in 1940 as an alcoholic and she as a drug
addict at Kankakee State Hospital in Illinois. When I finished
she said, "Jane, I've been in and out of these places all my
life. If you run, it won't be an escape. The police will always
hunt and haunt you. Don't go."

I was shocked, angered. Maude Oberg was the daring expert. I thought she would join me.

"What do you mean, 'don't go'? If I don't, how will I ever
get out of here? Who cares about me?" Maude didn't say another word, just looked at me.

From childhood my father taught me disbelief in God to
my believing mother's grief. "Jane," she would say, "God's
love is the only thing that endures." I ignored her. In my
teens, Mother died, and after that I began to get into trouble.
I flirted with crime.

My father, with anguish, implored: "Jane, don't. Don't...."

I mocked him: "Haven't you taught me there is no heaven,
no hell; no judgment, no God? If this little life is all I have,
why shouldn't I enjoy it?"

And so I sank, driven by impulsive desires. I needed the
stimulation of drink; I needed it more and more to dim my
guilty conscience.

Finally one doctor told me:

"If you continue this way, you will lose your health, your mind, maybe your life. Let me commit you to Kankakee."

I shuddered at the thought. To be caged! But by then I was so sick and tormented that I blurted out:

"Lock me up! Do anything! Only free me from this suffering."

In the hospital I was put into a ward with some 150 patients. They were alcoholics, drug addicts, psychotics subject to "disturbed spells." I was afraid of them until an attendant said, "I'll introduce you to someone who will be a friend."

When I learned that this "someone" was a drug addict and a murderer, my fear returned. For some reason, in that frightful moment, I recalled Mother's words: "God's love is the only thing that endures."

This helped me.

Led into another overcrowded, noisy ward, I saw some patients standing, a few sitting on the available chairs, some leaning against the walls. Others were walking around, some were dancing. The attendant pointed to a closed group in the center of the room and yelled: "Maude Oberg!" A towering individual detached herself from the group and came toward us.

When I saw Maude's broad smile I said to myself, "It's fake. It's put on." But then I knew, and I can't tell how, that the smile was real. When the attendant asked her to take me under her wing and show me the ropes, Maude slapped an arm around my shoulder. As I recoiled from the impact, she smiled: "Cheer up, kid. You'll learn to like it here. After a while it will be like home." I shuddered.

At 22, Maude had stabbed and killed a man. But this big, loud woman had an incredible softness. She seemed to splash all commonplace things with color and excitement. The patients, nurses, even the doctors sought her out for her gay ways, and her talent with the piano and song.

After that fateful conversation in which Maude with one

cold breath dashed my hope of escape, I tried with frantic concentration to think of someone to help me. I could think of no one. I withdrew into brooding silence.

Suddenly there came a telegram from my half-brother, Raymond, in Rockwood, Michigan: "Wire collect. Let me know how you are."

For the first time in my life I uttered something that sounded like a prayer: "God, I want to live differently."

Eventually, Raymond and his wife came, signed the release papers, and took me to their home. How, out of the forgotten past, did they suddenly think of me?

Raymond said he had been driving along a highway when an inner voice urged him to contact me because I needed help.

"It wasn't the still small voice of the heart," he said. "It was the Lord's voice."

As I left the grounds of the hospital, I turned for a last look at the walls and saw a hand waving from one of the barred windows. I couldn't see the face, but there was no mistaking the booming voice:

"Jane! Don't forget me! Come back and get me!"

How could I, an alcoholic, get Maude, a drug addict and a murderer, out of a state hospital? I tried to forget the scene.

But the thought of Maude gnawed at the peace I should have felt in my brother's home. Awake and asleep, I kept hearing: "Come back and get me! Come back and get me!" Added to this was the terrible uneasiness, a turmoil inside me which I did not understand.

One day I tried to explain it to my brother. "You have given me love and kindness," I told him, "and I'm grateful. But I'm still in a prison, a prison of my own misery."

"Jane," my brother said, "it's your soul that's imprisoned. Only Jesus Christ can set you free."

Raymond's words set me to thinking. And soon after I turned to Him. "My promises aren't any good, but Yours are," I prayed. "Please, God, set me free."

Bolstered by my new-found faith, I went to Detroit and shared a four-dollar-a-week room with my friend from the old days, Clara De Runtz. Clara listened to me, and quickly concluded that the hospital had been too much. So I stopped talking about my new way of life. But when she saw I had really changed, she began to ask questions. In time Clara, too, found Him. Together we determined to go back for Maude.

Clara worked as a waitress; I was drawing show cards as a free-lance artist. We bought an old $50 Ford on the installment plan and drove to the hospital. The superintendent was amazed. "How can I release Maude to you?" he said with disbelief.

He was fingering my records. "But Jane's not the same person that you have in those files," Clara said. "The Lord has her heart now."

He looked stunned. After a long pause he said, "I don't exactly know why, but I believe you."

Shortly after that we returned to get Maude. When she got into the car I think she rather expected us to pass her the bottle. Instead we bowed our heads in thanks to God. On the way home, when Clara and I sang "In the Garden," Maude thought we were surely demented.

"But how can two people go crazy on the same thing?" she wondered.

After ten days she told us she wanted whatever it was we had.

When Maude first went to church with us she overdressed like a peacock. But some of the people told her they were glad to have her and hoped she'd come back. She did. We told them our story and they asked us to tell it to others in different churches. After a while we told it in missions and then in jails. We did that for 12 years.

From our own bitter book we knew that most of the women we talked to in the jails and the hospitals would have no place to go when they came out. We decided that God wanted us to do something about them!

In Miami, Florida, in 1951, we opened the first Home of the Ministering Friends for these forgotten women. Three years later we opened another one in Brooklyn, New York. Maude and Clara run the home in Miami. I am in Brooklyn with Esther Walsh, who resigned her job as head of The Visiting Nurse Service for the Metropolitan Life Insurance Company, to devote all her time to the Ministering Friends.

They're not institutions, but private homes, where women of all faiths, or no faith, receive the help they sorely need. When they come to us they may have been drinkers, dope addicts, thieves, prostitutes. But they are sick; they are alone; and they need the love of a friend.

The women are given food, clothes, and care without charge until they're well enough to look for work or return to their families or children. We hold regular Bible studies while they're with us. Our spiritual teaching presents Christ and His love in word. Our material help presents Christ and His love in deed.

The Homes are a marvel to us because they are what God has done with us, in us, and through us, not what we have done in our own will and strength. It is only understandable in the light of God's word that He has chosen for His service the foolish, the weak, and base things that are despised.

This steelworker didn't realize he was ruining his life with his relentless drive to be a success. When he tried to reverse the situation he found himself in a bigger mess than ever. There seemed to be no way out until that unforgettable Sunday morning.

The Day I Cried

by JOE CSIKOS

I KNOW now that seven years ago on the tenth of May, Velma, my wife, had made her decision to leave me. Looking back, I cannot blame her.

She wasn't going because I drank or because I gambled away the grocery money or was in trouble with the law. I was in trouble with myself. Inside I was mean and bitter. Every day I would come home from my job as a foreman in a steel-mill with an anger as hot as the blast furnaces I had just left.

Velma never left me. The 11th of May, 1958, was a new day and I became a new Joe Csikos.

How did it happen, this change?

When I was a boy growing up on an Indiana farm 40 years ago, my family was poor. My parents were Hungarian immi-grants. They spoke what English they knew very thickly and badly. It was not surprising, therefore, that my brothers and sisters and I—there were 16 of us altogether—spoke an English that differed a little from our schoolmates! And to children, "being different" can make you an outcast.

I remember in particular the time my mother, who did all the sewing for us, made a shirt for me to wear to school. To save material, she had sewn the shirt in such a way that the stripes at the bottom were horizontal while the top stripes ran vertically. My classmates teased me so about this oddness that I was humiliated. Off by myself I vowed I would get ahead in the world. Success became an obsession.

At 18 I went to work as a laborer in the transportation section of United States Steel's Gary works. I loaded pig iron in a cart. It was hard work, but I doubt that the plant ever had an employee more determined to do well at it.

I was promoted in time to fireman. Then switchman and from that came a big jump to group leader. Then, consecutively, I was raised to relief foreman, assistant general foreman and by the time I was 44 years old in 1957, I had arrived at a pinnacle—general foreman with 18 foremen under me. With my particular background I had gone as far as I could go. The men addressed me as "Sir." In my terms I was the success I always had wanted to be. Then everything turned sour.

I think I had been general foreman for six months when I realized a startling fact. I hated my job! Especially did I hate the burden of disciplinary action, of reprimanding the men for minor negligence, of deducting pay for tardiness, of saying "That's your tough luck" to a guy who had had a flat tire on the way to work.

I started taking out my frustration on Velma and our two children. Yet, I hardly knew I was doing it. Even after I had sensed that my job and I were wrong for each other, it only added bitterness to the basic frustration. "Is this the reward for sweat and diligence?" I asked myself.

A year went by. Finally, after weeks of arguing with myself, I went into the front office.

"I want to be taken off this job," I said. "I want to be demoted." Nobody believed me. Then, when they did, they were confused as to what they should do about it. Eventually I was given the lesser job of steel movement co-ordinator.

But now everything was worse. My superiors could not help but have doubts about my value, and I could not help hating myself for going so counter to a lifelong habit of "getting ahead." My homelife was unbearable because I myself was so unbearable. Little wonder that Velma had come to the end of trying to get along with me.

Then came Sunday morning, May 11, 1958.

I had been on the midnight shift at the mill and had just climbed into bed when I heard Velma arguing with my eight-year-old son. She was trying to get him to go to church with her.

"Why do I have to go?" he whined. "Dad doesn't go."

At first I was angry. There they go again, knocking me for something else, I moaned. And after my working all night at the mill.

But what my boy said was true. No matter how often Velma tried to get me to go with her, I wouldn't. Suddenly I got up and strode into the living room.

"Wait for me," I told my family sternly. "I'm taking you to church."

I took them to a church that none of us had attended before, Trinity Reformed Church in the nearby town of Munster. From the moment we arrived there, I felt peculiar. Strangers though we were, we were met with a series of friendly handshakes and smiling nods. Instead of being warmed by the reception I only was puzzled.

We sat down in a pew. And that is when the most unexpected and profound experience of my life began to happen. I listened to the organ music. My eyes roamed the church until they came to a halt at a huge white cross set forth from the sanctuary wall and lighted from behind. I could not draw my eyes from that cross. I stared at it unblinkingly. I stared at the light diffused around that cross until my vision grew hazy. Only then, with the haziness, did I realize that my eyes were filled with tears.

The service began. The minister said, "This is a day of worship. Let your heart be still, and hear God, for He is saying *come unto Me all ye that labour and are heavy laden, and I will give you rest."* *

By now the tears were falling from my face. I was oblivious to everyone about me, and my eyes still were frozen to the

* Matthew 11:28

cross. The minister's words seemed not to be coming from his lips at all. It was as though God were speaking. And in that instant my heart did become still and the time had come to reach out my hand to Him and ask Him to accept me as His servant.

"Jesus, help me," I prayed. "Please help me. Amen."

Almost as instantly as I said "Amen," I had the sensation of someone taking hold of my hand, saying, "Come, follow Me." For a few precious minutes, I felt as though I were glimpsing Heaven. Everything about me was brilliant, all yellow gold. I seemed set apart from myself and family. Then, imperceptibly, I returned to Velma's side. The service was over.

Abrupt. Unexpected. Unheralded. In that one day, in that one Sabbath hour, I was reborn. I know for certain that I was reborn, for from that moment on, I was different.

"Is Joe sick?" my brother-in-law said later that afternoon. People, at first, did not comprehend what had happened to me. Velma did. I think she must have wept—with joy—for a full day.

What is the meaning of rebirth to me personally? Basically it is one of focus. Jesus—not my ego—is now the center of my life. Seeing things as He would see them gives me a new perspective on everything.

Now I am able to recognize the good in the people I meet. Now I realize that the material poverty I used to curse is not one jot as terrible as my later, impoverished spirit and that such things as dress and speech are but petty vanities, of no weight when God is your strength.

I am enthusiastic, too, about my job. It's the same one I had the day I went to church. But now I have real pride in our plant. One day, I was praising the mill as I walked alongside a fellow worker, a man known for his foul mouth.

"I get the same feeling here," I said, "as I get from church."

The man looked at me peculiarly, finally asking, "Why?"

"This whole, incredible mill," I tried to explain, "has been created to make steel—steel that will benefit people. So, in a way, through my job here, I have the privilege of serving people. I'm proud of that."

"But how's it like church?"

"Well," I said, "when I'm in church, I have a similar feeling of pride. I'm proud of the privilege of serving my Lord and Master."

We walked the rest of the way in silence.

When I see that man now, he always stops to talk. I have yet to hear a single swear word from him.

I mention this incident because it represents not only the way I think since that startling May day, but because it shows the way Jesus permeates every area of my life.

When one is born again, it is as though other people were reborn with you. Their goodness shines for you to see. Suddenly it is easy to see the Christ in other people. And suddenly, even a steel mill can look like a cathedral.

At the age of 24 Art De Moss was handling $10,000 a day in horse racing bets in his mother's attic. This indifferent, self-centered young "operator" was sure he had all the answers. Now if he could only get his mother to stop all this praying nonsense in his behalf.

The Most Amazing Day of My Life

by ARTHUR DE MOSS

THE day began no differently than any other. On this particular October day—Friday, the 13th, 1950—I slept until noon as I usually did.

I dressed sluggishly, bothered by a slight hang-over. The three telephones on my desk had been mercifully quiet. Now one of them rang. I answered it, wrote down some figures, hung up. Hungry, I started downstairs for breakfast when the phone rang again.

"Fifty on Dancer in the Sixth," I said and wrote down the figures.

My parents thought I had installed the extra phones in my attic room of their home for my insurance business. They would have been aghast if they had known that above their heads I was handling $10,000 a day in horse racing bets for people in the area of Albany, New York.

The phones kept ringing. Finally, I removed all three receivers, locked my room and went downstairs for breakfast—and my daily encounter with Mother.

Mother was small, vivacious, a Godly woman who read the Bible constantly; in fact, she was a saint. She needed all her virtues for she had a real cross to bear when it came to me.

Not that I realized it then. Or much cared. I was 24 and self-centered. I had my own insurance business, but my main interests were gambling, drinking and women.

17

Mother heard my footsteps and was waiting for me in the kitchen. "Breakfast or lunch?" she asked.

It was the usual disapproving way she greeted me when I slept until noon. But there was love behind the concern in her dark eyes. I kidded her, finally drew a smile and sat down at the table.

"Arthur, when are you going to start living like a normal person? It was four a.m. when you got home."

"Mother, I like my life." Wearily I prepared my usual defensive maneuvers.

"But you're thinking only of yourself. God didn't create you to be one of life's sponges."

"Now, Mother, Bob went to seminary, didn't he? I'm sure he will do enough good for both of us." Bob is my brother.

"Bob is as upset about you as I am. In fact, you may be interested to know that quite a few people are praying for you, Arthur. Bob, Dora, and your three aunts. And I've never seen your father so concerned. We believe in you, Arthur, and we are praying that Christ will come into your life."

I wanted to flee. The idea of all these people praying for me was preposterous.

"Mother, let me say again that I'm doing what I like to do. I'm happy. Understand. I'm happy!" Of course I wasn't really happy—and Mother undoubtedly sensed this.

She looked at me with reproachful eyes, and I realized suddenly that it was time I had my own apartment. It really wasn't fair to involve my parents with my "business." And these verbal sessions were becoming more uncomfortable.

I finished breakfast, joshed Mother into a slightly better humor and then drove into town to buy *The Racing Form*. After poring over this gambler's bible for a while, I placed a few bets of my own, then started back home to monitor the three phones and handle other business matters.

It was while driving back home that I noticed the publicity for Hyman Appelman, the evangelist, who was holding revival meetings in Albany. What intrigued me about this man was that before he had become a Christian evangelist he had been a successful lawyer. And my curiosity was further piqued by the fact that the meetings were being held in a mammoth converted horse stable. The idea of horses and religion under the same roof made me chuckle.

These revival meetings were in their second week. Twice, out of curiosity, I had planned to attend, but something better always came along. Considering my interests at the time, something better to do could be most anything.

As I look back now it was incredible that I actually did turn up at Hyman Appelman's revival meeting that evening. I took a seat toward the back of the hall and calculated the quickest way to sneak out if it became too boring.

There was hymn singing, a solo, and then the evangelist began to talk. Right away I was surprised at his approach. It was concise, logical. There were no emotional swells of tone and emphasis. He talked to us about sin, how we were filled with it, how it separated us from God.

As he described me as a sinner, I soon found myself agreeing and wondering how long it would take him to consign me to the pits of hell. It was this "hell and damnation" approach that I had found so repelling. I felt I would rather go to hell than be associated with the stuffy people who talked so much about it.

"Now the wonderful promise we sinners have is that we *can* be saved from our sinful lives," he continued.

I had heard the words, or ones like them before, but now suddenly in the context of his talk, these words had meaning. I found myself leaning forward with expectation.

The evangelist held up his Bible. "Here it says very specifically that Jesus Christ came into the world to save sinners.* Now when you really accept this promise and appropriate it, it is the most remarkable fact of all history. God sent His Son to this world, not to rule as a king on a throne, but to mingle

---

* Luke 19:10, I Timothy 1:15

among sinners and redeem their lives. He came for you—don't ever get away from this fact."

Suddenly everything Hyman Appelman said made such sense that I no longer seemed to have resistance to it. Was I dreaming this thing that was happening to me?

"Why are we here in this world?" the evangelist continued. "To live as we want to live, to do just what we want to do without responsibility to our Maker? God made us and He loves us and His heart aches over the way we ignore Him. How much patience is He supposed to have? How much patience would you as a father have if your child treated you as you treat God?

"There isn't much time," he continued. "Compared to eternity, our lives on this earth are a snap of the fingers. But with Christ we live forever. He tells us so. You can begin this new life right now by making your decision for Christ."

When the evangelist finished I sat there motionless. Then he issued the invitation to those who wanted to accept Jesus Christ: I found myself on my feet at once, walking into a new life.

During the rest of the city-wide crusade, I was at every meeting and one afternoon had a long personal talk with Hyman Appelman. Meanwhile, amazed friends kidded me at first. "You'll be your old self in a few days," they said. They were wrong.

Several days later I sought out Mother. She knew something had happened because my hours and habits had suddenly changed. And I was beginning to eat breakfast in the morning.

"Mother," I began, feeling unsure of myself for the first time in years. "I think you should know what's happened to me."

I paused, for an ashen look had swept over her face. "Oh Arthur," she said, "what have you done?"

When I told her about the revival meeting, the change in her face was remarkable to see. At first there was astonishment, then relief, then tears, then joy. And then she cried out, "Thank you, dear God. . . ."

Until that October night, gambling had been almost like breathing to me. What happened to me after that night is described in the passage *"If any man be in Christ, he is a new creature. . . ."*[*]

Actually I did not have to struggle to give up gambling, drinking and my loose life. As I began to pray and study the Scriptures my desires changed. The old habits and pastimes sloughed off. Since Mother and Dad both passed away several years after this experience, how glad I am now that they lived to see the change Christ made in my life. I only wish they could have lived to see me develop my own insurance business on a Christian basis.

I guess the most surprising part of the whole story is how long it took me to really understand how it all happened. For there is only one explanation:

Intercessory prayer.

It was the steady, concentrated, selfless prayers of other people organized by my mother and carried out by a group of about ten relatives and friends. How else do you account for the fact that a man, who was apparently without troubles, who was so indifferent to God and so self-centered, could experience such a change? The more I look back on it, the more remarkable it seems. How did I ever get to the meeting in the first place?

Why did Appelman's words move me so? I found out later that many people in the evangelist's organization were praying specifically that his words would reach the hearts of people in the audience. And they certainly reached mine.

Don't ever underestimate the power of your prayers to help —even to change—other people. With God, all things certainly are possible!

[*] II Corinthians 5:17

Paul Dietzel, head football coach at West Point, tried to separate his religion from his work. In what he calls the biggest decision of his life he discovered why he could not do this.

To Reach Your Goal

by PAUL DIETZEL

IT is 1:30 on a crisp autumn Saturday afternoon. Inside the locker-room at West Point the air is charged with the tension and emotion that precedes an important football game. Outside in the stadium 40,000 people are waiting impatiently. The Army squad is ready, but before we go there is a pause. There in the cluttered locker room with its smells of liniment, adhesive tape and football gear, 50 strong young men close their eyes and bow their heads.

"Lord, we have prepared for this game to the best of our abilities. We leave the outcome to You. Help us to play clean, follow the rules and use our skills to the maximum. Protect us and our opponents from injury. And may all that we do reflect glory on You."

The team then charges through the locker room door and out onto the field.

With the saying of our team prayer each Saturday afternoon during the football season, another week's preparation for the game is completed. I feel our team prayer is as much a part of getting ready for a game as the all-week physical conditioning process. Certainly it's as important for the mind to be in good condition as the body.

Yet I wasn't always so convinced of this. Once I tried to separate my religion and my work. When I became a Christian, I learned that this is impossible. Furthermore, I found that when I took my convictions into my job I was a better

22

coach than I had been before. But perhaps I am getting ahead of my story.

When I began coaching back in 1948, I paid only the barest lip service to my Christian background. My wife, Anne, worked hard on me, but it was slow going. On Sunday morning, for example, she would have to struggle hard to get me up and off to church, especially if the party the night before had been a late one.

Despite my lackluster attitude, God blessed me with a wonderful family life and growing success in the coaching profession. But not until 1959 did I really face up to the challenge of Christianity in my own life.

This came about with my participation in a conference put on by the Fellowship of Christian Athletes at Estes Park, Colorado. I was amazed at what went on at this conference. Over 700 young men attended, most of whom were there to commit their lives to Jesus Christ.

Invited to give a speech, I suddenly had to face myself in a way I never had before. How could I talk to these young men about Christianity and not be 100 per cent with it? There, in the space of a few days, came the most momentous decisions of my life.

First, came my own personal commitment to Christ as Lord and Saviour. Then came an evaluation of my life and habits; obviously changes had to be made.

Social drinking, for example, was one of those unnecessary and often negative practices that could go first of all. I decided to commit myself to church membership and activity. I also pledged myself to present my body as a living sacrifice to Jesus Christ; to seek His guidance through prayer; and try to be, myself, what I ask other young men to be.

Needless to say, this experience forced me to place under the microscope every coaching principle and technique I used. The measuring device became: is this policy compatible with the Life and Person of Jesus Christ?

This is a tough standard. Try it in any field of endeavor and you will see what I mean.

Soon I realized that I had to know more about Christ Himself, which meant a fresh study of the New Testament.

So I began to read the Bible. I was captivated by Christ's all-out, wholehearted and complete concentration on winning people . . . *I am the way, the truth, and the life: no one comes to the Father but by Me.**

Jesus chided timidity . . . *Why are ye fearful, O ye of little faith.***

I particularly was interested in the way He prepared Himself thoroughly for His work. For 40 days and nights He fasted and prayed to be able to be disciplined completely in what He had to do. Then He went about His ministry with complete singleness of purpose. With His disciples Christ showed great patience indeed, but also firmness and authority.

As a football coach making this study of Christ's life, I saw many an analogy with my own profession . . . the value of preparation and purpose—singleness of purpose. I did not change my philosophy about the importance of an all-out will to win—I did get new perspective on it.

Before each game our staff spends literally thousands of hours in preparation. There are reports from scouts on the strong and weak points of our opponents to mull over, practice on the field which, important as it is, is only one of a hundred phases of the preparation needed. There are such matters as the diet of players, equipment, publicity, student body spirit and the details of being good hosts to the opposing team. The preparation is everlasting and continues all year round.

I remember one season when we practiced a certain play all year long. From early in the fall till near the end of the season we drilled on this one particular play. It required a very special situation on the field before it could be used.

---

* John 14:6
** Matthew 8:26

Some of the players complained, "Not that one again, Coach. We'll never use it."

"Maybe not," I told them, "but let's have it ready just in case."

Then one Saturday the right moment came late in the game. We surprised the opposition with the play we had worked on all season but never used. It resulted in a touchdown and victory. The players learned a lesson not only about football but also about life.

When the day of a game comes, I begin it as I begin every day: with a recommitment of my life to God. My prayer involves my own imperfections which I lay before Him. I do not pray for victory in the game that afternoon.

Then at the stadium, after the squad prayer, I get off somewhere by myself for a moment. First, come a few deep breaths to relax the body. My senses then become alert to smells, sounds, busy sights. You almost can taste the excitement, feel the myriad of emotions that go with the day of the game.

The stadium is alive with color and people. How many other stadiums are there across the country where this same picture is developing, I ask myself? I feel a sense of inner joy about it all. Then I realize that God is looking down at all these busy stadiums. Does He care about who wins in each one? I doubt it. But He does care about *how* His people live and act.

With this realization, comes proper perspective for the game ahead.

America's Junior Miss of 1963 describes her persistent quest for truth after she found she could not answer the disbelief of another with a strong belief of her own.

Bird on My Shoulder

by DIANE SAWYER

NOT long ago I was sitting alone in my room at Wellesley College trying to write on the subject, "Why I Believe in God." After hours of walking in circles—both mentally and physically—I decided to try out my ideas on some of the other students in the dorm. A lively argument began. I sensed in those girls the same confusion which I've felt so often. Yes, and the same need for answers.

Perhaps it's different in the adult world. But it seemed to me in my last year in high school—and now in college too—that when we young people set out to find God with our reason, we reach a dead-end every time. For me, truth is like a parakeet let out of its cage. I chase it around my room, across the campus, into the chapel itself, but it flies farther away all the time.

And then when I've stopped racing after it, perhaps when I'm not even thinking about it, it will come gently and light on my shoulder.

I had one of these inexpressible nudges from something outside myself the day before the Junior Miss Pageant began in March 1963. I was driving into Louisville late that afternoon on some last minute errands. Suddenly a rabbit was under the wheels of the car—before I could even begin to use the brakes. I knew I had hit the animal although there was no impact. I drove on.

Then, inexplicably, I was blinded by tears. An impulse that

was not my own said, "Stop. Go back. Don't leave the rabbit on the road."

"That's silly," my rational self replied. "You just don't stop to pick up a rabbit. Besides, it wasn't my fault."

But the tears blinded me so that I hardly could see ahead. "I won't turn around," I repeated. Everything human in me said "drive on."

Yet that something stronger kept insisting. And finally I obeyed. I turned the car around and drove back to the spot where the rabbit had streaked from the underbrush. There it was, lying beside the pavement. It was dead. Gently I picked it up and laid it beneath a bush, well back from the road.

And with that act the tears stopped just as suddenly as they had started.

What was the truth that had touched me so compellingly? Was it a message about the oneness and importance of all God's creation? At a moment when my own plans and affairs loomed very large, hadn't a whisper come to me from the Love that included rabbits—and even the two sparrows which were sold for a farthing?

After the exciting experience in Mobile, there was a lot of travel for the Pageant. One Sunday in a large city, my chaperone and I slipped into a church near our hotel. The sanctuary was almost full—not quite. When it came time for the announcements, the pastor solemnly stood up and here is what he said as best as I can remember:

"I have witnessed the disunity resulting from recent attempts of Negroes to worship in a nearby church. In order to avoid what happened down the street, I called a special meeting of the board of directors. We have informed the ushers to tell any of these Negro agitators who come and try to attend our worship service, that we haven't room enough for our own members."

That was all. Just a simple announcement. I looked around at the people. Theirs was a routine reaction. Again, I know that the emotion I felt was larger than my own.

I am no crusader. I think I understand some of the complexity of this problem. But suddenly I knew that I could no longer take up this pew space that was so valuable.

The minister was reading some more announcements, but the words that crashed in my ears were different: *Though I speak with the tongues of men and angels and have not charity, I am become as sounding brass. . . .* * It was that other Voice impelling me to action once again. With my astonished chaperone gathering gloves and pocketbook, I got up and walked from the church—wondering if I ever would be able to explain it to her, or to myself.

Back in the hotel room I tried to describe it. It was as though something more concerned and more dedicated than I had reached down and made a decision for me that I might not have reached by myself. For I often had wrestled in my own mind with this question of integration without reaching a very clearcut conclusion.

A friend to whom I told this experience said he had no doubt that it was the Holy Spirit. He believes that the Spirit daily tries to reach each one of us with His perfect counsel. "The key," he said, "is our obedience. As long as we obey that subtle prompting, it will come ever clearer and more frequently. But if ever we begin to stop our ears, it will grow faint and then disappear."

That made sense to me, because nine or 10 months before there had come a moment when I was sure the Holy Spirit had revealed a new truth to me. It was during a period in my life when I had pulled away from the religious training I'd received as a child.

I think most teenagers go through a time like this, and when adults ask why, the nearest I can come is the word *embarrassment.* Teenagers are terribly self-conscious. And Jesus represents a kind of simplicity and humility that is not at all attractive if you're primarily concerned with what people think of you.

* I Corinthians 13:1

Furthermore, I'd use the word *vulnerability*. There is something about Christ's life of sacrifice and service that made Him totally vulnerable to people. Whether we admit it or not, young people pull away from situations where we can be hurt. And so we pull away from identifying with Christ who was hurt.

I hadn't realized how far it had gone in my own case until one of the boys in high school said some things that bothered me. He, too, was reared in a Christian home, yet he had become a doubter.

"I could step on a Bible right now and not feel a thing," he said. Then he scoffed at church ritual and the idea of a divine Christ.

I tried to talk to him, but inside I was more upset than I showed. What bothered me was not as much his attitude as mine. For I'd realized suddenly as he talked that I could not counter his disbelief with a really strong faith of my own.

That night I could not sleep. A feeling of despair surrounded me. Why must I be so confused? It was nearly four a.m. before I dropped off to sleep.

The next night it was the same . . . a great feeling of depression . . . inability to sleep. I was tortured by questions about Christ. Was He a myth? Was He God? Did He really perform those miracles? My thoughts seemed to start off in one direction and end up back at the starting point. There the big question was always waiting: was Jesus who He said He was?

I've wondered since why I did not turn to my parents for answers when I needed them so badly. Mother and Dad are the kind of Christians who live their faith and had tried to teach my sister and me to live it too. Perhaps that was just the trouble. What faith I had, had been given to me, with no effort on my part. Perhaps it was time to earn a faith of my own.

For five nights the torment lasted . . . sleeplessness . . . emptiness . . . straining to know . . . reaching out for something. On the fifth night it happened. I can't describe it in any other way than to say that a cloud about me seemed to lift, the answer of Faith formed a pathway to light: He was! He is!

I got up and began to read the New Testament. I had read the entire Bible through twice before, but never like this. Once I'd read it as a lover of literature, once for its history. Now I read as a seeker. Words leapt at me from the page, thrilling and true. I read on and on, excited, with a feeling of great joy.

When I arose the next morning—to the same breakfast of eggs, the familiar school routine—the feeling of elation and belief was still there. But I had no idea as to how to share it or use it.

There have been other whispers from God, not as loud nor as clear as that night's revelation, but enough to keep me remembering that He seeks us even more fervently than we seek Him. Sometimes in my search for truth I feel as if I'm climbing a ladder up the side of the Empire State Building. At the 100th floor there is great vision and wisdom for the climber. Right now I'm up to the fifth floor and sometimes when I look up and see the distance to go, my heart sinks.

Then a bird lights on my shoulder and I remember that it's really not like this at all. It's not a long climb that we must accomplish alone. The distance was overcome when Truth came down to our level. Now He stands outside each separate heart, and we must only be ready to fling wide the door when we hear His gentle knock.

George Romney, Governor of Michigan, was once a Mormon missionary in Europe. He tells, honestly, how he often fumbled, and sometimes failed—but describes how the experience so profoundly affected his life that he was never the same again.

Doors Slammed in My Face

by GEORGE ROMNEY

IF I were asked to name the one most rewarding period in my life, I am quite sure that I would answer: the two years I spent having doors slammed in my face.

Nobody, of course, likes to have a door slammed in his face. I know it was true of me when I was 18. I can recall, vividly, when to earn pocket money I sold light-bulbs door-to-door. But my venture collapsed because I simply wasn't tough enough to withstand the continual scowl and the rude sound of a door being slammed.

Yet, a few months later, I was out knocking on doors again. I did not find it easier than before. In fact, it was harder, because I was 6,000 miles from home, living on $12 a week in a strange country, and I was talking to people about a subject that leaves almost any teenager shy: religion.

"I'm-a-missionary-for-the-Church of Jesus Christ of Latter Day Saints-sometimes-known-as-the-Mormons," I'd say quickly as a face appeared in the doorway. Most often that's as far as I got; the door would close and I'd be left standing on the stoop with a tract in my outstretched hand.

Why, then, was this the most rewarding time in my life? Because during those two years I learned the immense value of talking to others about one's own closest beliefs. I learned, in fact, some important lessons, but before telling about them, I think I should try to explain just what it means to be a Mormon missionary, and especially what it meant to me.

It is the custom of our Mormon church to choose missionaries from among our young people. To be selected for this service is a great honor. If selected, they agree to serve two years and to go wherever the Presidency sends them. (I counted myself lucky to have drawn an overseas assignment, the British Isles.)

The youngsters go at considerable sacrifice. The only expense the church pays is the missionary's return-home passage; even the literature he passes out is paid for out of his own pocket. I earned $700 for my expenses by lathing and laying hardwood floors near my home in Salt Lake City. Usually the missionary must interrupt college for his two years. And, perhaps worst of all, it is a standing joke among the young men and women that, when they get back, their sweethearts will have found somebody else. I know I was deathly afraid my girl, Lenore, would not wait so long for me.

The effectiveness of this custom is undeniable. But perhaps the biggest value of the experience is not so much what it does for others, as what it does for the young people themselves. They return home to start their mature lives with broad lessons in believing, lessons and convictions which stay with them forever.

The first lesson that I took away from my life as a missionary was perhaps the most important of all. It was, simply, that you cannot inherit faith; each individual must discover faith for himself.

If faith could be inherited, I would have had a strong, personal faith from my parents. I had grown up in areas where people of my faith predominate. My childhood had been steeped in the lore of the L.D.S. (Mormon) trek across the plains and mountains. I had played with L.D.S. boys, dated L.D.S. girls, come across the ocean as an L.D.S. missionary, only to discover that what I had inherited was not faith, but a background.

The difference between a religious background and a religious faith, it seems to me, is the difference between the passive and the active. A background can be absorbed passively, but faith is the result of active experience, struggle and challenge.

To convey my beliefs to others, I found I had to be certain of them myself. I could not depend on the thoughts of my father or grandfather. I had to know for myself.

Fortunately, I had been taught that there is a proven formula to test religious principles. It consists of these steps, (1) a desire to know, (2) a willingness to study, (3) sincere prayer, (4) obeying the principle being tested.

In the early months of my mission, I made effective use of this spiritual truth-testing formula. Because of my desire to know the truth or error of my message, I studied diligently. Many hours were spent in the Glasgow public library studying other religions as well as my own. I prayed hard for understanding, and I lived the principles I was testing. Through this came conviction about life's most important truths.

Another lesson I learned was that we all need help, and frequently it comes from unexpected sources. In London I discovered that no one was particularly interested in hearing me talk about my religion. Few were talking religion, but nearly everyone was talking politics and economics. Ramsay MacDonald had recently been elected Prime Minister, and the labor movement was the lively issue of the day. When I stood up on my soap box near the Tower of London and tried to talk about the restoration of the Gospel, few cared.

An unexpected friend became the solution to my problem. I noticed that each day a colorful, old, red-bearded Socialist came to Tower Hill to stump for his beliefs among the clerks and secretaries who came to the park for their lunch. One day he began to heckle me. We soon began to argue with each other; he for Socialism, I for my Christian convictions. Our discussion was friendly but became intense, and soon the clerks were listening and taking sides. Every day after that, he would question me. This drew large crowds. His unsolicited questions helpfully created interest on the part of others in my religious message. Thus an unexpected obstacle became a source of real help.

This was our life for two years, knocking on doors, arranging meetings, speaking on street corners, passing out tracts. Hard as we worked, however, I feel sure that our efforts had more effect on us than they did on the people around us. And this, in fact, is the third lesson: you cannot teach without learning.

At the end of my two years, I sailed for home with a belief that was far stronger than I had brought with me.

True faith comes from such experience. This, I am sure, is one fundamental reason behind the Mormon tradition of sending young people abroad to tell others about our church. I shall always be grateful for those two years of effort and struggle, which enabled me to convert background into understanding and faith. The result has helped me every day of my life.

The "Lady Preachers" patiently issued The Call *each night at the Revival meetings in the little village schoolhouse. Then they waited for the villagers to come to the altar. No one ever did. Was it all for naught? The Ozark boy who wrote this story has a surprising answer.*

She Never Knew

by James Hefley

THE ancient car wheezed to a halt. Two young women stepped into the single dusty street that cut through our Ozark village of Mt. Judea, Arkansas. They climbed the steps to the porch of my father's store where I was sitting with the teen-age members of the spit-and-whittle club.

"We're the new missionaries," one of them said. She was a frail little blonde, and as she spoke—with a crisp Eastern accent—she kept adjusting the spectacles that perched on her freckled nose. "Could you boys tell us whom to see about getting the schoolhouse for Monday night?"

We boys exchanged grins. I whispered to a friend, "Lady preachers."

"And Yankees too," he replied. But not to disprove traditional Ozark helpfulness we directed the young women to my uncle, a member of the school board. A short while later they were back.

"We can have the schoolhouse," the freckled one said. "Will you boys come? We'll have a good time—games, and singing, and Bible stories."

I nudged my friend on the bench beside me. "Sure we'll come," I said, winking, "and have a good time."

Monday night the two young women were back. With no organized social life in the community, about 30 mountain boys and girls showed up. We older boys had our good time that first night. We scuffled during the hymns, jerked chairs from under unsuspecting girls, laughed uproariously at the wrong places in the stories. But Florence and Helen, as the two missionaries asked us to call them, plodded patiently through the meeting. Not once did they call us "ignorant hill-billies" as we had expected.

And the next Monday night they were back. And the next. In time we exhausted our bag of tricks. We eventually became rather fond of our two missionaries. I especially liked Florence Handyside, the frail blonde one. Florence was from Rochester, New York. She had attended the Moody Bible Institute with the idea of becoming a missionary to Korea, and then the war had come along. So, while waiting, she joined the North Arkansas Gospel Mission. All in all Florence Handyside served our churchless Ozark communities for four years.

I suspect that in her own opinion those years were a failure. In my village of Mt. Judea, Florence and Helen ended each Monday night with an altar call, but not one of us ever went forward. I remember one hot summer night in 1946, the last time I saw her. The games were finished and Florence stood in front of the torn stage curtain and talked about Christ's love for us. I sat at an uncomfortable desk and fidgeted and blinked back the tears. Love and patience were trying to pierce through my young indifference and callousness.

Florence looked right at me and asked, "Is there here to-night some boy or girl who will trust in Christ?" Helen began pumping out a hymn of invitation on the battered organ. I wanted to walk forward, yet an invisible wall stood in my way.

The organ stopped. Florence waited a few moments longer, then closed with a prayer. Ten minutes later she and Helen got in their old car and clattered away in the dark.

I walked down the hill toward home. For years my cherished dream had been to run a big-time gambling casino. I used to pore over an illegal catalog that pictured roulette wheels, faro tables, crooked dice and cards, and big slots. Already, in my Dad's store, I operated punch boards and a small slot machine. It was a good start, and I wasn't about ready to give it up. By the time I reached home, the fresh breeze had swept away the emotion I had sensed earlier, and I felt better.

It was nearly a year later when an itinerant preacher came to our mountain and again issued the call to accept Jesus as Saviour and Lord. I remember nothing about his sermon, except that it was a poor one. But four years' patient work by the lady preachers had borne fruit. At the close of his talk several in our little town, including me, came forward and gave our lives to Christ.

An ax disposed of my slot machine and a fire took care of my stock of punchboards. I went on to college and a writing career and never again did I dream over a catalog of roulette wheels.

But Florence never knew. Her call to Korea had come at last. On her arrival there she had fallen ill and died almost at once. Florence's total career as a foreign missionary lasted less than one month.

Florence Handyside died without knowing the influence her life had been during her four years in the Ozarks. Besides me, many others came to trust in Christ. My sister is now in full-time Christian work. Another of Florence's hillbilly kids became a registered nurse; another a college professor. In a neighboring town a church was organized by the people to whom Florence preached.

*One soweth, and another reapeth,** said Jesus. It is one of the hardest lessons of the Christian life, to work steadily on, to continue faithfully when we cannot personally reap the harvest of our labors. I can see Florence now: frail, bespectacled, slight of stature. She is standing by the torn stage curtain in the old schoolhouse. Her crisp Yankee accent sounds so out of place in the Ozarks. "Isn't there some boy or girl

* John 4:37

here tonight," she is saying, "who wants to let Christ come into his life?"

The organ stops. Florence waits. And no one comes forward.

"Yes, Florence," I want to tell her, "we are coming. Too slow for you to see. Too shy for you to know we love you. But we are coming, slowly, surely, the way that you have pointed."

Both were deeply in love yet their romance was at the breaking point because religion stood between them. When Rilla Scott finally made a choice between her faith and her romance, events took a startling turn.

Stormy Hearts

by RILLA SCOTT

O N my first day at work in the features department of a big Sydney newspaper, I collided head on with Peter Scott in the corridor.

Peter was everything I admired in a man. He had an attractive English voice, intelligence, a quick wit. And I soon learned that he shared my interest in theater, literature, music.

After being agonizingly aware of each other for about ten days, we dined out together. It was a perfect evening. In fact, the whole future looked perfect. Soon, we were radiantly in love.

Then the flaws began to appear. Cynical office jokes, in which he joined, hurt me—but because of my deep love I kept silent. It bothered me the abrupt way he spoke to simple, well-meaning but perhaps slightly inefficient people. And I was embarrassed to tell him that it was attending church which kept me from seeing him on Sunday evenings.

Only several weeks before I had gone to a meeting of the Billy Graham Crusade in Sydney, drawn into the auditorium by depression over my failure to find work as an actress, plus fear of the future. When I walked forward to give my life to Christ, I realized it was the first time I was doing something for myself about faith in God, rather than simply accepting certain beliefs as an inheritance from my parents.

After this spiritual rebirth, I was given the courage to seek a job in a new field—journalism. But Peter was so brittle, so sophisticated, so witty, I was sure he would laugh our romance out of existence if I showed my true religious feelings. And yet the ringing pronouncement of the Crusade, and of my beloved church, was to put Christ first.

Put Christ before my hopes of marriage, before my love of Peter? It was a real test of my faith.

I couldn't make the challenge to Peter directly, not right away, not the way I could to other people I met. However, I asked him to dinner at my flat, and deliberately left my Bible and some religious papers lying about.

At first, he didn't notice them, but after dinner he casually picked up some Bible notes and read them. "What's all this rubbish?" he asked lazily. "Don't tell me you're one of those 'churchy' people?"

So began what turned into months of arguments, discussions, fights, tears, furious departures from each other and later phone calls of contrition. Then new fights.

He wanted and needed me, but couldn't accept my "religious cant" as he called it. I desperately wanted and needed him but couldn't accept his cynical approach to God.

Then came the dreadful day at the office when I saw him open some bills, smile, and toss them into my waste basket.

I was horrified at his lack of responsibility and cried out, "But you can't do that!"

"Why not?" he asked. "The system's worked so far. If things get too bad, perhaps I can pass around a plate in your precious church." My whole world seemed to collapse.

"I suppose there's no question of your marrying me now," he said. "You'd have to buy cheap cosmetics and bargain basement dresses."

Then, there came that one wild, violent, unbelievable night. We had another argument. Furious, Peter seized a favorite lamp of mine and smashed it to bits. He stormed out of my flat and, as he crossed the street below, I grabbed a script he had left for me to read and flung it out the window.

If it hadn't been so tragic, the scene would have been ludi-crous—my lamp in pieces, his typewritten papers fluttering down two stories to the rainy pavement.

Weak and shaken, I lay on my bed and succumbed to great racking sobs. Was this what God had led me to? Loss of Peter just because I had tried to keep true to Him?

Then there was a knock at the door, and hope returned for a moment. Peter was coming back.

I opened the door, but from the fierce, tense fury in his eyes I knew that Peter was far from penitent. He wanted a book and some papers.

Not a word was spoken. We often had threatened to break up before. Now all links seemed to be broken between us. I sat quite still, watching as he looked for his things.

At that moment, I almost hated God for destroying, so I imagined, any chance of happiness with Peter.

But then I thought, had I *really* opened my heart to God when I'd been with Peter? It suddenly became clear that al-ways I had kept God out of my relationship with this man I loved. I realized that this had been the reason we had had no harmony between us.

Then I knew I had to do something I had never done be-fore, not with anyone, and it was doubly hard in Peter's pres-ence.

But with that extreme relaxation which sometimes comes from despair, I just knelt by the chair and prayed. I prayed fully and aloud I think for the first time in my life, with heart and soul and mind utterly committed to God.

Words poured out, and I'll never know quite all I did say. I know I asked God to forgive us, to pour love into our hearts and to fulfill His plan. Finally, I stopped but kept my eyes closed, waiting I suppose, for words of sarcasm from Peter.

The silence became so pressing that I had to look up—and there was Peter, sitting on the couch with tears in his eyes. . . .

Looking back, I am overwhelmed at the sudden change God worked in our hearts that night. But it did not happen until I had removed the obstacles of pride and fear which kept me from being the type of person God could use.

When we were married, it wasn't all hearts and flowers, with problems automatically solved. In fact, some things became harder. Just as we were overcoming the last of the considerable debts, a joint business venture of ours failed, with the loss of borrowed money. Peter tried to get back into journalism, only to find it a time of recession.

Yet it was Peter now, and the fervor of his prayers, who brought us both through.

Slowly, bit by bit, we are finding power and guidance to overcome the debts and the flaws in each other's character. My fears and doubts about being a good wife and mother, after years as a career woman, are each day gently but firmly being removed. And Peter's tenderness, sympathy and understanding toward others is miraculous to see.

Recently, we became the happy parents of a sunny-natured, beautiful baby daughter. The christening was a memorable occasion—one of the highlights of my life. Peter and I stood side by side in church and dedicated to God our first-born child, vowing to guide her, by prayer, teaching and example toward the deep joy and fulfillment we have found in the Christian life.

Most people want to keep their religion at arm's length. To know Jesus Christ, really know Him, might call for some changes in personal behavior. Here's the personal story of what happened to Guideposts' Executive Editor when he kept seeking for a deeper relationship with the Master.

The Five Christs I Have Known

by LEONARD E. LESOURD

TEN people at a dinner party began to discuss a movie about Jesus Christ. A gay young woman, bored by the subject, said blandly:

"Why would anyone ever want to be like Him?"

There was silence for a moment, then the conversation veered into another direction. Yet I found myself fascinated by that silence. What thoughts, unexpressed, went on in the minds of the other nine people? How many wanted to state their feelings for Christ but did not because of embarrassment? How many shared the girl's boredom? How many simply had no thoughts about Him at all?

I can think of at least five different reactions I would have had in the past 40 years. In my youth, I couldn't have cared less about Him. Today I think that what an individual does about Jesus Christ is the most important decision he can ever make.

At 10 the *first Christ* I knew was the pale, anemic face on the Sunday school wall. "Gentle, mild Jesus" did not inspire this boy whose obsession was athletics. As a youth, I believed in God, went to church, became a perfunctory Christian but outside of church never gave Him a thought.

In college I encountered the *historical Christ*. Now here, I found, was a comfortable position to take toward Him. The

43

historical Jesus is usually set far back from the stream of life.

With this approach, one is not likely to be shunned or considered a fanatic for his beliefs. He can join the intellectual chorus and recite the words, "Jesus was a good man. He had some good advice for us, but let's be realistic about those myths and fairy tales in the Bible."

In my case, putting Christ in this setting was a simple solution during college and four years as an Army Air Corps pilot. The historical Jesus did not interfere with anything I wanted to do.

True, faced with the cold, clammy fear of death during World War II, I desperately needed a philosophy. The historical Christ was too remote to be of any help. And so I settled on an attitude of nonchalance which meant that nothing was really important, not even life itself.

My drift from this "historical" relationship with Christ to a third stage—*Christ the Teacher*—began in 1946. I had been out of the Air Corps for a year, wandering around the country collecting material to write a novel. But the novel did not materialize; my philosophy of nonchalance left me unadjusted to face the competition and realities of the post-war world.

Through the guidance of my parents and an unusual chain of circumstances, several months later I found myself applying for and accepting a job I did not think I wanted. It was to write articles for a small new religious magazine named Guideposts.

Soon a spiritual change began to take place inside me as I interviewed for the magazine people of achievement who had at the core of their lives a strong faith. I began to want what they had.

"Christ is the greatest Teacher," a sales manager for a paint company told me one day, "and there is practical value in the Gospels for us today." I began to see that what the Master said nearly 2,000 years ago could be applied to me, now. For example, His words, *Ask, and it shall be given you; seek, and*

*ye shall find; knock, and it shall be opened unto you.** Here
was helpful advice for an ambitious young man. I was also intrigued by the passage, *I can do all things through Christ
which strengtheneth me.*** Christ the Teacher was a good
psychologist. He understood people. The phrase "spiritual
technique" entered my vocabulary. All this was fine as far as
it went. The unfortunate part was that I became interested in
Christ not for what He was and is, but for what He could do
for me.

It took a fellowship group to nudge me into the fourth
stage—where I encountered *Christ the Person.* I walked into
the Young Adult Group of Marble Collegiate Church one
night in 1947, 28 years old, cynical and lonely.

As I entered the door, I told myself that these church meetings were a waste of time—stuffy people talking about a stuffy
religion. To my surprise, instead of pious types, I found attractive, intelligent people who were genuinely friendly.

Before I knew what had happened, I was pulled into some
of their activities. They obviously found Christ to be more
than a teacher. Through them and through books, particularly
The Man Nobody Knows by Bruce Barton, my concept of a
pale, meek and mild Jesus changed to one of a virile Man with
great stamina. I also began to picture the sense of adventure which the Disciples must have felt following such a Man.

Then I attended a week-end retreat in June, 1948, with
some of these young adults. This particular affair combined a
series of discussions, quiet meditation, and some recreation.
The central theme was on the importance of making a personal commitment to Jesus Christ.

At first I decided that I already had done this. After all, I
was a member of a church. Soon I began to realize, however,
that they were not talking about church membership, but a
specific personal step that for most people went beyond this.

When one of the group described how he had gone into a

* Matthew 7:7
** Philippians 4:13

small chapel nearby, knelt at the altar and made this commit-ment, I became uneasy. This was an emotional religion which I always had avoided. It was the threat to my self-control—to the veneer of sophistication carefully built up over the years.

Yet, I felt myself drawn to a quality of life I was seeing in these "committed" young people.

Before the weekend was over I found myself in this chapel, on my knees before the altar, saying a simple prayer, "Lord, I don't know how I happen to be here, but I want to give my life to You. I do so now. Show me how to be a good disciple."

Immediately there was a great sense of release and exhil-aration; also a kind of cleansing. This experience climaxed my growing relationship to Christ the Person.

The years which followed this "surrender" experience were full of exciting creativity. I felt close to Christ. I had an en-thusiastic witness for Him which I gave regularly. What more was necessary?

Yet somehow I was not spiritually undergirded at all for a calamity in my personal life which unexpectedly came when I was 39. The breakup of a marriage is devastating. The ques-tion I asked was, "Why?"

I had turned over my life to Christ; had worked hard at being a good Christian. Behind my self-pity was the feeling that all this Christian effort somehow should have made me immune from a personal disaster.

In the period of discouragement that followed, I came face to face with the spirit of evil. Never again will I think of the Devil as a comical red-robed figure with a pitchfork. He is subtle, suave and persuasive. I discovered one of Satan's best tools for the conquest of a human being is self-pity.

When one is falling, the instinct is to reach out for some-thing to hold on to. I did this and found one handle to clutch— my commitment experience kneeling at an altar 10 years be-fore. This was still very real to me. And so I knelt once more and sought Him again as I had before.

With this act of submission came a new recognition and acceptance of my frailty. Before I had, in effect, congratulated Christ for having found me. Now I realized that it was not enough to have Him just as a Leader, or a Guide or Presence. I needed His Spirit within me.

Thus began my fifth and most meaningful relationship with Jesus—my contact with the Holy Spirit or the *Indwelling Christ*.

I see now that the first disciples likewise had their moments of great defeat. Humble, dedicated, they had all committed their lives to their Master, yet their commitment was not enough. When trouble came, Judas betrayed Christ, Peter denied Him; the rest fled in panic when Jesus was arrested and crucified.

Yet the great miracle of Christianity is what happened to these confused and inadequate men at Pentecost. Christ appeared and said, "You shall receive power when the Holy Spirit has come upon you." *

The Disciples gathered in the Upper Room and prayed deeply for many hours. The Bible describes the "rush of mighty wind" that came, and how "they were all filled with the Holy Spirit." What a sight this must have been! How indescribable the joy, the elation, the resurgence of power as these men were reborn! The Holy Spirit filled them all with such power that they were able to go forth and bring Christianity to the world in spite of ridicule, beatings, imprisonment and execution.

Is the same power available to us today?

I believe so with all my heart. Though only a beginner in my experience with the Holy Spirit, during the past five years my life has been blessed in ways I could never have believed possible during my deep despair back in the mid-50s. My feeling now is one of overwhelming gratitude and joy—the kind of deep joy that can even bring tears unexpectedly. And also love—love for my family, for friends, for work, and most of all for Him.

* Acts 1:8

Prayer

ONCE a change has taken place and your spiritual growth is under way, the next step is to establish regular communication with God, the source of all power. This is done through prayer.

"How do I make this contact?" you ask. Prayer can take many forms: a frantic plea for help by a woman alone in a plane she can't fly; a silent, wordless reaching out of one man's heart; the simple conversation of a woman while she irons a dress.

You may want to talk to God through your church worship service or while taking a stroll in the country. When you pray—where, how or why you pray—does not matter as long as you establish the contact. It is my conviction, after 40 years in the ministry, that something withers up and dies within the person who does not find a way to commune with his Maker.

In the following stories you will meet people who found that prayer was not only essential to their spiritual growth, but in some cases to the maintaining of their sanity, and even to preserving life itself.

NORMAN VINCENT PEALE

Her husband gasped, clawed at his chest, then collapsed at the controls of his private airplane. His frantic wife was his only passenger. They were 2,000 feet up in the black night—and she didn't know how to fly. An unforgettable story of fear and faith and the power of prayer.

S.O.S. Anyone, Anywhere!

by BETH BLACK

IT was a perfect night for flying. Two thousand feet below us the friendly lights of the Dallas suburbs made an endless necklace against the dark earth. Above us, the soft spring sky was spangled with stars. The engine of our little airplane, the *Blue Bird*, droned steadily. My pilot-husband said happily, "I love flying at night, don't you? Just the two of us. It's so beautiful."

I nodded, too contented to speak. It seemed to me that I had everything in life that a woman could ask for: an adored husband, a houseful of children waiting at home, security, happiness. . . . And then without warning, like a hammer smashing down on a crystal vase, came panic and terror. I heard Spence gasp, felt the plane lurch. I saw him clutch at his chest with one hand. "Darling!" I cried. "What's wrong?" There was no answer. The look of pain faded from his face, his head fell back, his shoulder sagged against mine. His other hand slipped from the wheel.

"Spence!" I screamed. I leaned across him and grabbed the wheel with both hands, trying to steady the plane. Even as a passenger, I knew that if you pushed the wheel forward, the plane would nose down. If you pulled it back, the *Blue Bird* would rise. If you turned it like the steering wheel of a car, the plane would bank to the right or left. But that was all I did know. I was two thousand feet above the darkened earth in a plane that I didn't know how to fly.

The gauges on the instrument panel were a menacing jumble of needles and figures. But in those first dreadful seconds all I could think of was Spence. His eyes were half open; he seemed to be breathing faintly. I took one hand from the wheel and groped for his pulse. I knew that Spence was still alive, but some deep instinct told me that this was a fatal heart attack.

Suddenly something in me seemed to cry out, if Spence is dying, then let me die too. Let me go with him, and not hurt anyone else by crashing into a house, or—worse, perhaps —colliding with another plane. I twisted the wheel, turning the plane, heading for the dark areas away from the lighted suburbs, away from the crowded airlanes between Fort Worth and Dallas. Above some open field I could shove the wheel forward, or just let go. . . .

This was my first reaction, but then, right on its heels, came a more rational thought: what about the five trusting children waiting at home? Did I have the right to rob them of *both* parents? Of course I didn't! I had to get back to them somehow.

I knew that if I was to have any chance at all, I would have to get through to the control tower at the Dallas airport. I picked up the radio microphone and pressed the sending button as I had seen Spence do. "S.O.S." My voice was shrill with grief and terror. "S.O.S. Love Field! This is Nine Seven Charlie calling Love Field. I'm in trouble, terrible trouble. Please help me."

Static crackled from the loudspeaker-receiver above my head, but only static. Perhaps I was sending on the wrong channel. Frantically I twisted the selector switch and tried another frequency. "S.O.S. Love Field. S.O.S. anyone, anywhere! I need help! Oh, God, won't someone help me?" It was more than just a question. It was a prayer, the most desperate and urgent prayer I had uttered in my life.

And although I didn't know it, the prayer was being answered. In the tower at Love Field, the traffic controller, Donald C. Potter, did hear me faintly. Instantly emergency measures were taken. Potter's supervisor, Lester Reece, ordered his radar room to try to get a fix on the *Blue Bird*. Two airliners and a private plane waiting to land were sent into a holding pattern away from the field. Crash trucks and firemen were alerted. Don Potter kept calling to me, asking me to identify myself, but I could not hear him. In my panic I was switching frequencies so rapidly that he could not get through to me. Eventually Lester Reece realized this, and gave orders to start calling on all 16 channels.

Now a bumpy wind sprang up, buffeting the little plane, making it swoop and lurch more wildly than ever. Once the lights below came rushing up at me. In terror I tugged back on the wheel and saw the stars glitter as the *Blue Bird* climbed. Reaching across Spence to hold the wheel was awkward and difficult. I knew the controls could be swung over to the passenger's seat, but I was afraid to attempt this, afraid I might lose control altogether. "Help me, help me!" I sobbed into the microphone, but my only answer was static and a jumble of faraway voices.

Below me I saw a brighter light and, looking down, I recognized the 22-story Southland Life building. I was over downtown Dallas. Now, at least, I knew where Love Field was. I headed for it, pushing the wheel forward.

Now the altimeter read 1,000 feet. Now it was 800. Ahead of me I saw two parallel rows of blue lights. A runway, I thought: this would have to be it. Down, down. . . .

"Pull up! Pull up!" A frantic voice from the loudspeaker suddenly ripped into my ears. "Aircraft south of Love Field, pull up! You're going into the downtown area!"

For one heart-stopping second, I was paralyzed. Then I knew. Those blue lights below me didn't mark a landing strip. They were the parkway lights of an expressway! In a frenzy of fear, I yanked the wheel back. The *Blue Bird* climbed steeply. Below me I saw cars and the massive shadow of an overpass. I don't know how close I came. It seemed like inches.

"Turn around!" cried the loudspeaker. "Turn around!"

Somehow I turned the plane back toward Love Field. This time I picked an actual landing strip, Runway 31. I was coming in cross-wind, and I still was frightened, but a strange thing had happened in the darkened cabin. I could feel Spence's shoulder solid against mine, and suddenly some of the panic left me. A surge of strength and determination seemed to come from outside me, as if God had heard my prayers, as if Spence were somehow helping me too. It was an extraordinary sensation, this feeling that God and my husband were with me, two separate, strengthening spirits trying to calm and reassure me, give me courage. . . .

I reached out and punched the button marked "flaps," as I had seen Spence do. I punched the one marked "landing gear." The plane was weaving badly; I couldn't control it. I knew I was going too fast, but I was still afraid to touch the throttle. I decided the only way to slow down was to cut off the engine. I reached out and turned the ignition key. In the sudden silence, the wind shrieked and the voice on the loudspeaker kept calling instructions, but I could do nothing except cling desperately to the wheel. I saw the ground rushing up, but I didn't feel the plane touch the concrete. I didn't feel or remember anything. I don't to this day.

They tell me that the *Blue Bird* slammed into the ground at an angle of 25 degrees, bounced 40 feet in the air, then slid another 300 feet in a screeching mass of tangled wreckage. The horrified watchers were sure that no one could have survived. But when the crash trucks pulled alongside, I was sitting on the edge of a crumpled wing, jaw cracked in three places, left arm smashed above the elbow, dazed and bleeding, but alive—and asking for help for my husband. But Spence was beyond all help. The doctors believe he died before the crash. I think so too.

• • •

Has this experience changed me inwardly? Of course it has. Until that night of May 14, 1960, I was what you might call a casual Christian. I considered myself a believer, but there was little depth or intensity to my beliefs. I never stopped to wonder whether the Power that rules the universe cared about me, or had a plan for my life or a purpose for my existence.

Now I'm convinced that there *is* a purpose. Why else was I spared? By rights, I should have been killed in the crash at Love Field. I was injured, it's true—and the doctors thought that despite the bone grafts I might lose the use of my arm. But I *needed* that arm, to care for the children. Slowly strength has come back until now I have 95 per cent of normal use.

I still remember that extraordinary sense of being sustained and protected by a power beyond all human comprehension. That was the contact that brought me through the worst crisis of my life. That's the strength I'm living on today.

The wife of a famous comedian tells the warm personal story of a prayer that came from a friend—and how it changed her husband's life.

Danny's House of Thanks

by Mrs. Danny Thomas

IT happened in Detroit in 1934. I was on "The Happy Hour Club" radio show when the announcer walked me over to the new singer, and said:

"Rosemarie, I'd like you to meet another singer, Amos Jacobs."

His grin was boyish and uncertain. I liked it. Most of all I liked his eyes. They were bright with truth.

Two years later we were married.

Somewhere along the line he decided to change his name, so he took the first names of his two brothers and called himself Danny Thomas. Danny was a singer then, who later became a comedian—by accident.

In 29 years of marriage we have shared all the ups and downs of an actor's life, and been blest with three children. Yes, we've had our quarrels, too, but underneath it all there has always been the abiding promise, "Till death do us part." It's pretty hard for Saturday's quarrel to go very far when you're kneeling next to each other at mass the following Sunday.

Danny's success on television has made it possible for him to keep a promise he made a long time ago, a promise to a saint named Jude. Looking back, it seems to me that the meeting between Danny and the Saint was inevitable. . . .

Danny was born in Deerfield, Michigan, into a home of few material possessions, but one that had a wealth of love and mercy. Come to think of it, these are the real roots of our happiness today, not anything that came later.

He got these traits from his parents who were Lebanese. Danny's mother was a woman of remarkable strength, of a simple and undeviating faith. She raised her daughter and eight sons on stories about the old country. "In the old country," she would say, "people were measured in only one way; either they had hearts and souls or they didn't. Their wealth or lack of it, their power or their weaknesses were never mentioned. Such things didn't matter."

When Danny was 10 he sold candy in a theater. There the acting bug bit him. By 16 he was a performer, a singer; at 18 he worked as a factory hand and as a night watchman so he could buy a new suit for a job on "The Happy Hour Club" radio show in Detroit. He had hitchhiked there.

On that show he became known as "The Tin Horn Cavalier," partly because he used a gas pipe and a funnel for his act, "Trumpet Impressions," and partly, I suspect, because of his nose. One night he was so broke he had to break a date with a girl, who became so furious that she wrote a letter to the radio station, asking: "Is that his nose, or is he eating a banana?"

Danny read it over the air that night, and suddenly found himself a comedian. That brought him a few more theater jobs than before, but he still had to struggle.

Even after we were married and had our first child, he was earning only $35 a week—when he worked. He struggled, bitterly, trying to find his level. I begged him to quit this crazy, uncertain business, and get some kind of a job, any job, with a steady check. I used to pray at night: "Dear Lord, let Danny open a grocery store, or anything that will be steady and keep him at home."

On one of his blackest nights, when he was working in a small club, Sam,* an employee he knew, burst in on him raving about how St. Jude had cured his wife of cancer. Danny asked who this Jude was.

* Name changed for obvious reasons.

Sam explained that Jude was really Judas Thaddeus and that he was one of the apostles, but was called Jude because they didn't want to confuse him with that other Judas. Sam went on to say that his wife was given up at the hospital, but that he knelt down on the marble floor at midnight and stayed there until dawn, asking St. Jude to intercede with God for her. Just when the sun came up, the doctor walked out, lifted Sam up, and said: "I don't know whom you're talking to, but thank him, because things are happening that I can't understand. I've called all the doctors over to see it. Whatever cancer there was is no longer there."

Before Sam left, he pressed a card into Danny's hand. It was a prayer to St. Jude. "Ask him to help you, Danny," Sam said. "He helps all the helpless and hopeless."

Confused and happy for his friend, Danny put the card in his pocket.

The next night Danny was passing a church, and stopped in. When he put his hand in his pocket to get something for an offering, Danny felt the card. He knelt and had a long, friendly chat with Jude, and asked him if he thought God wanted him to go on trying to be a comedian or to give it up and open a grocery store. Danny then promised that if God showed him which way to take, he would build a shrine for St. Jude.

Not long after this, Danny got his first important job: one week, for $50, at a small Chicago night club. He stayed there for two years. For the first 26 weeks he got a $10 raise every two weeks. Then he was offered a half-interest in the place.

When Danny went to church to give thanks for all this, he sat down for a moment to think, and next to him on the seat was a little pamphlet. On it was a prayer to St. Jude.

Danny felt good and bad at the same time; bad, that he had forgotten all about his promise to St. Jude, and good, that Jude had reminded him so gently about it.

Danny came home and told me that being a partner in a night club was no way to build a shrine to Jude, and that he had decided that the shrine was going to be a research hospital for children's diseases.

I said he was a religious fanatic, and he said, "Honey, I love you, but this I must do."

It wasn't long after this decision that Danny found his real place in the entertainment business; first in movies, then in television. Meanwhile he never quit on his promise.

After talking to the experts, he learned that one of the most practical locations for the shrine was in Memphis, Tennessee, next to the State University, because the medical college had the largest student body in the country and one of the best faculties. He also learned that it would cost $2,000,000 just to build the hospital, not to mention maintaining it.

It took Danny over ten years to get most of it; by his own contributions, through endless benefits he played, and by raising it among all the Arabic-speaking people in America. These people are of all faiths—Catholic, Protestant, Jewish, and Moslem—and they represent all walks of life, from plumbers to psychiatrists. But I believe it was the first time they had ever done something together, as an ethnic group, here in America.

On November 2, 1958, in Memphis, Tennessee, Danny dug up a spadeful of earth to break ground for the St. Jude Hospital Foundation. One friend has called it: "Danny's house of thanks." It will soon be open. The labs are already busy researching leukemia.

Part of that first spadeful of earth is encased in a jar in our living room. And Danny still carries in his pocket the thumb-worn card with the prayer to St. Jude on it.

It began as a short cruise away from the heat of the tropical shore. Then came the explosion. What followed was a night of terror and pain—and triumph.

Faith in the Fire

by Don Powell
as told to Maurice Berquist

NIGHT comes down like a velvet curtain in the tropics. Our boat, the Bahama Star, was anchored just off one of the white sand beaches of Andros Island, in the Bahamas. For two years, with my wife Jane and our three small children, I had been serving as a missionary to the natives of that lonely, poverty-stricken place.

We lived on the boat. It was a hard life, brutally hard: heat, insects, violent storms, strange tropical infections that blistered the skin. No refrigeration. No civilization at all, really. Still, I was doing what I thought God wanted me to do: I was preaching the Gospel in the most obscure and remotest place I could find.

It seemed like the last straw when the stove broke down on that day—May 20, 1960. We couldn't cook. Money was running out. I hadn't been able to order supplies. I thought that things were about as bad as they could get. Little did I dream of the ordeal that lay before us.

At about six o'clock I decided to move the boat a little farther from shore in an effort to get away from the insects that were tormenting us. When I turned the ignition key to start the engine, I heard a peculiar sound. The boat was moving, but a strange feeling came over me that something was wrong, terribly wrong. I spun the wheel back toward land and shouted to my helper, Carl Whitehouse, "Something dreadful is going to...."

That was all I had time to say.

I was blown through the roof, straight through one inch of plywood, whether feet first or head first I do not know. In about 30 seconds when I came to my senses and opened my eyes, I saw that the top was blown off the boat. The windows were blasted out. Flames leaped around me. There was not a soul to be seen. "Lord help me," I cried. "Lord help me!"

God must have given me supernatural strength. I ran to the back of the boat. The cargo hatches had been blown away; the interior of the boat was an inferno. I looked down into the flames and saw my three children lying there.

I leaped into the cargo hold and snatched up three-year-old Donny. I caught seven-year-old Donna by the arm and pulled her out of the flames. I carried them to the bow of the boat and went back for five-year-old Kathy. By the time I got back to the bow, Jane was there. It was the only part of the boat not in flames. Most of our clothing was burned off. Our flesh was blackened, cooked. Jane looked at us, her family, and she moaned, "All of us will die." That was the first thing she said. I tried to give her a faint ray of hope. "Don't worry," I said. "All of us will live."

Time was to prove that neither of us was right.

Crewman Carl Whitehouse had been blown overboard. Somehow he got to land and came back with a small boat. We got the children into it and made for shore. Behind us, the *Bahama Star* blew up with a blast that shattered the night. Three miles away, people saw the flames. The heat charred the wooden timbers of a pier 100 yards down the beach.

On the shore, a terrible period of waiting began. Someone radioed for a plane to come from Nassau and take us to a hospital. There was nothing else anyone could do. Donna was the worst; from the back of her neck to her heels, her skin was gone. Kathy, Donny, and Jane were burned. I couldn't tell how badly. Much of my own body was covered with severe burns.

It was a nightmare. I felt that I was going out of my mind.

Then, incredibly, something happened. I heard Jane praying. I don't know what she said, but that prayer changed everything. Before it, there had been the terrifying screams and moans. Then all was hushed. Even the children grew still. We stood in the Presence of God. It was more real than the earth under our feet; more real even than the pain. There are no words to describe this Presence. It was as if loving arms were around us, comforting us, banishing fear. . . .

The plane came. It brought two nurses, but we had to leave them behind. There was room in the plane only for the pilot and my family. In Nassau, a jeep waited to take us to the government hospital, but I persuaded the driver to take us to the Rassan Clinic. I had heard of the famous surgeon, Dr. Meyer Rassan. I thought he might be the only man in the Bahamas who could save us.

The attendants at the Clinic hesitated admitting us. I must have looked like a madman. Finally, I managed to persuade them to telephone Dr. Rassan. When I told him about Donna, he said, "I'll be right there."

I went out in the street to wait for him. I remember a man in a sports car saw me, screeched to a halt, ran up to me. "What happened?" He was trembling. "What are you doing?"

"I'm waiting for Dr. Rassan."

He couldn't understand how I could walk at all. I must have looked like a walking dead man. Then he pulled out a handful of money, shoved it at me, ran back to his car and sped away. One hundred and twenty dollars he handed me—apparently trying to help in the only way he knew.

A moment later Dr. Rassan drove up. I led him to the jeep, and when he saw Donna, he reached in and picked her up. I never shall forget this. He was immaculately dressed in a good suit and a white shirt. But he held the burned body of my little girl against him and ran into the hospital like a man possessed.

They treated Donna for an hour and a half. Then they tended to Kathy and Donny. Jane and I were last. They couldn't give me a general anesthetic because I had lost so much blood. I don't know how much I had lost, but they gave me a number of transfusions. Then they began cutting away the burned flesh. I was fully conscious through it all. Finally they covered me with a yellow salve and swathed me in bandages until I resembled a mummy. Then they wheeled me back to my room.

All that night, I talked to God. I talked out loud to Him, thanking Him for saving us, for bringing us to Dr. Rassan. The nurses urged me to keep quiet and go to sleep. I couldn't be quiet, and I couldn't sleep.

Soon after daylight, Dr. Rassan came in. He looked exhausted. He told me that everything possible had been done for Donna, but that it was no use: she was dying. I couldn't believe it: our little Donna who wanted to be a missionary "like Mummy and Daddy."

Despite the nurses' protests, somehow I got out of bed, ran into Donna's room and looked down at her. They were right; she was dying. "I feel like I'm going away," she said. "But don't cry. Everything will be all right."

I tried to hold her, but my bandaged arms would not go around her. I laid my head on her little breast. When I looked up I saw that the nurses were weeping. I knew, then, that she was gone.

For several days we held our breath as Kathy and Donny fought off the effects of both the burns and shock.

My mother arrived from Jamestown, New York. I remembered what Donna had said while we waited on the beach. "If only Grandma would come and pray. . . ." Now she was here and how we needed her.

Shortly after she arrived a phone call came from the United States. My mother held the receiver to my ear, and I heard a voice saying, "Don't worry, people are praying for you here. You all are going to get well." We discovered later that a number of churches in Nassau had groups praying for us too.

Seventeen days from the time I stood with blackened flesh

and sought entrance into the Rassan Clinic, I was on a plane headed for the United States. Though the loss of Donna tore at our minds, our souls were filled with unbounding gratitude. God was not only healing our bodies, but our hearts.

A few days later, I was preaching in my father's church in Jamestown. I say that I preached, but that is not quite true. For weeks, as I stood in front of congregations, I could do little more than weep. But God used even the weeping.

Little Donna's death has meant the salvation of many souls. Hearts were touched; people were converted. And so, looking down from her Heavenly Father's house, Donna can see that she is a missionary after all, as she wanted to be.

Today, we are back at work, continuing our mission. At times, I find myself wondering if the tragedy I have described really took place. But I know the story is true.

I can look down into the waters of Andros Harbor and see the shattered hulk of the *Bahama Star*. And I can go to a grave, where the body of our little missionary lies.

God does not cause the evil and the sorrow in this world. But He can take pain and suffering and even death, and turn them to wonderful use. As long as He chooses to use it, then, this story is not ended. All I know is that "He is no fool who loses what he cannot keep to gain that which he cannot lose."

This charming cameo of a story offers some practical advice to those who think that the ritual of prayer should follow a formal pattern.

I Always Pray Standing Up

by Elna W. Daniel

As a small girl I was taken to pay the melancholy but customary "last respects" to a young cousin who was not expected to live. The family lived on a farm remote from hospitals, and medical science was not then what it is now.

I remember that as we walked into the house, somebody shushed me, saying that they were having prayer in the parlor. My mother and father joined the other grownups who knelt there, and I took the opportunity to slip down the hall and into the kitchen. There I found my great-aunt, the child's grandmother, wringing out cloths in a pan of water.

"Why aren't you praying too, Aunt Sarah?" I asked.

She looked down at me without stopping her work. "I always pray standing up," she said, picking up the tray of wet cloths and hurrying into the sickroom.

My little cousin got well. His illness was never diagnosed, and I do not pretend to know what saved his life, but I often heard my mother speak of the dogged way Aunt Sarah packed wet cloths around the boy to bring his fever down and dropped liquid into his throat with a medicine dropper hour after hour when the doctor had said there was no use. Perhaps my cousin would have lived without either the prayers sent up in his behalf from the parlor or the ones from the kitchen. But I always had the feeling that if I needed prayer, I'd rather have Aunt Sarah's kind.

Many times when I feel that prayer is the only thing that can help, I remember Aunt Sarah and take a last look around to see if there's anything I can do *while* I pray.

When my husband died suddenly of a heart attack, I felt that there was no answer to death. Looking around I saw that there were business affairs to be settled and decisions to be made in regard to my children's future as well as the physical demands of my two-month-old baby. I didn't know which way to turn. Then I remembered Aunt Sarah's words. So I set to work and by the time all the decisions were made, my prayers were partially answered. Time itself had dulled some of the agony of grief.

Aunt Sarah's "I always pray standing up" had helped again.

The flatcars were speeding down the track, cameras were grinding, when 15,000 pounds of logs hit stunt-man Bob Morgan on the back. An incredible story of how one man's courage and prayer overcame unbelievable odds.

"Hang On, Bob"

by Bob Morgan

FOR 17 years as a Hollywood stunt man I lived with danger. A stunt man is paid to take risks, risks that the studios won't let their high-priced stars expose themselves to even if they're so inclined.

To be a good stunt man you have to have three qualifications: good nerves, good physique, and a liking for your job. Of the three, good nerves are probably most important, for every time you go to work you face danger. I have learned that a man's body can be broken in a few minutes. In the past few months I learned something else: a man's soul is a lot less fragile.

My career started a short time after I got out of the navy. Over the years, carefully made up to look like one Hollywood star or another, I have performed all sorts of hair-raising feats —and never got hurt. I never got hurt because I never took unnecessary chances and always kept myself in top physical condition. Like a boxer or a football player, I'd actually go into strict training three or four weeks before we'd start shooting a picture.

That's what I did before we went on location in Arizona with the Cinerama epic, *How The West Was Won*. And everything went well until one sunny day in April, 1962, when we were filming the train robbery scene.

The train was an old-fashioned, narrow-gauge affair consisting of an old-time big-funneled locomotive, one or two passenger cars, several flatcars carrying enormous logs and a caboose. With my hair dyed blond, I was supposed to fill in for actor George Peppard in a risky scene where he clings to the big logs and dangles over the coupling between two of the flatcars.

The script called for the huge load of lumber to be spilled eventually into a ravine in a spectacular wreck. The chains that held the logs were designed to be released hydraulically at a given signal. The trouble—and it almost was fatal trouble for me—was that the signal was given too soon.

I had finished my scene, but the cameras were still on me, and turning. I still was between the flatcars, just over the coupling, when the logs were released. Fifteen thousand pounds of timber hit me in the back. I was hurled onto the track directly in the path of the speeding wheels. Two flatcars and the caboose went over my body.

I suppose people have fallen from moving trains, landed *between* the rails, and come out alive. But I was *across* the rails. I remember thinking, "This is it. What a way to die." One of the flatcars hit me so hard that it jumped the track.

When they picked me up I understand that I was more like a mangled rag doll than a human being. The right side of my face was torn away. My body was a twisted nightmare. Later they took a piece of cross-tie about a foot long out of my back. Nobody thought that I'd be alive when they got me to the nearest doctor in the little town of Superior.

I was, just barely. My injuries were beyond the scope of a small-town hospital, so I was rushed by ambulance to Phoenix, 70 miles away. There, nine doctors struggled frantically to keep me alive. Dozens of pints of blood were pumped into me. Even so, the doctors told me later my heart stopped twice while they were working on me. Something got it going again. By this time a lot of people were praying for me, so maybe it was prayer.

My wife, Yvonne De Carlo, is a fine actress. But she's much

more than that: she's a tremendous person. She flew to Phoenix with my daughter, Bari Lee, leaving our two small sons at home in California. I was such a wreck that she wouldn't let Bari Lee see me—she said afterward that she was pretty sure I was dying and she wanted the child to remember me the way I had been. But Yvonne stood by that hospital bed looking down at what was left of her husband, and when I managed to open one eye I saw her there smiling and telling me that everything was going to be all right.

Now, I have a theory about faith. Faith isn't just believing in God, although it certainly includes that. Faith is also a reaching out toward a goal and believing, despite all the evidence to the contrary, that you can arrive at it, that you *will* arrive at it. It's an act of will, like closing your fist around an iron bar and holding on no matter what happens. When Yvonne came into that hospital room I was so weak and in such a state of shock that I hardly could think at all. But when I looked up and saw her, I knew I wasn't going to leave *her!* In other words, in that moment I made up my mind not to die. I had a goal. I reached for it and touched it. "Now hang on, Bob," I told myself. I like to think—and I believe it was—an act of faith.

For a long time, I hovered between life and death. Gangrene set in: they had to amputate my left leg and thigh. This was a blow, a terrible psychological blow, because all my life I had prided myself on my physical strength and skill at sports —especially golf. But the doctors had no choice; it was that or death.

Gradually, I began to come back. I got used to pain but there were other demons: depression, despair. I found that I didn't want to eat. And so, I had to set myself another goal. "Get that food down, Morgan," I'd say to myself. "Get your strength back. There's no use achieving the goal of life if you're going to be weak and helpless." So I forced myself to eat—and later to exercise. The trick, I found, was not to reach for everything at once. Just one thing a little beyond your grasp and keep fighting until you touch it.

One goal I set myself was to get out of the hospital in time to see Yvonne open in a new show in Chicago. That was in September, almost six months after the accident. And somehow, thanks to inspired medical men like Dr. Paul Jarrett, I was there. Not all in one piece, exactly. But there.

It's a strange thing how adversity opens your eyes to the beauty and wonder of human existence. People have asked me if I am bitter. How can I be bitter when I've been helped so much by so many people? Blood donors who never had heard of me. Letter writers who never knew me. Doctors and nurses who worked themselves past the point of exhaustion for me. People who offered financial help. People who prayed. . . .

I'm back with my family now, slowly working out a new way of life. I wouldn't be much good in a hundred yard dash, but I can stand up on my artificial leg and hit a golf ball quite a distance. And I think I've been able to help a few people too; people who have encountered tragedy or loss; people who have had to endure the hammer blows of life. "If I did it," I tell them, "you can do it. Pick a goal just beyond your grasp, reach for it, touch it and then hang on. Hang on until it's time to reach for another one!"

*Here is the fascinating story of a new organization—
Employment Anonymous—which helps discouraged
job-seekers find the right work.*

Job Hunting on Your Knees

by WILLIAM G. DELAHAN

EIGHT unemployed men—all hesitant and skeptical—
showed up in the church for the first meeting of what
was to become a unique experiment.

It began in the Fall of 1961 when three laymen of Pitts-
burgh's Memorial Park United Presbyterian Church, Paul De
Motte, Kirwan Flannery, and Donald Rehberg, set out to help
men in the parish who were out of work. They invited the unemployed to a meeting. The eight who came discovered to
their surprise they could help each other.

"I didn't know Frank needed a job," one said, "but I know
where they need a man just like him."

Another said, "Joe is a construction man, and they're planning a new set of houses on the other side of town."

With those helpful and hopeful comments "Employment
Anonymous" was born, an experiment that since has ranged
beyond the parish where it started, and sometimes beyond
its original purpose.

But finding jobs was only part of it. It became apparent
right away that most of the people had more than a job problem. Many had made themselves unemployable by becoming
bitter and belligerent. Their confidence was low or non-exis-
tent; they had lost their initiative, their friendliness, even
their faith in God.

"We asked them to try prayer," says Kirwan Flannery, "a
special kind of prayer. We asked them to pray for 30 days
for just one thing—a mind to work."

At the second weekly meeting the number of men doubled, then tripled and after that kept increasing. Other communities heard of the project and formed their own employment anonymous groups.

Though it always wasn't easy to persuade men who had rejected prayer to try it, the results often were startling when they did.

Twenty days after he began praying, one man, unemployed for eight months, got a better job than he ever had held or hoped for and was so convinced that prayer did it, he persuaded a jobless neighbor to try it. The neighbor found work on the 29th day.

"One of the more amazing things about all this," says Paul De Motte, "is that the job each man found exactly fits his qualifications. Yet none of the dozen men in our church who now are working with Employment Anonymous has any experience in personnel work at all."

How does prayer change and continue to change all of them? When they begin to pray, they always find it necessary to take a new, deep look at themselves. Soon they fervently pray not only for work, but for a stronger faith.

A steel worker, jobless for over a year and a half, admitted to the group that he would sit at his window every morning bitterly cursing "the lucky men" he saw on their way to work. At first he scoffed at the idea of praying for 30 days. Even after he finally yielded, it took a time before he could get himself to acknowledge the hate in his heart. But it was a new beginning when he did. He soon found himself praying for an end to his hatred, as well as for a job. He achieved both.

The men and women in Employment Anonymous discovered when they helped one another they found a new joy in life, and their own problems seemed less important.

But the best effect of all this is that each person finds a new and rich relationship with God. And all of them quickly would agree, "Prayer has changed us. It can change other men, it can change the world."

*Fired from his job as school principal, this man fought
a bitter battle inside himself. The release came suddenly and unexpectedly through one line of a familiar
prayer.*

The Bondage of Hate

by Lawrence H. Davis

THE moment my friend stepped through the door, I knew
this was no social visit. "L. H. . . ." he said, staring out into
the schoolyard, "there's been a meeting of the School
Board. . . ."

I laid down my pen and said, "What are you trying to tell
me?"

"He's done it at last, L. H., you're out. Harvey's forced the
Board to vote for a new superintendent."

I finished out the day mechanically and walked slowly
home. Verna met me at the door. One look and she knew
something was wrong.

"What's happened?" she said.

"I'll tell you later, after dinner."

"No, I want to know now. Children, you run upstairs and
wash."

Above the racket of our four children's feet on the stairs, I
told her:

"Harvey's got control of the Board—I'm out."

Verna sat down heavily on a kitchen chair. I probably
shouldn't have told her so suddenly: neither of us was that
young anymore. "What are we going to do?"

"I just don't know."

In earlier years, my chances of finding another job might
have been better. I'd been in school work since 1902 when I
began teaching in a little one-room school house on the Indi-

ana plains. Thirty years of teaching and managing experience. Plus the less measurable fact that schools were my life, my love. These were my qualifications. But this was 1932 when the depression was in full swing.

All that spring and all that summer, each time I ripped open a reply to an application, it was *No*.

One job in a little Iowa school drew 165 applicants.

"That makes some contest, Verna," I said handing her the letter. "Maybe I shouldn't have told them I'm 51."

When it became evident that I would not find a job in my profession, I began to look for other work, any work. I walked the streets and knocked on doors and always the answer was the same: "Sorry."

My age, the depression . . . but there was still another reason for my not finding work; more subtle, but just as devastating. People instinctively kept away: they sensed that I was charged with hate.

Have you ever known what it is to hate a man: the feeling works away at you, inside, gnawing like a hunger pain. With me it was so intense that whenever I had to go uptown, I took the back streets because I was afraid of meeting Harvey. I was afraid of what I might do.

There's a perverse kind of satisfaction in returning over and over to the source of pain. In my case I relived the events that led to my dismissal. They began, I told myself, the day we didn't buy that refrigerator. . . .

Harvey, the president of the Board, was in the kitchen appliance business. Shortly after I was named superintendent, he said, "It seems to me, Davis, that our Home Economics class needs a new refrigerator." He winked. I didn't understand that wink and answered that I would ask the Home Economics teacher. At the next meeting of the Board I had her reply: she would rather have two sewing machines.

"Fine. Fine," said Harvey jauntily. But I noticed that his hands were clenched into tight fists. Later as we were leaving, he spoke to me again. "Some day, Davis, I'm going to control this Board." He was smiling when he said it; it took me four years to understand that smile.

How I loved to chew on that story as I walked about looking for work. I think without realizing it, I was glad not to find a job. Because the harder things were, the more Harvey became a villain.

Many of the townspeople were on "my side." There was one thing, however, that puzzled me. Late one evening our minister called and after visiting on the porch for awhile he arose to leave. "I know you're having a hard time," he said. "Just keep close to God and you will see your way clear. . . ."

Keep close to God! God? It was almost as if He stood against me. I could understand feeling far from Him if *I* had been the one to hurt Harvey. But Harvey had hurt me: why should I feel so unable to pray?

The summer leaves turned to brown and dropped and we were down to the last few pennies of our reserve. By the first killing frosts, we were living on skim milk, an occasional egg and bread. The children got the eggs and milk. Verna and I lived on bread.

I mean it literally. Morning, noon and night Verna and I each took one piece of bread and then said the usual blessing: the Lord's Prayer.

And yet it was this prayer which gave me freedom from my slavery to hatred.

I will never forget the day. It was cold: snow already had fallen. The night before a friend had paid us a visit and when he found us all sitting around in our heaviest clothes, he offered to let me cut two large elms from his farm for fuel.

Before daylight the next morning I shouldered my ax and saw and was off to his farm down the river. The snow made the five mile walk difficult. Inside the pocket of my jacket was my one slice of bread: it was all I would have to eat until I returned home that evening.

When I reached the fields and saw those two giant elms my heart sank. I was a schoolteacher, not a woodsman! Still . . . I picked up my ax and took a mighty, hate-filled swing. Four hours later the trees lay stretched across the snow. Then I took out my piece of bread and sat down on one of the tree trunks.

Mechanically I began to recite the words Verna and I always said before meals. "Our Father which art in heaven, hallowed by Thy name. Thy Kingdom come. . . ."

I looked out over the gray, icing river, not really paying attention to my words. ". . . forgive us our trespasses as we forgive those who trespass against us. . . ."

I stopped short.

What was this I had just said? Forgive us in the same way *we* forgive? Suddenly I was shaking from head to toe, and not from the cold. It was a physical reaction to a gripping and powerful insight that swept over me. I saw with a brilliant kind of clarity why I had felt so far from God. I was blocking my own path to Him with my own unforgiven sins. I saw that in His prayer Christ put a condition on forgiveness: first we had to forgive others, *then* we could straighten out our own relation to God. Specifically, I would have to forgive Harvey before I could shed the depression of my own unforgiven sins.

"Father," I prayed, almost joyously, "help me to learn to forgive."

After a while the most penetrating peace settled over me. I was relaxed and spent. But I felt wondrously clean too. In the gathering shadows of darkness that afternoon, I started home. I sang all the way.

I do not feel it was coincidence that I found work shortly after this experience. Nor do I feel it was coincidence that in the years which have passed since this incident, I have never again allowed myself to hate. I know what damage it can do.

There was a particular moment when I *knew* I was free. For several days I worried about meeting Harvey. I thought I had forgiven but I was just not sure. How would I react when I saw him again?

Then, one bright, cold day I deliberately put myself to the test: I walked uptown—by the main streets. There must have been a new spring in my step, because people turned to stare as I walked past. Up ahead was Harvey's store. My pulse beat faster as I drew near.

And suddenly there he was.

He came out of the store and turned to close the door behind him. Thus he had his back to me. I could easily have turned around. But—I will never forget this next moment—I did not *want* to turn around. I walked up to Harvey and greeted him like an old . . . well, "friend" would be too strong a word. But the point is I held no ill will toward him.

"Harvey?" I said.

He swung around abruptly and saw me. His jaw dropped. A startled, puzzled look came on his face.

I held out my hand. Harvey grasped it hesitantly, then firmly—and in that moment I knew the last barrier had been removed between God and me.

Do long-winded discussions about religion often block us from God's real power? "Yes," says a man who has led Faith at Work conferences for many years. Here is a dramatic story which proves his point.

Too Much Talk

by BRUCE LARSON

IF your church is not as alive as it should be, ask yourself this question: has there been too much *talk about* Christianity and not enough *doing* it?

A group of us ministers faced this matter several years ago while we were together for a two-day retreat at a church in New Jersey to discuss mutual problems and to pray about them. As so often happens, the discussion part predominated. It was late afternoon of the final day when a startling event occurred.

Suddenly the door of the meeting room opened and a stranger walked in. The pastor of the host church knew the man and greeted him. Self-consciously the man seated himself at the fringe of our circle. Though there was no more than a momentary pause in the discussion, the experienced eyes of the other clergymen present took in the situation—the watery eyes, the sagging shoulders, the seedy clothing. Obviously the man was an alcoholic.

The discussion continued, while the stranger listened. "It seems to me," a crisp voice said, "that all we have been talking about can be summed up in our need for God's power—the kind of power that changes lives, heals, restores, that. . . ."

He stopped, his attention arrested by the agitated movements of the stranger.

"That's it! That's what I need. I could use some of that."

There was sudden silence. While everyone watched, his

bleary eyes filled a bit more and the quavering voice continued:

"My name is Ernie. I drink too much. People have tried to help me . . . doctors, hospitals, missions, and all that. But I—I can't seem to stop. How do I get this power you're talking about?"

The question hung, quivering in the silence. Despite the fact that we all had had some experience in dealing with people in need, the intrusion was embarrassing. Closing time was at hand. There were trains and planes to be caught, families to get back to, next Sunday's sermons to think about.

Finally, a white-haired man spoke up. "Ernie, all of us have problems too. It's a problem-filled world."

The voice of the elderly minister was gentle as he sought to help the stranger.

"As to how we can get God's help. Well, that isn't always too easy. It takes patience, time. There are many roads to God, many avenues by which. . . ."

"Damn!" The interruption was explosive, passionate.

"Damn—Damn—Damn—Damn!"

The quiet of the room was suddenly being blasted by Bob, a young minister and a former businessman. Anger and impatience were written clearly on his face. Again and again he beat his fist down on the seat of the empty chair beside him.

"This man doesn't want to hear about our problems," Bob said vehemently. "He's asked us a question—how can he get God's help to stop drinking? We haven't answered him. If we don't know the answer, then let's adjourn this meeting, stop our endless talking, go home and tell our people that the church hasn't any answers for today. In that case, we'd better stop being hypocrites and shut the church doors for good."

There was a shocked silence, but the impassioned words had cleared the air. Almost simultaneously, five or six men— including the angry preacher and the white-haired minister— rose and walked over to Ernie.

Bob knelt in front of the alcoholic. "Ernie, do you believe that Jesus Christ can come into your life and change it?"

The watery eyes looked down, childlike. "Yes. Yes, I do."

"Then we're going to pray right now, Ernie, that He will do this for you."

The young minister took both of Ernie's hands in his. The white-haired preacher stood behind, placed both hands gently on top of the alcoholic's head. The others stood around in a semicircle, each one with his hands on the stranger.

Bob's prayer was short, hard-hitting. He asked for Christ's healing power for Ernie, for the forgiveness of sins, for the beginning of a new life.

"Now, Ernie," Bob said, "you pray too. Just thank God that He has heard you and healed you."

"I hope so," Ernie quavered.

"Not hope so. He *has!*"

"I—well, I'd like to believe that."

The answer was gentle, but firm. "Ernie, thank Jesus that He has already come into your life."

The room became completely still. And then in wavering sentences Ernie's voice reached up to God. "God, I'm a tired, weak old man. I don't see what use I am to anyone. But I'd like to find the new life they talk about. Please help me."

His plea was real, vital. Every one of us in the room knew it, felt it. We had been talking about power. This was power.

Forgotten were train schedules, plane reservations, other obligations. For the first time in two days, real contact had been made with God through one of the least likely of persons. The air was charged with emotion. Out from the depths came some of the deep needs of the ministers themselves.

A pastor from New England began it. At first his words seemed unrelated. "I was driving down here several days ago, feeling lonely and apart from God. While crossing over Bear Mountain Bridge, I looked in the ice-clogged river and saw a small boat locked in the ice.

"That boat fascinated me. For my life has been like that.

Frozen, isolated, shut within myself. I'm frozen with the fear of other people's opinions, the fear of not being a success, the fear of not pleasing people."

Suddenly his eyes filled with tears. "Would you pray for me, that I'll get thawed out so I can really help people again?"

There was no hesitation now. The men quickly gathered around him. All but Ernie, who hung back, shyly. But the young minister walked over to him.

"Ernie, come on over and pray with the rest of us."

"Oh no! I couldn't do *that*. . . ."

The minister took him by the hand. "Look, Ernie, you've received; now you must give. And *we* need *you* now."

So Ernie knelt beside the minister and prayed with the others. The prayer was very simple. And in that room, miraculously filled with power, every one of the ministers found a new closeness to God with a childlike renewal of their commitment to Him.

Later the pastor from New England was marveling to me at the turn of events. "As long as I live, I'll never get over it," he said. "What had happened to Ernie minutes before was the real thing. The proof was that it was Ernie, with his winey breath in my face, who was God's channel for transmitting the power. It was like electricity flowing through him to me."

This experience points out so clearly that any individual—rich or poor, old or young, pastor or layman—who has made a decision for God—is at that moment a disciple of His. And if the Kingdom of God is to move ahead, lay people as well as clergy, must be a part of the total ministry of the church.

Why do we waste so much time talking about religion when Christ's call to action is so clear: *go out into life . . . heal, teach, pray, repent, love, forgive. . . .*

This account of the journey under the frozen sea, across the top of the world, by the Captain of the Nautilus *discloses the loneliness of his momentous responsibility—and what he did about it.*

Under The North Pole

by WILLIAM R. ANDERSON

IT was the greatest adventure of my life, conceived in prayer, planned in prayer, attempted in prayer, and achieved in prayer. It was the 1958 voyage of the nuclear submarine *Nautilus* under the frozen Arctic seas to the North Pole. It was my privilege to command the *Nautilus* on that historic occasion and I am convinced that if we had not asked for and received Divine help and protection, we never would have made it.

That voyage from ocean to ocean across the top of the world was an event of critical importance in the history of our country. To understand this, one must remember the circumstances that prevailed at the time. In October, 1957, the Russians startled the world by putting the first man-made satellite into orbit. In November, they launched an even larger one. With two Sputniks circling the planet, it looked as if the Russians had seized a commanding lead in the Cold War. Throughout the world, confidence in America's weapons and military power was badly shaken.

During that summer, before the Sputniks went up, the *Nautilus* had carried out some experiments under the ice pack on the Atlantic side, north of the Greenland Sea. We had discovered that in places the ice was twice as thick as it had been assumed to be—and had bashed up our periscopes in the process. On my return to Washington, I had discussed with Cap-

tain E. P. Avrand, then Naval aide to the President, the possibility of the *Nautilus* making a polar transit. Now suddenly,
in January, 1958, I received an urgent summons from the
Pentagon to report for discussion of a subject "too sensitive
to talk about on the telephone."

At the Pentagon I learned that the White House had in-
quired if it would be feasible for the *Nautilus* to attempt a
voyage from the Pacific to the Atlantic Oceans by way of the
North Pole. If successful, such a feat would produce a vast
amount of scientific information and would dramatize the
range and power of our small but growing fleet of nuclear sub-
marines. Clearly, such a voyage would lift the morale of freedom loving people everywhere.

When the President was advised that the Navy favored
such an operation, he insisted on one thing: complete secrecy.
The proposed trans-polar voyage of the *Nautilus* was one of
the most closely guarded secrets in the history of the Navy. I
don't think that more than a dozen people knew about it. My
own superior officer in the submarine service didn't. My wife
didn't. My crew certainly didn't. When we finally left Seattle,
they thought we were on a routine training cruise.

This secrecy heightened my sense of loneliness and responsibility to a degree I have not known before or since. There
was only one thing I could do to lessen it: pray. Whenever I
did pray, I felt less alone, and I prayed often—prayed that
whatever happened I would not fail my crew or let down our
country.

We knew that the most difficult part of the voyage would
come after we passed through Bering Strait and began to
grope our way under the ice of the Chukchi Sea north of
Alaska. The Chukchi Sea is shallow; its average depth is only
120 feet. If the ice was thick, could the big *Nautilus*—4,000
tons submerged and as long as a city block—get through? This
was the question I lived with.

One thing I *didn't* have to worry about was the calibre of
my crew. Of the 116 men aboard, no two were alike. Some

came from big cities, some from small towns. Some had Italian ancestors, some English, some Irish. . . . To a man they were skilled, good-humored, responsible and brave. People say to me sometimes, "Weren't there a lot of psychological problems?" To such a question I can give an honest answer: No, we were too busy to be bored. And you aren't likely to get problems in a team where each man is an individual working in his own special way to achieve a common goal.

We made our first attempt to reach the Pole in June. For eight days, all went well. But suddenly, near midnight on June 17th, the voice of my conning officer, Lt. Bill Lalor, rang through my cabin speaker, sharp with urgency, "Captain, will you come here, please!"

Instantly I snapped up and raced to the control room. When I looked at the tracing of the sonar pen, I felt my heart pound. The ice above us was 63 feet thick and getting thicker. Only eight feet of water separated the jagged, granite-hard under-surface from the top of the *Nautilus*. As I watched, the margin dropped to five feet. Close under our keel was the bottom of the Chukchi Sea.

We were driving ahead at ten knots; there was no time to think. I had dodged torpedoes in the war, but I had never faced anything like this. There was not even time to pray. And yet I must have prayed, because in that split-second of time a decision was made—not *by* me but *for* me. I actually felt, on my left shoulder, something like a great, reassuring hand, pressing—*down*.

"Take her down 15 feet!" I heard my voice give the order. Then I stood there, bracing myself for the grinding crash of steel against ice or the sickening shock that would mean we had hit bottom. But there was none. I ordered the rudder put hard over, and slowly the *Nautilus* swung around, carrying 116 men away from the deadly ridge of ice. Few of them knew how close we had been—a prayer's breadth, I truly believe—to disaster.

So the ice defeated us on that first attempt. But later that summer we tried again. Cautiously, gingerly, we probed our way through the shallows of the Chukchi Sea into the deep waters of the Arctic basin. On August 3, cruising in comfort below 400 feet, we approached the Pole. Above us was the vast wilderness of ice, gray and chaotic. Below us the sea was more than two miles deep. In the control room, our navigators tensely made their final calculations.

Then, at 11:15 p.m., E.D.T., we reached the top of the world. Picking up the microphone of the public address system, I told the crew that we were at the Pole. "And now," I added, "I would like for all of us to give our thanks to Him who has guided us so truly, to pay a silent tribute to those brave men who have preceded us here whether in victory or in failure, and finally to offer our prayers for lasting world peace."

There was silence for a moment. Then I heard cheers in the crew's mess. Our navigator was noting down our official position: *U.S.S. Nautilus: Latitude 90 Degrees North; Longitude Indefinite.* If there really had been a north pole we would have run right through it.

Two days later, after 96 hours under the ice, we surfaced northeast of Greenland and were able to report our success by radio in a momentous three-word message: "Nautilus 90 north." I was picked up by helicopter, flown to Washington, greeted by the President, then allowed to fly to England to meet the *Nautilus* and share in the tremendous welcome she received on her arrival there. There is nothing in the world more thrilling than the feeling that your country is proud of you.

I also was grateful—grateful to the Power that watched over us, the Power that ordained and sustains and rules the universe.

*What can a monarch possess that is worth more than
a kingdom? A famous author traveled all the way to
Tonga Island in the South Seas to find the answer.*

A Queen at Prayer

by Catherine Marshall

IN the summer of 1962, on a remote South Pacific island, a
tall, stately Polynesian Queen taught me some fascinating
truths about the workings of the Holy Spirit.

For over a year my husband, Len, and I had been planning
a trip to the South Seas. We were delighted when an invitation came from Her Majesty, Queen Salote Tupou of Tonga,
the chief island of the Friendly group, located halfway between Tahiti and Australia.

I often had heard of this Queen in connection with the
World Day of Prayer. Since the International Date Line is
drawn almost directly through the Friendly Islands, the
World Day of Prayer begins its global circuit in Tonga with a
service at dawn over which Queen Salote presides.

Then, too, this Island Queen became world-famous at the
time of Queen Elizabeth II's coronation in 1953. During the
procession from Westminster Abbey to Buckingham Palace,
a world television audience had watched Queen Salote ride
majestically in an open landau drawn by four horses. Despite
a pelting rain which soaked her, the Queen's good humor and
warm smile had never wavered.

As our small British De Haviland Huron flew low over the
turquoise water of the Pacific I was wondering what this
Queen would be like.

A few minutes later the plane set down on a grass field and
pulled up in front of the quonset hut terminal. A tall Polynesian man wearing a vala (the wrap-around skirt traditional to

much of the South Pacific) and a tailored black coat stepped forward.

"I am Ngalu, Her Majesty's aide-de-camp," he explained. Just behind him was the Reverend George Harris, the Methodist missionary who would be our host in Tonga.

When we had our preliminary audience that afternoon with Queen Salote, we were quickly won by her graciousness.

But most of all, her warm brown eyes drew me irresistibly. Through them radiated unmistakable signs of spiritual vitality. I wondered if the Queen later would reveal to us the secrets of those spiritual springs.

On the next day, following a Tongan feast on the grounds of her summer palace at Kauvai, we had a private interview with the Queen. How does one ask Her Majesty about personal beliefs? We began with a question about the World Day of Prayer. To our delight she was soon talking simply and directly out of her own experience.

She described how her prayer life had begun when she was a four-year-old princess. Her beloved mother, Queen Lavinia, had died when she was two. The little princess cherished every scrap of information about her mother. She had learned that it had been Queen Lavinia's habit to go by herself into the Royal Chapel for prayer every day at 12 noon.

Remembering this, one day shortly before noon she slipped alone into the big white church. For a moment she stood just inside the door wondering what to do next. Out of her loneliness flowed a strong yearning toward God. But she had no idea of how to put this into words; indeed, the only prayer the little four-year-old knew was a grace.

Day after day at the stroke of 12 noon she said the grace. And God heard not only the words, but also her deep desire. The Holy Spirit, the Comforter, crept into the little princess' heart to allay the pain of her mother's death. Then He made Christ real to her, a Person with Whom she could share everything. Thus for the little girl prayer came to mean her "personal conversations with Jesus."

"Today, I always begin with silence," she told us, "which is a gathering of my own thoughts and a time of worship of the greatest Person I know. Then quietly I go through a process of emptying myself out before God. If there is grief—and there often has been in my life—I tell of my grief; if there is a problem, I pour out the problem. Sometimes in my inadequacy I stand there shivering. So often I've found that I have to come down to complete helplessness before God can get through to me. But He has never failed me. Always there is help, always an answer." The brown eyes became thoughtful, then the Queen chuckled. "Sometimes the answer is not at all what I want to hear."

For the Princess Salote, as for all of us, the process of growth came via the overt events and challenges which life handed her. When she was 18, her father King George Tupou II died. Amid her grief, the ministers of state entered to inform her that she was now their Queen.

"As strange as it sounds," Queen Salote told us, "I had given no thought to the succession. My reaction was an astonished, 'Isn't there anyone else?'"

There was no one else. When the ministers had gone, the new Queen had but one thought, "I must go and talk with my Friend about this. He will help me."

There were many other crises through which He helped her. . . . The death of her husband in 1941, and soon after that the death of one of her three sons—a young teenager who had had rheumatic fever in earlier childhood.

The day after the funeral found the broken-hearted mother bowed, alone, over the boy's new grave. Then through her tears, the Queen gradually became aware of a humbly-dressed woman moving hesitantly toward her.

"Your Majesty," she said, thrusting some flowers into the Queen's hands, "I lost a child too. I understand how it is. I want you to know that many of us are praying for you."

"I felt a great bond with that unknown friend who had made a special trip to the cemetery for me," the Queen told us. "Through her I came to see how much grief there was in the world, but also how much compassion. Deep peace flowed into my heart."

Over the years there has been an increasing bond between the Queen and her subjects. She had needed this bond, too, in the guiding of her island kingdom's constitutional monarchy, for it has presented the Queen with some perplexing problems. On one occasion a European occupying a high position in the Tongan Civil Service became irresponsible, even defiant to the Queen. He tried to turn the Tongan officials against her. She found it impossible to deal with him directly.

Then she tried a carefully worded communique to the overseas department through which he had been appointed. This resulted in an investigating committee being sent to Tonga. But through lies the commission was deceived. Thus the Queen's position was made more difficult.

"This was one of those occasions when I was reduced to helplessness," she told us. "Finally the clear answer came in prayer that I was to have patience and wait. Patience was hard just then."

By going back again and again to talk to God about the problem, the Queen was given the inner strength not to crumple under pressure and to maintain her quiet dignity. Soon after, a second investigating committee uncovered so much evidence against the official that he was promptly replaced. It worked out exactly as the Holy Spirit's guidance had said it would.

Through such experiences, both the European and Tongan people have come to hold Queen Salote in high regard as a woman worthy of the fealty due a queen—worthy not just because of the right of succession, but because of a voluntary taking upon herself the role of a servant to her people.

Leadership of such a caliber is not possible without spiritual disciplines. The Queen joins some of the Tongan people in a pact to rise as early as 4 a.m. each day for personal prayer.

Queen Salote is also an active member of a small group that

meets once a week for spiritual nourishment and prayer. In
the town of Nuqu'olofa alone there are five such groups (including men and women) with an average of 20 persons each.

"More and more leaders in business and government are
joining these groups," Queen Salote explained. "Niuvao, the
sergeant of the police, heads one of them. I have seen many
lives changed because of these meetings."

We talked about this process by which one's life is drasti-
cally changed and turned toward God. Usually the Holy
Spirit works through one human being to reach another—
what Jesus meant by being *fishers of men.** But certain things
have to happen to us first: the giving up of our own will and
a surrender of self to Christ.

Next, His Spirit comes to live in us where self was before.
That Spirit brings us alive at the emotional level. Joy comes
surging through, and, sometimes, tears. We should not resist
tears, for it is only the old ego in us that is ashamed of intense
emotion.

Then, no longer wrapped in the insulation of self-absorp-
tion, for the first time we have the ability really to communicate with others. And across the bridge thrown out between
two persons, the Holy Spirit walks into the heart of yet another human being.

There was indeed a bridge between the three of us sitting
that July day in the Queen's drawing room in Kauvai.
Warmth flowed from this woman, to us. Yes, and there was
even that touching of the emotions, as I later was to discover.

Months after, as I sat at home composing a letter to the
Queen, to my astonishment I found tears falling on the paper.
The tears had nothing to do with sentimentality, nor was
there a trace of sadness in them. In fact, here was pure joy . . .
joy that a Queen has had the courage to obey Christ in the
affairs of a modern state . . . joy at the greatness of the living
Christ as I had glimpsed Him in the heart of another human
being.

* Matthew 4:19; Mark 1:17

Guidance

JUST as we know that the language of prayer is a universal language, and that prayer is as essential to man as food, so do we also know that when man prays, God listens.

But too few of us realize that it follows logically that if God listens to our prayers and pleas, we should, in turn, wait to see if He has an answer for us. How many times have you prayed to Him for help, then immediately turned to something else without waiting to see if He had some specific guidance to offer?

The guidance we receive from God is a very essential step on our spiritual climb. We can't go very far without it and we shouldn't try. Especially since God is ready to give it to us if we *really* want it.

How does guidance come? Jerome Hines began to receive it once he had made a decision for Christ, then began to have regular prayer and Bible reading. George Plume received it unexpectedly in a moment of great peril when he unfroze long enough for God to get through to him. John and Elizabeth Sherrill came to depend on God's guidance during a year's trip to Africa on a teaching mission for Guideposts.

The following stories will help you understand how and why guidance is another step to a vital faith. But don't let yourself get bogged down in technique. Remember that God wants to help you. He will find a way to reach you if you have an open, receptive heart.

NORMAN VINCENT PEALE

A remarkable behind-the-scenes story by a famous opera basso, who was in Russia during a grave international crisis. Jerome Hines did not realize it at the time but his final performance in Moscow enabled Nikita Khrushchev to communicate to the world a political position of great importance.

A Voice for God

by Jerome Hines

IT was 3 A. M., Moscow time, October 23, 1962, when President Kennedy went on the air to announce the American quarantine of Cuba. My wife Lucia and I were asleep in Moscow's Metropole Hotel. Two blocks away lights were ablaze in the Kremlin.

For me it was the last day of a five-week singing tour of the Soviet Union. A final performance of *Boris Godunov* was booked for that evening at the Bolshoi Theater.

At breakfast, Bill Jones, a friend and traveling companion, told us that he had heard a rumor about a new crisis between Russia and America. Four hours later we had lunch with Foy Kohler, the American ambassador. He confirmed officially that the United States had established a quarantine of Cuba.

Immediately, we wondered what effect all this would have on our evening performance of *Boris*. Would there be demonstrations against Americans? The ambassador, however, had reassuring words, "The Russian people have not been told about the crisis."

The rest of the day was tension-filled. Back at the hotel, we packed, made a few phone calls and then tried to rest. About 3 P.M., I left the hotel for the half hour's walk I take before each performance.

As I walked past the Kremlin, past St. Basil's Cathedral, I

was thinking about the many occasions in my life when I had needed God—but, how the steady flow of His guidance had always been dependent on my obedience. . . .

Thirteen years before in 1952 I first had learned to listen for His help. At that time there was a great conflict going on in my life. On one hand, I did not want God interfering in my life, upsetting my plans and my desires. On the other, I found myself pulled strongly toward Him.

Meanwhile, it was in this year of 1952 that a performance of *Boris Godunov* was scheduled by the Metropolitan Opera. More than anything else I wanted to play the role of Boris. I felt that I was ready for it. The opera manager did not agree. We argued, and I threatened to quit.

But in the end, I received the role. When self-doubt took over, however, it became a hollow victory. For now that I had won this great responsibility, I was obsessed by the fear of failure. And a failure in this assignment could ruin my career. In desperation I conceived an idea for a publicity stunt. Near the end of the opera Boris, dying, plunges down the stairs. With this fall I would feign a back injury.

"Opera star injured in fall." I could see the headlines. What a boost all this publicity would be to my career.

That night in a hotel room in New York, I wrestled with the still small voice of God in my heart.

Is it honest to fake an injury?

"Honesty hasn't anything to do with it," I countered. "What would You have me do?"

Would you be willing to give up the publicity stunt?

"No!" was my instant reaction.

For long agonizing moments I argued with myself. Finally, I realized that either I had to surrender myself to God or separate myself completely from Him.

"All right," I said. "I'll do what You tell me."

Then came the inner instruction: *open the Bible and there will be your answer.*

When I had checked into the room I noticed a Gideon Bible

on top of the dresser. Obeying the order, I got out of bed, opened the Bible and my eyes fell upon these words:

Who shall ascend into the hill of the Lord? . . . He that hath clean hands, and a pure heart; who hath not lifted up his soul into vanity nor sworn deceitfully.*

Give up your silly, egocentric publicity scheme and get on with your work. How much clearer can guidance be!

The result was that when I did sing *Boris Godunov* at the Met**, newspaper reviews could not have been more generous.

This experience of obedience to God revolutionized not only my career, but also my entire life. And yet spiritual growth was so often blocked by my ego. Time after time I would charge ahead on my own steam, only to fall on my face. On each occasion, I would tell myself once and for all to get out of my own way and let God guide my life.

Now I realize that guidance comes to different people in different ways. Some people obtain it through meditation and Bible reading. To others it arrives at odd moments in the form of quiet mental nudges.

There are times, to be sure, when I want direction, but all I can hear are my own thoughts clamoring for control. Yet I know it is not real guidance when I keep asking over and over, "Now, God, is this what I am supposed to do?" For if God is trying to tell me something, I feel it so strongly that there is no doubt.

The challenge of a lifetime came in 1962 when I was invited to sing *Boris Godunov* in Russian with the Bolshoi Opera Company in Moscow.

Lucia and I felt that our trip to Russia involved much more than the fulfillment of my long-time dream of being the first American-born basso to do *Boris* in Russian at the Bolshoi. Here was an opportunity to take a stand for Christ in various ways before the Russian people.

* Psalm 24:3, 7

** Mr. Hines was the first American-born basso to perform the role of Boris.

How can you do this in an atheistic country? We had some definite ideas. But our witness would not amount to anything unless my performance of *Boris* was effective.

That is why we both were so upset by what happened to me when we arrived in Moscow. I came down with a throat infection three days before my opening performance of *Boris* at the Bolshoi on Sunday, September 23. The Russian doctor said that I could not sing. I took the pills he gave me and went to bed.

But the big question was not what the Russian doctor ordered but what God wanted. I opened my Bible and read this passage:

You then, my son, be strong in the grace that is in Christ Jesus . . . Take your share of suffering as a good soldier of Christ Jesus.*

A soldier is under orders. He must obey if the mission is to be accomplished. I knew then that nothing was to be canceled. I was to go ahead despite the doctor's orders, trusting God to provide the voice and the strength.

But Sunday night when I arrived at the theater, my throat still was a question mark. And by the last act, I had little voice left.

Before the last curtain I went behind some scenery in the wings to wrestle this crisis through in prayer. If my voice fails, I thought, the whole Russian trip is finished. Had I mistaken my guidance? Or was my faith being tested to the limit?

In my extremity, I saw clearly that I was to go on stage in God's strength—not mine. And at the moment I needed it, the promised help came. My tension vanished. An energy from beyond myself revitalized me. My voice was clear, strong.

Later, Lucia and our associates told me this was the finest act of *Boris* I ever had performed.

In the weeks that followed, the inflow of energy and help continued. Facing an impossible schedule of 12 performances

* II Timothy 2:1, 3

and 12 rehearsals in a 30-day tour of Russian cities, I felt the Holy Spirit guiding me, giving me strength and courage.

There were ways to show our faith in God too. Lucia and I long had made it a practice to say a quiet blessing in public restaurants before eating; we did this throughout Russia. To the Russian people assigned to help us during the tour, we found occasions to talk about Jesus Christ. We attended church services when possible and invited our Russian contacts to go with us.

During one performance in Leningrad the chorus applauded me backstage. Impulsively I told them in Russian "Give God the credit, not me." For a moment there was stunned silence, then louder applause than before. . . .

And now we were down to the last day, the final *Boris* back in Moscow with the threat of nuclear war over us all.

At 6:15 I was in my dressing room and nearly finished with my makeup. Curtain time at the Bolshoi is 6:30 P.M. Suddenly there were excited voices outside and the stage director burst in.

"Khrushchev's here."

Bill Jones and I stared at each other. Two weeks before we had both felt an odd premonition that this last *Boris* at the Bolshoi would be surrounded by unusual circumstances. How right we had been!

The first act went well. Between acts Lucia and our interpreter rushed backstage. "Jerry," she said, "are you trying to start an international incident? Khrushchev led a standing ovation for you. But you didn't acknowledge it."

"I didn't see him."

"He's in the right hand box."

I calmed them down and promised them I would find a way to acknowledge him.

The opera is set in czarist times at the turn of the century. Boris has committed murder to gain the throne. In the final scene, guilt-ridden, insane and dying, he cries out to God, "Forgive me," and then dies.

I saw a chance to inject a note of Christian hope, to show that Boris, after asking forgiveness, finds salvation and peace through Jesus Christ. So, after the words "forgive me," with radiant uplifted head as his plea is answered, Boris—as I interpreted him—cries gratefully "Oh, my God."

At previous *Boris* performances in Moscow, Kiev and Tbilisi, the Russians had responded to this additional emphasis with enthusiasm. How would Khrushchev, an avowed atheist, feel about it?

Everything built up perfectly to this climax. When the final scene came, Boris weakly then exultantly finds repentance and, dying, plunges down the stairs.

Instead of waiting for the postlude before applauding, as is customary, this audience broke all precedent by rising at this point. Pounding his hands together in front of them all was a familiar baldheaded figure.

I walked over in front of Premier Khrushchev's box and bowed.

It was a day later when I realized the significance of Khrushchev's presence at the Bolshoi that night. Papers throughout the world reported that by paying a tribute to an American singer, he was indicating the future conciliatory role his government would follow in the Cuban crisis.

If this is true and God was able to use me in this emergency, I am very grateful. For I know that God wants to reach the Russian people. He does have a plan to bring Christ into our hearts. But that plan needs obedient disciples. This means me—and you.

Two large families were struck by tragedy. One lost a mother; the other a father. Because the surviving parents believed in God's guidance, there is a happy and unusual conclusion to the story.

No Room for Selfishness

by F. L. BEARDSLEY

EVER since the Garden of Eden, I suppose, wise men have sought for an answer to the sorrow and trouble in the world. I don't consider myself particularly wise; in fact, I think of myself as a simple man. But I've found an answer. Or rather, the answer found me.

For the past 29 years I've been in the navy. During World War II, I met and married a girl I loved very much. By 1960 we had 10 children and just had built a home—a very happy home—in Carmel, California. But in November of that year, with no warning, my wife became ill. Four days later she died.

Frances' death left me stunned: I just couldn't believe it. In my meditations and my prayers, I often had tried to express to God my willingness to accept any trials or burdens He might see fit to send into my life. But certainly I hadn't dreamed of as grievous a blow as this.

My children were wonderful. The older ones took over most of the housekeeping chores and the care of the younger ones. And I tried to hide my grief from them and pray my way to some sort of acceptance of what I knew must be God's will. But I would wake up in the mornings and see Frances' shoes still in our closet and the thought would sweep over me like a black wave that nobody would ever be able to fill those shoes, nobody....

Thus the months passed. I went to work. I tried to comfort my children. But in a way, time stood still.

Then one day I had a letter from my sister, Mary Eleanor, who is Sister Superior of a parochial school in San Leandro, California. She enclosed a copy of a prayer that had been given to her by a young widow named Helen North. Helen's husband, a naval flier, had been killed in a plane crash, leaving her with eight children. She had come to enroll them in school, learned from my sister about my wife's death and asked her to send me a poem she had found helpful in her own sorrow.

I must have read that verse a thousand times. Its message did comfort me, but there was more to it than that. This may seem hard to believe in the light of what followed. Even then I had a queer feeling that something was being worked out: that beyond all my misery and loneliness there was a *plan*, and that this poem was a dim shadowy part of that plan.

Well, at first nothing happened. I wrote Mrs. North a note thanking her for the poem. No reply. While I had no intention of remarrying, what I didn't know was that Helen North had decided not to remarry. She had been deeply in love with her husband. She was not interested in corresponding with strangers.

But then tragedy came to another navy family. Dick North's best friend also was killed in a flying accident. Helen wanted to send the poem to the widow, but she could not find her copy. So she had to ask my sister to ask me to return it.

When I received this request, the strange sense of destiny, of hidden purpose—call it what you will—became stronger than ever. I sent the verse back to Mrs. North, along with a little poem from a consolation card I had received that expressed much the same idea—the idea that our vision of everything, even what seems like tragedy, is limited, and that God will work out things for the best if we only have faith and don't give in to despair. Along with these two items I sent some pictures of my children and myself. Helen says I was pretty cagey: I asked her to return the pictures so that she'd have to write me! Well, maybe, but I think I also was acting out my part in the plan.

When Helen returned the pictures, she sent a snapshot of herself. I remember staring at it and thinking how pretty she was, and how much she reminded me of Frances. Then I sat down and wrote a note inviting her to dinner. I had a hunch that she would accept. She did.

By this time, my children were almost as excited as I was. The older boys cooked an extra-fancy dinner. The girls had the house spotless. I took our guest out for a drive after dinner, and when we came back the kitchen was immaculate. "Well," said Helen, "I don't think anything should interfere with a household as well organized as this one!"

But already she knew—and I did too—that the good Lord did intend to mend our broken lives . . . by leading us to each other.

There were so many *little* things that pointed that way. That first evening I discovered that Helen not only resembled Frances in her warmth and humor and sparkle but, like Frances, had studied to be a nurse in the same Seattle hospital. Another thing: when we came back to my house for coffee, Helen looked at her cup and began to laugh. "What's so funny?" I asked her. "This pattern," she said, indicating a wheat-sheaf on the china. "It's exactly like mine!"

That's the way it went: all the jagged broken edges of our lives fitting together. Between us, we had 18 children. Yet there was no duplication of names. Actually, when we finally became engaged, it was the children who pushed us into an early marriage. They couldn't wait to adopt one another—and after we were married they did, in a proper legal ceremony before a judge, each one standing up in turn and swearing to adopt and love and cherish the other.

As you might expect, our marriage got a lot of publicity. This may have been because we sent out the wedding invitations in the children's names, all 18 of them requesting "the honour of your presence" at the ceremony. "Look at all those kids," cried one reporter when we had our picture taken after our marriage, "enough for two baseball teams!"

Hundreds of people wrote us letters. Most offered congratulations and good wishes. A few took a dim view. There were some too, who disapproved when we said we hoped we would have children of our own. Since then we have had two— a boy and a girl. So now we have 20 reasons for happiness instead of just 18. As Helen said to a newspaperwoman after the birth of our first child, "The Good Lord has blessed our family so with health and happiness that we would be pretty selfish not to welcome another little soul to share all we have."

Sure, it's a bit chaotic, but it's a joyous chaos. Everybody helps everybody; in a family as big as ours, there's no room for selfishness. Of course, there are occasional squabbles; now and then someone drops the ball. But there's always someone to pick it up. We try to fit chores to personalities. We arrange bedrooms according to congenialities.

We've learned to simplify too. Sorting out laundered socks was a real headache, for instance, until we decided to have nothing but white socks for all the girls. They go from the dryer into a big basket. Each child simply takes two that match—more or less. It works fine.

Many people seem to be interested in the mechanics of how we live. We have added three bedrooms and two baths to the five-bedroom home that Frances and I built back in 1960. We buy food in bulk whenever we can: five gallon tins of peanut butter, hundred pound sacks of sugar and flour. At a typical breakfast we'll eat maybe three dozen eggs and drink four quarts of milk. The navy, fortunately, takes care of medical expenses. Next year I'll be eligible for retirement— a 30-year-man. I hope I can find a job to supplement my retirement pay.

Often I've been asked how I keep from worrying about finances. Part of the answer is simple: we have enough with my Navy pay and Helen's service and social security benefits to live comfortably, if we manage our money intelligently. But there's a deeper reason than that. I don't worry because I trust the Power that brought us together to keep us together.

If I do my part, I know He will do His. We all believe this: it runs through the grace we say at every meal, through all our family prayers.

So, you see, I've found my answer to the problem of sorrow and trouble in the world, or perhaps—as I said before—it found me. And the answer is this: God has a reason for everything He does, even if our limited vision always can't see it.

Helen's Poem

God would not send you darkness, Dear
  If He felt you could bear the light,
But you would not cling to His guiding hand
  If the way were always bright.
And you would not care to walk by faith
  Could you always walk by sight.
'Tis true He has many an anguish
  For your sorrowful heart to bear,
Many a cruel thorn-crown
  For your tired head to wear.
He knows how few would reach Heaven at all
  If pain did not guide them there.

So He sends you the blinding darkness
  And the furnace of seven-fold heat,
'Tis the only way, believe me,
  To keep you close to His feet.
For 'tis always so easy to wander
  When our lives are glad and sweet.
Then nestle your hand in the Father's,
  And sing if you can as you go,
Your song may cheer someone behind you
  Whose courage is sinking low:
And what if your lips do quiver?
  God will love you better so.

An enemy bomber roared in for the kill. "Dive—Dive!"
came the order. As the USS Harder *crash dived, sea-*
man Plume's job was to close the conning tower hatch.
But it wouldn't close. As he struggled, death was only
minutes away.

The Sea on My Back

by George Plume

EVERY submariner lives with one terrifying fear: in a life
or death situation he might have to shut the hatch or
close a watertight door on shipmates, thus abandoning them
to death—or even suffer the same fate himself. It is something you accept and never think about.

Certainly I wasn't thinking about it as the submarine *USS
Harder* surged smoothly through the Pacific off the coast of
Japan that night in 1944. It was a routine evening on war
patrol.

Yet, after almost 22 years I can still see that night, hear it,
feel it . . . even smell it.

It was the night I *knew* there was a God: the night I experienced His *real* power and felt the indescribable wonder
of His presence.

We were slipping along at ten knots, using the hours of
darkness to recharge our batteries and air banks while patrol-
ling on the surface. Lieutenant Sam Logan was the Officer of
the Day on the bridge; a lanky whiz of a submarine officer.
The second section had relieved the watch at 2000 hours (8
P.M.) and I had taken over as quartermaster on watch.

The lookouts changed at staggered intervals, to prevent
clogging the hatchway in the event the bridge watch had to
come scrambling down. There was a man coming and going
every half hour. Up through the control room hatch, turn,

two steps over to the bridge ladder and up, using the dog-wheel on the open hatch cover as a handle to pull themselves through the manhole.

On diving, the last man off deck yanks a lanyard which brings the cover slamming down. The quartermaster must then reach up and swiftly spin the dogwheel to extend the dog levers under the hatch rim into locking position.

Except for scattered rain squalls, visibility was good that night. With the enemy coast only an hour's flying time away, our lookouts were "keeping their binoculars warm."

I had just come back down into the conning tower after a topside look around when a low-flying Japanese patrol bomber burst out of a rain squall directly behind us, roaring in for the kill.

The after-lookout screamed the warning, "Clear the bridge!"

The three lookouts came tumbling down the hatch. As quartermaster on duty I leaped for the forward corner to be ready to help Logan secure the cover.

"Dive—Dive!" bellowed through the speakers. Down came Logan, lanyard in fist, pulling the hatchcover closed.

"He's right on top of us!" Logan panted.

Then he swiveled his head and shouted to the control room, "Take her deep . . . FAST!"

With the trip latch apparently engaged, Logan spun away to jump down the control room ladder and take over the dive. There wasn't *time* to wait for a "green board" signal below, which would signify all hull openings closed. Thirty seconds from the diving alarm our decks had plunged beneath the sur-face.

In those 30 seconds my surprise at the suddenness of the bomber attack turned to utter shock as water poured down upon me from the partially closed hatch. It was stuck and would not close.

I gripped the wheel desperately, twisting back and forth with all my strength but it was immovable. Fighting water that all but blinded me, I looked over my left shoulder frantically. The helmsman had gone below, right behind Lt. Logan. I was alone.

There was a wild shout from below, "We still got a red light on the bridge hatch!"

But I couldn't answer. The descending water was a fierce torrent and I was choking as I kept up my maddened twisting and jerking at the dogwheel. Roaring in my ears, the terrible noise of the in-rushing sea increased.

A thunderous explosion sledgehammered the hull, then another, causing the *Harder* to jump convulsively. The submarine lurched sideways under the smashing blow of a third Japanese depth charge.

Then, over all the terrifying noise, I heard a heavy clang as the control room hatch slammed shut below. They had abandoned me!

Surfacing, to stop the uncontrollable flooding and save me, meant destruction for the *Harder* and death for every man on board. But I didn't think of that. I didn't think of anything. I tried to scream for help. And then I went berserk as I wrenched and tore at that jammed dogwheel. All *I* knew was that I didn't want to die—not alone in here—like this. The awful force above tore me away from the hatch mechanism, while inexorably from below, the water rose in that tiny, steel cubicle. I grabbed for the ladder. . . .

I was paralyzed by fear beyond description, a miserable fright born of complete helplessness. Yet, deep within me was the recurring thought *God help me, God help me.* It was not an uttered or conscious prayer. My panic had carried me past such intelligence. I couldn't fight. I couldn't think. I couldn't *ask* for God's intervention.

And that is when it happened.

Suddenly, through the chaos, there came a quieting and a strange feeling of reassurance. It seemed, inexplicably, that in the few moments I had left there was plenty of time. Then from the calm within me came these words which I shall hear for the rest of my days, "George, *open the hatch!*"

Without question or thought, obediently, and with strength that had left my body, I reached up. This time I turned the dogwheel *back*, to open the hatch. The dogs stuck for a heart beat then slid back, easily . . . and the monstrous sea pressure immediately pressed the hatch tight on the rim! Instantly the crushing downpour dwindled to a trickle.

Methodically, I slowly reversed the wheel and secured the hatch. The trickle stopped. I turned to look about me in wonder. Then I forged through the water to get my hand on the speaker "talk" lever and said, "It's okay. The hatch is closed. You can pump this place out now."

I've marveled for years, in thinking back, that even then, without conscious thought I did *not* say, "*I* closed the hatch." The truth bespoke itself. The hatch *was* closed, but not by me.

The conning tower was pumped out, the hatch below opened and I climbed down to rejoin my backpounding, joyful shipmates. Commander Sam Dealey, one of the finest men I shall ever know, had quiet words of commendation as the boat cruised safely in the depths.

But through all of it there was that one question . . . that single, small, lingering doubt. I turned to Lt. Logan and asked, "Did anybody down here use the speaker to tell me to open the hatch?" The looks of surprise around the control room told me what I guess I already knew. Someone else had helped me.

Today, almost 20 years later, I still feel the mighty power of that reassurance—that He is a practical, physical, ever-present God, that He has a plan for each of us. And in that knowledge I have a serene, indestructible, immovable faith which I, simply, humbly and gratefully, try to share with those about me.

*TV and recording star Anita Bryant has made five
Christmas trips with Bob Hope to entertain the Armed
Forces at bases throughout the world. Yet Anita almost gave up her career before it had begun. A story
of an important decision and how it was made.*

When You Don't Know
Which Way to Go

by Anita Bryant

EACH of us can look back on his or her life and remember
standing at some important crossroad and wondering
which direction to go.

Making a decision about a school, our field of work, or our
marriage partner are three of the most crucial choices in life.

I am 25-years-old and already have made all three decisions.
The first one came at 16. It was the toughest one I ever have
made—and I would like to share with you what it taught me
about guidance.

But first let me explain the circumstances that led up to that
crossroad. I think I was only a little more than two years old
when I first sang in public—it was in our Barnesdall, Oklahoma, church.

When I was 10-years-old we moved to Oklahoma City. I
auditioned for a local television show one day and did well
enough to be asked to come back again. I became a regular on
the program and eventually was given my own TV show
when I was only 12. Later, when Dad's work took him to
Tulsa, I sang on television there.

It was in Tulsa when I was 16 that I auditioned for Arthur
Godfrey's Talent Scouts program. When word came that I
had qualified for the finals and would be flown to New York
City to appear on a national network, I was ecstatic.

That was until some people whose opinions I respected told me they thought I would be making a mistake to go to New York.

"Why?" I asked in disbelief.

"If you go to New York," one person in our church reasoned, "you will discover that singers of popular music often are called upon to compromise their Christian position. Are you willing to toss your convictions overboard for a career?"

In the few weeks before I was scheduled to appear in New York, I wrestled with the decision night and day. Would I be deserting Christ if I pursued such a career? Wasn't it assuming a lot to think this one show would lead to a full-time career? But even if it did, wasn't I strong enough to resist these temptations people were telling me about?

My preparation for the New York date was going badly. I lost sleep and worried a lot. Finally, one night in my room, I defiantly told the dresser mirror, "I am going to New York. No one's going to stand in my way. I'll walk there if I must."

I stood firm with that decision until about a week before I was supposed to leave. One night after singing at a church revival meeting, I wavered. Singing at revivals is something I have done since I was a youngster, and I still enjoy doing the old Gospel hymns best of all.

That night after I arrived home, the words of the hymn, *I'll Go Where You Want Me to Go,* kept revolving in my mind.

I'll go where You want me to go, dear Lord,
O'er mountain, or plain, or sea;
I'll say what You want me to say, dear Lord,
I'll be what You want me to be.

Was New York and a singing career Christ's choice for me or was it just an ego-stuffed little girl's will holding sway? The answer didn't come easily. Finally, I did what I should have done at the start: talk my dilemma over with Mom. I had tried to keep my oscillating emotions to myself because Mother and Dad both were proud of me, and I knew they both were anticipating my appearance on the Godfrey show.

Mother was to fly to New York with me and be my talent scout!

After I told Mother what some of the church people had advised, and how confused I was, she made a statement that I shall never forget as long as I live.

"Anita, always listen to advice," Mother said. "Weigh the facts with an open mind. Then sincerely pray for God's guidance. But always remember, don't ask God to bless your wishes; rather that you do with your life what *He* wishes."

That night I prayed a different prayer. Not "Tell me it's all right to go to New York, Lord," but "show me what You want and *I'll do it.*"

This was the prayer God wanted to hear, for suddenly a great burden was lifted from my shoulders, and soon I felt relaxed and reassured of His love. A serenity encompassed me and I knew I was to go ahead. I never have felt more certain of a decision in my life.

But in retrospect, I know that what was important was not going to New York or staying home, but that I had fortified myself from within by putting my life in God's hands.

So I went to New York, appeared on the Godfrey show and my career was in motion—a career which in nine years has taken me many times around the world and given me thousands of opportunities to witness for Christ.

There have been many other decisions, but Mother's advice about seeking God's guidance *always* has been the answer! Recently, I saw some of the things Mom told me in a list of steps on guidance attributed to Henry Drummond who said when facing a decision you should do the following:

First, think about the facts.

Second, pray.

Third, talk to wise people, but don't regard their judgment as final.

Fourth, beware of the direction of your own will, but don't be too afraid of it. God never unnecessarily thwarts a man's nature and likings.

Fifth, make a step in the direction God seems to be leading —even if it's a small step. For doing God's will in small things is the best preparation for doing it in great things.

Finally, when decisions and action are necessary, go ahead —boldly, confidently, trustingly.

I don't know if Mother ever read Henry Drummond's list, but she knew this truth and gave it to me when I most needed it.

In the years ahead, when my children turn to me for help, I pray that God will give me the wisdom to direct them properly. I hope they will find meaning in my mother's advice. If they do this, they can make any decision—boldly, confidently, trustingly.

Here's the story of how one of America's outstanding medical missionaries was led to an unusual mission— the treatment of lepers in India.

Doorway to a New Life

by Dr. Paul Brand

HOW does a person receive "a call from God" to undertake a particular task in this world? Those who have received one know that the experience is like walking through a door into a new life. Yet many seek the door and never find it, while others walk in without ever knowing that they have passed through. The latter must surely have applied to me.

Back in the fall of 1946 I boarded a ship bound to India from England. In my pocket was a cablegram which had uprooted my plans for a medical career in England and started me across the continent in pursuit of what seemed a rather unattractive duty.

"You must come at once," the cable had read. "We need you here desperately. Signed—Cochrane." Dr. Robert C. Cochrane, then head of the Christian Medical College at Vellore, India, is a great missionary-statesman. I had never met him personally though he had known my mother. If Cochrane said he needed me I felt it my duty to respond.

Arriving in India, I told Dr. Cochrane good-naturedly, "You have bullied me into coming. All right, I'll stay, but only for a year, to see you through this shortage on your teaching staff."

Because of my wartime surgical experience in rehabilitation I was asked to instruct in Orthopedics.

One day while visiting a nearby hospital devoted to treating leprosy, I stopped to examine one patient whose hands showed the paralyzed, claw-like deformity typical of the dis-

111

ease. The hand had lost all sense of feeling and the fingers were curled tightly against the palm.

"What is being done," I asked one of the hospital staff, "to rehabilitate these deformities?"

I was absolutely astounded to learn that no rehabilitation was considered possible for leprosy patients. At that time perhaps two out of every 100 persons in that part of India were in some way suffering from leprosy, and many, like this patient, showed the paralysis and deformation caused by the disease. They were outcasts, considered incurable, and permitted to beg, or just shift for themselves. Up to that time leprosy patients were not admitted to any general hospital, even Vellore had no ward for them. A few homes and special hospitals existed to give them some care, love, and a place to stay when families would no longer accept them.

Curiously I pried open the fingers of the patient's hand, placed my own hand in his and said, "Clasp my hand, squeeze!" Immediately the patient's fingers closed on mine in a grip like a steel spring. Long nails cut into my flesh.

I drew my hand back in pain. And then suddenly I experienced a wonderful thrill. I realized that the patient's hand still retained life, and *some* muscles that worked.

Excited by the discovery, I discussed the possibilities with our research staff. These doctors, biochemists and laboratory technicians began making extensive tests of the damaged arms and legs of leprosy patients. The results showed: nerves responsible for the sense of touch were dead, some muscles were damaged, others untouched. Most important, the deformed limbs showed no traces of live leprosy bacilli. It was a clue.

About this time a patient saw me trying, unsuccessfully, to turn a key in a rusty lock. Offering to help he took the key and turned it hard—the lock opened. As the smiling patient proudly handed the key back to me, I saw that the flesh of his fingers was torn to the bone. Apparently he did not realize the great pressure he exerted because the nerves were dead and he had felt no pain.

Following this discovery, we devised tests to measure the pressure used by patients in walking and working. Results showed that it was the use of strength, with no feeling of pain, that did most of the damage. Torn flesh, from walking on sharp objects, cuts to limbs, and burns on unfeeling hands, all resulted in simple infections which, because they could not be felt, became serious, sometimes turning to gangrene and ending in permanent damage to the body. *This* was a most important discovery: the leprosy bacilli, itself, was not the deforming agent.

And then we began to try for rehabilitation. First we operated on hands. Tendons from undamaged and little-used muscles in a patient's arm were grafted to the tendons of the fingers, to provide a new source for activation. The graft took, and for the first time in years a patient was able to open his hand and grasp the tools and articles of daily life.

Since that day we have performed this operation on hundreds of others. Each day brought new challenge, new progress, new excitement.

My original contract lengthened into two, three, four years. Gradually I realized I had at last found my "call." Truly, I believe, I was one of those who had to be literally "pushed through the door" to the new life.

Recently I have been lecturing on the work which we are doing in Vellore. In Switzerland I met a group of young people who were studying for the missionary field. One of them asked:

"How can I *know* when God has 'called' me?"

My reply was to tell them my own story!

Born in India, of missionary parents, I was sent to England to complete my schooling. Undecided about a career I knew only that I wanted to work where I could be of service to people. So I prayed, earnestly, for God's guidance in the matter.

While waiting, though I did not feel called to follow my parents as missionaries, or to return to India, I joined a building firm where I learned carpentry, plumbing, architecture and some agriculture. Then I took a course in first aid. It was this that made me decide to study medicine.

I had just finished medical school when World War II cut across my life, and I found myself drafted to remain in London, caring for air raid victims. Much of the surgery I performed was concerned with the rehabilitation of shattered hands, arms, legs and faces. Little did I see, then, how God was quietly preparing me for His call. At war's end I had decided to settle myself in London for practice when Dr. Cochrane's cable arrived.

Today, I told my young listeners in Switzerland, there seem to be increasing numbers of persons anxious to receive "a call from God" to guide their life's work. But often some of these dedicated people use the excuse of "waiting for the call" to avoid shouldering the responsibility of routine duty which stand immediately before them. It is too bad, for of this I am certain, God *will* find us, and make His will known, wherever we are. The story of John Parthasarthy is a beautiful example.

John had not only the claw hands of a leper but he was blinded as well. The old man came one day to ask that we perform the tendon-graft operation on his hands. Now, there are literally thousands of persons in India with this deformity so we have tried to select those who, when healed, could be taught a trade and returned to useful service in their communities.

"What work would you do?" we asked him. "Though we can open your fingers, we cannot return the sense of touch—and you are blind."

"I once played the organ," replied John Parthasarthy. "I have faith that I will make beautiful music again."

With great misgivings, but unable to resist John's pleadings, we operated on John's hands. Weeks later, when the incisions had healed and the claws returned to a semblance of normalcy, we led John to the organ in the chapel.

John's nerveless fingers caressed the keys, his sightless head bent to one side as though listening, then the hands moved—

and discord filled the silence. Without the sense of touch the fingers would not obey.

Unhappily, we drew away, leaving John to his broken dream. He tried a few more chords, without success, then paused—and began again. This time the melody mended, the stray notes fluttered, then fell into place and the lovely strains of an old hymn, *Jesus Shall Reign Wherever The Sun* filled the room with a glorious sound. John's sightless face was a beautiful thing to see. We will never forget it.

John is now in the sanitarium at Hyderabad. But every afternoon there he plays the organ, bringing cheer and inspiration to the patients and staff. How glad we are now, that God inclined our hearts to have faith in John's faith.

Faith—it is such a simple and beautiful word. I often look about me here at Vellore and think: the work being done in this medical college is a most remarkable example of faith. For here we are striving to live the compassion that Christ taught—and finding that it passes all barriers of individual belief.

Vellore is a tremendous cooperative venture linking scores of Protestant denominations. And the students at this College training to become doctors, surgeons, nurses, and technicians represent many races and come from many countries in S.E. Asia, and although not all have personal religious convictions yet we are striving, together, to experience and to express the transforming power of Christ in our individual lives as we work together to help our fellow men.

When a man quits a good job to take a position that pays little and has no security, he is either a fool or an idealist. Russell Cone was no fool. He loved dogs and felt guided into a career that could save lives.

"Man Gone, Daniel!"

by RUSSELL K. CONE

IN the gray dawn of June 26, 1957, Mrs. Libby kept saying: "All night, he's been out there all night."

I was standing at the door of a little vacation cabin on Dinky Creek, 6,000 feet up in the High Sierras. The Libbys' three-year-old son had been missing since one P.M. the afternoon before. Forest rangers had started searching within one hour. At midnight the sheriff had phoned me at my home 150 miles away and told me to get there fast with my best bloodhound. I chose my old veteran, Daniel Boone.

Now I asked Mrs. Libby for something her son had worn the day before. "Pick it up with silverware so you don't confuse the scent."

I opened the rear of the station wagon and Daniel Boone lumbered down, sneezing and yawning in the cool morning air. I snapped the long tracking leash to his harness. Mrs. Libby came out with a small brown shoe held between two forks.

"He took his shoes off just before he went out. Just think, barefoot all this time. . . ."

I held the shoe to Daniel's nose. "Now, Daniel," I said, "Randy Scott Libby is out there in those hills and I want you to take me to him."

That was for Mrs. Libby. In Daniel's long ear I spoke the command I had trained him to understand.

"Man gone! Man gone, Daniel!"

In an instant Daniel was all business. His tail tensed, his nose quivered, he dashed from side to side of the narrow dirt road.

For six hours we zig-zagged through that wilderness country. Then we came to the foot of an almost perpendicular rock slide. I looked at Daniel incredulously: could a three-year-old have climbed it? But Daniel had already started up, sending a river of sand and rock down on me. We struggled up, panting and slipping until at last we reached a broad plateau.

Faster and faster Daniel tugged and then he dove into a clump of manzanita. A little boy was there.

"Hi, Randy," I said.

Looking at Mrs. Libby's radiant face late that afternoon, I thought: I almost gave up this work with bloodhounds. I almost kept a good job as appliance service-man for Sears-Roebuck; I almost let doubt talk me out of God's will for my life. . . .

A message had come for me while we were searching for Randy. A little girl was missing in Yosemite National Park. Please hurry.

Yosemite was a hundred miles away; Daniel and I set out for it at once. As we sped over the miles, my mind went back a few years. I tried to recall when I had first suspected the job that God had in mind for me. I think God has a certain job for every person on earth. The first trick is to discover what it is. The second is to trust it. Mine, it seemed to me, was especially hard to believe. A dog handler? It seemed so off-beat.

And yet, how else could I explain the things that had happened? In 1949 my wife and I had bought four and a half acres of trees and undergrowth in the Santa Cruz Mountains and hauled our house-trailer there.

"You know, Thanis," I said to her, "We could have a dog up here."

"What kind of dog?" asked Thanis.

"A bloodhound," I said. I'd never wanted one before; I'd

never even seen one. But suddenly it had to be a bloodhound.

"I wouldn't know where to look for one," the man in the pet shop told me. "There aren't more than four or five hundred in the whole country." But I kept looking. When at last I heard of a puppy for sale for $100, I bought him sight unseen. A hundred dollars—when we were saving our money in quarters and dimes! It was hard to explain to Thanis but harder to explain to myself.

We named the dog Daniel Boone. I'd had him about a month and was walking him one day when Sheriff Hendrick's car pulled up.

"Is that a bloodhound?" he shouted as I hurried over to him. The sheriff was almost shaking with excitement. "Is he trained?"

I looked at him blankly. "Trained for what?"

"Tracking! Trailing people!"

"Why bloodhounds haven't tracked people since 'Liza crossed the ice!"

"That's true," he said, deadly earnest, "because people don't train them much for it any more. For the past 60 days we've looked for a man. Found him yesterday—what was left of him. A bloodhound might have taken us to him in a couple of days."

That was the beginning. There was no one to teach us how to train a bloodhound, so Thanis and I devised our own system with a can of dog food and one of Thanis' slippers. In time, when I thought we were ready, I phoned Sheriff Hendrick. Four days later he called back. A 77-year-old lady was lost on Madonna Mountain. It took us five hours to find her. One look at her face as Daniel and I emerged from the trees and I knew I was a bloodhound man for life.

In six years we found more than 100 lost persons, from a 92-year-old man to a 22-month-old baby. I bought more dogs. The more I learned about them the more I saw the hand of God on these homely, ungainly creatures: many breeds of dog can follow a trail two or three hours old; three separate times my bloodhounds have picked up a trail five *days* old.

When the search was for a child I would tell his parents my favorite Bible story. In it Jesus describes a shepherd's joy when he finds a sheep that was lost. *Even so,* He says, *it is not the will of your Father which is in heaven, that one of these little ones should perish.**

I sincerely believed that this was God's work. And yet, it complicated my poor human existence so! My boss at Sears-Roebuck was understanding and let me off whenever there was a search. But of course they couldn't pay me for that time; one month I was gone 11 of 22 working days.

Sheriff's offices sometimes paid my transportation to and from the search scene. But I was buying $90 worth of dog food a month. As for the families of the people we found, I couldn't ask them for help. Deep joy just doesn't express itself in dollars and cents, and shouldn't have to. But meanwhile our first son had come. Another child was on the way. It seemed to me that I had to choose between being "practical" and being Christian.

Then one night I sat bolt upright in bed. If this was God's work, why not trust Him?

The very next morning I walked boldly into the front office of The Calo Pet Food Company in Oakland and asked them to sponsor me. They did. From that moment on I have spent full time working with these dogs, not only searching, but breeding them and teaching others to track with them.

Overnight, people everywhere seemed to know about our dogs. Even the Air Force called: "We'll fly you any place you can't get by car." Nowadays we fly over 1,000 miles to many searches.

And whenever the dogs arrive, new hope lights up sleepless faces. It was that way when Daniel and I arrived at Yosemite that June night. The little girl, Shirley Ann Miller, had been missing for 32 hours and searchers were now pouring back to Bridal Veil Falls campground; searching at night

* Matthew 18:14

was out of the question in that rugged terrain. Men who had not slept for two nights set out eagerly with us at dawn on June 27. Shirley's silent, pale-lipped father brought along a map showing the areas already searched. All day we pushed back through incredibly treacherous country, keeping in touch by radio with the other search groups.

Late in the afternoon we reached the foot of a tall ridge. The map showed that both sides of it had been searched. Daniel wanted to climb it. It looked like a waste of precious time; the whole face of the ridge was clearly visible from below. How could she be up there?

Arduously, we followed Daniel. Twilight came as we reached the top. There was just enough light to see that what showed on the map as a single ridge was actually two ridges. Between them lay a small pear-shaped valley. But another dark night was upon us. We tried not to look at Mr. Miller as we made camp.

Next morning before sunrise all 200 searchers had gathered on top of that ridge. With Daniel in the lead we started down into the valley. It was almost noon when we came out of a thicket of chaparral. On a log in front of us sat the blondest little girl I'd ever seen.

The men rushed to her, picked her up, hugged her, wrapped her in blankets. For a moment I hung back. I was offering up a prayer—a prayer of repentance that I had ever doubted that God Almighty would fail to provide our few material needs as long as we were seeking His will.

Then Shirley saw Daniel. "Hello, doggie," she said. "Who brought you here?"

The men laughed. "He brought us here, honey," her father said.

I didn't laugh though. I think it was a good question. I kept thinking about it as 200 men, one dog and one little girl started back to camp. I kept thinking I knew the answer.

The desire to be noble—even for God—can lead to selfishness and stubbornness. Surprising events happened one day when this nurse took a searingly honest look at herself.

Where Does God Want Me?

by ANN MOODY

THERE is a rose above the mirror in my car this morning as I drive about town. I am a visiting nurse, and there are many other things in the car: charts, instruments, medical supplies. But it is the rose which tells a story. . . .

I was in the eighth grade when I first heard about the disease and suffering in a far-off country called India. Right then I made up my mind that I would be a nurse in that land. God had given me so much that I longed to do something for Him.

To some it might not have seemed that I had been given much. Our tiny farm in the mountains of Eastern Kentucky grew barely enough to feed my parents and their seven children. But youngsters, when they are loved, are not aware of these things. Our home life was happy and deeply Christian.

In 1934 I graduated as a registered nurse and went on to a school of missions to study Indian languages. I was ready for God's service! But the call to India didn't come. It was then the height of the Depression: rather than sending out new missionaries, many churches, lacking funds, were recalling ones already in the field.

For a while I was a public health nurse in the Kentucky hills where I'd grown up; later I did nursing work in other parts of this country. The years passed. I knew that the board of my church did not send out new missionaries after the age of 35. And so at 36, still puzzled over God's refusal to use me in India, I met a fine man and we were married.

And now a new work for God seemed to unroll before me. Next to nursing in India, my second ideal always had been a true Christian marriage. But this was 1942 and Dwight had enlisted in the Marines. Two months after we married, my husband was in combat on Guadalcanal.

It was three years before he came home, badly disabled and frighteningly changed. For a year after his return he stayed in a government hospital recovering from injuries. When at last the hospital released him, the affectionate, kind, Christ-centered man I had married had disappeared. Instead a silent stranger had moved into my home, a man who had stopped praying, a man who believed in nothing.

This was not the marriage God wanted! How hard I tried to make Dwight see this! I wept, pleaded, scolded. Our home life became a nightmare, my daily round of nursing visits a welcome escape.

One Saturday night Dwight did not come home. I knelt beside my bed for my nightly prayers. "Dear God," I began as I always did, "how can I make Dwight see the truth? How can I convince him that I'm right—I mean, that You're right. . . ." My voice trailed off. The truth which I had asked for Dwight seemed suddenly very close. But it was an ugly truth, something I didn't want to look at. God was showing me a willfull, stubborn, self-centered woman.

In all the years I had sought to serve God, had I ever asked first, "What do You want, dear Lord?"

Standing up, walking fitfully about the room, I forced myself to look at my cherished dream of India. It had been daring, heroic, sacrificial. "But oh, Lord," I whispered, "was it ever Your dream?"

My marriage: I made myself look at this dream too, in the burning light of God's truth. Was it possible that I had made the ideal of Christian marriage a wall between me and the actual flesh-and-blood person God had given me?

The desire to be noble, especially to be noble for God,

dies hard. It was early morning before my outraged feelings and hurt pride were quiet enough to hear that small tender Voice telling me, "No, no heroics, no distant places, no perfect marriage. My work for you is nearer at hand, at your neighbor's sickbed and with the very human man who needs you."

I knelt beside the bed again and used the words of Christ which I had repeated so often but understood so little. *Father . . . not my will, but Thine, be done.**

Dwight came home a while later, but he didn't come into the bedroom. I went to the living room and saw that he had fallen asleep on the sofa. As I laid a blanket across him I was conscious of really looking at him, perhaps for the very first time. And looking, I saw not a stubborn, uncaring man, but a badly hurt one. I thought suddenly how much I loved him and how much he needed to know it.

Monday morning I set out in my car on my familiar round of patients' homes, but it was a different journey! Across every threshold God's real work stood ready for me to do. My first call each morning was always to the home of an enormously obese woman who needed injections for her overworked heart. She was a sharp-tongued, complaining person and I usually made my visits there as brief as possible.

This morning, though, looking at the huge form propped in the chair where she spent her days, I thought with a sudden pang, "Why, she's lonely!" I took her pulse as usual, then on an impulse continued to hold her hand when I had finished, just pressing it with mine. She looked up at me and, to my amazement, tears began to roll down the great creases of her cheeks. With the tears came a flood of bitter words: her husband traveled too much; her daughter never came to see her.

One little act of compassion had opened a door. Over the weeks she poured out a story which began to be clear even to her: a story of her own demands and unreasonableness which had driven both husband and daughter away. I con-

* Luke 22:42

tributed nothing to this self-awakening except an ear to listen. From new closeness with her family, it was not far to wanting it with God. I began to read favorite Bible passages to her and pray aloud with her. At last this woman who had hated "churchy people" asked a minister to come instruct her and she was received into the church.

I mention this experience because it was the first, but there are so many more! There is the elderly couple facing separation in different welfare homes, the diabetic learning a new way of life, the crippled child struggling with fear as well as braces. What a miracle that through the humble medium of medicine they may glimpse the Great Physician who heals not only our bodies but our souls. Turn me down as a missionary? God gave me so much work to do, once I stopped insisting on my own way, that the days seem too short to hold the joy and meaning in them.

As for my husband, once I stood out of God's light, he found his way back from his war experience in a remarkable way. He has a regular job now and teaches Bible class. But, to me, the most meaningful thing is the flower. Each morning as I get into the car to start my rounds, I find a fresh rose above the mirror. It is the gesture of a man in love with his wife, and it delights me, as it would any woman.

But to me it says even more. It says that God is able to bring beauty from us wherever we are; that a life given to His service can flower as fully in Oregon as in India. That is why, in my heart, Lord, I lay the rose at Your feet.

A wise man once said, "Too often people call on God for guidance and then hang up the receiver in His face." This story by a Guideposts roving editor, written while he and his family were in Uganda, Africa, was an adventure in an unusual sense of the word—it was an adventure in trust.

Our Year of Discovery

by JOHN L. SHERRILL

THE car gave a violent lurch and came to a stop. "What was that?" the children called out. My wife Tib looked down into the draw below us. "I think we've gone through the bridge," she said.

It was true. As soon as I stepped out onto the narrow log-and-dirt bridge which straddled the 15-foot deep gully, I saw that our rear wheel had fallen through the rotten timbers up to the axle.

Tib and the children ran back to solid ground. Gingerly, I jacked up the car, intending to fill the hole, then let the wheel back down and drive off. But searching produced nothing but small twigs and pebbles which fell right through when I put them in the hole. Nowhere in this bush country were there rocks or logs big enough to fill the hole.

Since we had come to Africa we never had been in clearer need of help. We were still 15 miles from the village where we were to spend the night. Behind us were miles of bush; all afternoon we had met one car on the winding dirt track we were following in this little-traveled district of Uganda. A storm was building up over the Nile; night would be upon us in half an hour. We couldn't stay in the car for fear the rest of the bridge might go. We couldn't stay out of the car:

this was lion country. A mile back we had passed a fresh hippo carcass.

And so in this emergency we did what we had done frequently since arriving in Africa: we asked God for guidance. We used a principle we had used before, thanking Him ahead of time for the answer which we confidently expected would come. Then we simply waited.

And in the strange calm which follows this attitude, the answer was there, simple and perfect. I got the spare tire, slipped it beneath the jacked-up wheel and found that it straddled the hole exactly. I let the car back down and, to the cheers of the children, drove off. Just in time, too, for with night came the first wave of a driving tropical storm.

Now it would be possible, of course, to say that we had not received guidance at all, we were just using common sense. A year ago I would have been inclined to agree. But not today. For our African year, from beginning to end, was above all else an intriguing experience of guidance. In Africa where so much was strange, we found ourselves minute-by-minute asking God's direction. And living like this month after month we discovered four principles that make His directions clearer to hear.

The *first*, which we used in the anxious moment on the bridge, is thanksgiving *before* the guidance is received. There is something about a grateful heart that crowds out fear and quiets the mind to receive instructions.

A *second* principle which we found helping us again and again can be summed up in four words: pay attention to coincidence.

Among the many letters we wrote to people in Africa before we went there was one to Dr. Morton Hanna. I had known Dr. Hanna when I was a small boy growing up in Louisville; to me he was a name my parents mentioned more than a face. But when I learned that Dr. Hanna was teaching at a Kenya seminary, I wrote asking if we could visit him.

Back came a letter; he was sorry but he was returning home just a few days before our arrival. It seemed an indication that we were not meant to do anything at this particular seminary and we dismissed it from our thoughts.

On our way to Africa we passed through Rome. One evening we went to the opera in a small, out-of-the-way theater. A few rows away sat a man who looked familiar. By the end of the second act the mystery was too much for me: I went over and introduced myself. It was Dr. Hanna, passing through Rome on his way home from Kenya!

The more we thought about it, the more we were impressed with the coincidence of this meeting, in this little out-of-the-way theater, 4,000 miles from the place we had intended.

Next day we had lunch together and spent the entire time talking about the need at St. Paul's Seminary for a course in the kind of religious journalism Guideposts represents. In the end we did go to St. Paul's to teach a seminar which was one of the most fascinating and fruitful of our African experiences.

At other times it was harder to see the indications of God's will. Whenever it was a question of deciding between alternatives, we borrowed a technique from the Old Testament which constitutes the *third* principle we learned about guidance. The soldier Gideon, wanting to know God's choice, placed a lamb's fleece on the ground, as a sign to him.* "Putting a fleece before the Lord," this practice is called by people who use it, and we had not been in Africa long before an occasion arose when some such clear direction was needed.

In our case the choice was between working for the bulk of the year in Nairobi or Kampala. We could have worked on a Christian newspaper in either town. Personally, we leaned toward Kampala, in Uganda, but the drawback to living there was housing. With embassy staffs pouring into the new capital, houses in Kampala were scarce and very expensive.

* Judges 6:36-40

There was a missionary guest house in Kampala where we could stay for one month. And so this was the fleece that we put before the Lord. If we were intended to stay in Uganda, let us, before the month was over, find an adequate house, at a rent we could afford.

We started work at *New Day*, the Church of Uganda newspaper in Kampala. Regularly we called on real estate brokers and searched the newspaper for house ads: nothing. We even asked help from the American Embassy without any luck.

Twenty-five days passed, 28. The time was almost at hand when we would have to leave the guest house, and Uganda. Both Tib and I found that we were sorry.

On the next to last day, I paid one final visit to the American Embassy. "Still nothing?" I asked. The officer looked at me for a long time.

"Well," he said, "we do have one house ourselves. I've never told you about it. It's so far out of town."

We went to see it, and knew instantly that this was our house. It was exactly the right size for our family, sat on a hill overlooking Lake Victoria, and to New Yorkers used to suburban commuting, the half hour trip into town seemed downright homelike. We made a suggestion. If the Embassy would let us live in the house for the Guideposts' budget, we would take care of it for them, and while they'd be losing money it wouldn't be as much as if the house stood empty.

That evening, the 29th of our 30-day "fleece," there was a note waiting for us at the guest house. The house was ours.

The *fourth* principle came much more naturally: it has to do with the value of an impulse. Since we'd arrived in Africa, Tib had wanted to teach English in an African primary school —if possible, one where missionaries had not been teaching before. This, however, proved a problem. There were plenty of schools but they were mission schools where the children already spoke English.

When we first moved to the house on the hill, we'd stop for

the children along our daily route to give them a lift—but we soon learned why no one else did. We'd stop for one child and a dozen would crowd in before we could get the door closed, making driving almost impossible.

So we were no longer doing this when one day, driving home from the newspaper office, my eyes were drawn to two African children, a girl about 13 and a boy around 11, walking along the road lagging slightly behind a group of about a dozen children. To this day I am puzzled by the strength of the impulse to stop and pick up these two children.

When we reached the foot of our hill I stopped. "This is as far as I go," I said. "I'm afraid you'll have to walk the rest of the way."

"But," said the boy, in delightful English, "this rest of the way is accomplished." He pointed down a track leading through the banana plantation to a low mud-walled building.

"I am Ddungu," he told me proudly, "son of Muwanga, who is master of this school."

"School?" I said. "I'd like to meet your father."

And a few minutes later I was shaking hands with Muwanga himself. His was not a missionary school, he told me. The son and daughter I had picked up already had graduated and now walked to a secondary school in town. He had 100 students, and one other teacher besides himself. Yes, they tried to teach English—it is Uganda's national language—but neither he nor his teacher spoke it well. Yes, he would very much like to meet my wife.

And so began Tib's nine-month teaching experience. It still seems remarkable to me that out of all the children who troop along the road to Kampala, I should have stopped for the very two who held the key to Tib's teaching assignment.

And now that we are home again, do we still need God's guidance? We think we do. We think He has a perfect plan for each day and we try to discover it wherever we are. We will watch for the coincidence which, as someone has said, is "God's universe caught in the act of rhyming." We will dare to ask for signs. We will be more responsive to our impulses— provided we can imagine Christ's yielding to them. They may be nudges from an insight beyond our own. And above all else we will thank God, thank Him before we see the pattern, knowing that though we can see it only dimly, it is there waiting for us in all its perfection.

Here's a young man who saw life and matters of faith as being as orderly and logical as everything he was learning in his Yale University physics class. Then events took place which caused his carefully structured attitude toward life to crumble.

Logic Is Not Enough

by ROBERT MORRIS

IT was January of my sophomore year at Yale when Jim dropped his bombshell into our group.

There were 20 of us in the Yale Christian Fellowship, undergraduates getting together in the evenings. Here, on our own, we thrashed out the great questions of God and faith. We came from many Christian backgrounds: fundamentalist and liberal, Presbyterian and Roman Catholic, drawn together by a common search for reality.

Some of us had been afraid that what we learned in college would make it hard to go on believing. Instead, we'd worked out together concepts of God as logical as anything we were hearing in physics class. It was very comforting.

It was comforting, that is, until that first meeting after the Christmas holidays, my sophomore year.

There always had been a few boys who wanted to discuss healing and guidance and other things that had no place in intelligent religion, but we wrote them off as non-intellectuals. Jim was another matter: the best student in the group, very careful about his facts . . . feeling intellectually superior to him was just out of the question.

While he was home on Christmas vacation, Jim told us, Agnes Sanford had come to his parish church to hold a healing service.

Among the people attending was a crippled woman Jim

had known all his life. She suffered from deterioration of the discs in her spine, and had come to the service in a wheel-chair. At the close of Mrs. Sanford's prayer, Jim said, the woman sprang up out of the wheelchair and literally ran up the aisle, healed. "I saw it with my own eyes."

There was total silence. Objections crowded my mind: it had been a psychosomatic illness; the cure wouldn't last; it was a fake. But mostly I was angry with Jim. We'd spent a long time working out a religion acceptable to college students and Jim had knocked the whole thing over! But before I had a chance to speak, another boy was on his feet, talking rapidly.

"Something happened while I was home too," he said. Then he went on to relate how just before the holidays his mother had the feeling while she was at prayer that God wanted her to write to a neighbor's daughter, who was away at college. She was to caution the girl about the boy she was dating, because it seemed that God had other plans for her.

"My mother had had these 'messages' from God before," he said, "but she really fought this one. It seemed like the worst kind of meddling in someone else's life. Besides, she knew nothing about the girl's social life—maybe she wasn't dating at all." But at last his mother had given in and written the letter. Back came a lengthy reply. How had she known? The girl had told no one about a promise she'd made a certain boy in desperation, because she had no one to talk to, no one who cared. Now she realized that God cared!

Jim looked around the circle of faces. "How are you going to explain that letter?"

We looked away awkwardly. Somehow no one felt like explaining, though it was usually what we did best. I walked back to my room beneath the cold midnight sky, profoundly frightened. Was it possible that all this time the God we had spoken of so freely was not a principle—but a person? Did He move into situations to change them?

No! God didn't *do* things—that was the kind of superstition that had Indians out dancing for rain. Prayer didn't change facts, it changed people. Prayer brought our minds and wills into harmony with Divine Mind, operating serenely and remotely above us. "Oh God!" I pondered, "how close are You?"

A small incident the following day helped answer this question. Late in the afternoon, I felt a sudden and sharp need to talk to an upper-classman, a friend named George, about some of these spiritual questions. The only time I could see him was from five to six p.m., before dinner. But I knew that George always was in the library during this period.

"Lord, I don't believe You're interested in small matters like this, and I'm embarrassed to ask for help because it seems like testing You."

Yet I called George's room. His roommate answered. No, George was in the library.

Feeling a little foolish and almost relieved, I hung up. God was firmly placed back in His inaccessible heaven.

A few minutes later the phone rang. It was George. "My roommate told me you called," he said. On an impulse he had returned to his room.

Perhaps it was coincidence—that this once in the entire year George had broken a pattern. But our conversation that night at a small table in the rear of the dining hall was tremendously important to me—so important that coincidence hardly seemed to account for it.

As I stumblingly progressed toward a more personal relationship with God in the weeks that followed, I soon stopped making an obstacle of specific intervention. For what confronted me instead was the Specific Himself, a God so large He needed every detail of every life in which to express Himself.

Nor was I the only one experiencing these things. Many others in the Yale Christian Fellowship were being led to the same encounter with a God whose laws expressed Him but did not bind Him. No longer did we discuss God: now we spoke to Him, we listened for His answer, we asked His help.

And to our amazement, His help was granted. During my junior year a local minister many of us had admired was rushed to the hospital with double pneumonia compounded by pleurisy. The entire Fellowship assembled and this group, who a year earlier would have exchanged scholarly insights about the relation of prayerful states of mind to healing, spent the evening on our knees, begging God's touch on a man's chest.

By morning there had been a dramatic improvement in his chest. The next night we concentrated on the lowering of his fever; we learned later that it broke as we were praying. Now someone suggested the ancient technique of the novena: nine days of prayer with a single object. So for nine days we concentrated on a rapid healing. Doctors had predicted he would be in bed three months: on the ninth and last day of the novena the clergyman walked out of the hospital ready to resume his ministry.

Nor was this the only kind of prayer He honored. The healing of a good and kind man had not been hard to ask; we were shyer about requests that concerned our personal lives. But as we grew bolder in His love we found ourselves face-to-face with a God who cared even about the pleasures in our lives.

By my senior year I had decided that I wanted to become a minister in the service of the God I was discovering. But this meant seminary after college, and that meant another summer selling underwear. From Yale I'd gone home to Detroit each summer to take a job in the men's underclothing section of a big department store to earn tuition for the following fall.

Then, just before I graduated, I was offered a job as counselor at a boys' summer camp in New Hampshire. But the top salary offered by the camp was $350: to start seminary I needed $500. I told the camp director I needed more; only to God did I rather shamefacedly mention the exact amount.

The end of the year came. Goodbys were finished at Yale.

I stood for a long time in the doorway of my room, reluctant to leave it for the last time. Then I started down the hall for the airport and Detroit. The phone back in my room rang while I was still in earshot. It was the camp director: would I consider $500?

And so I went to New Hampshire, to a summer of mountains and white birches—but to so much more besides. To the God described by Evelyn Underhill as "higher than our highest yet more inward than our most inward part."

That God is high my generation has no trouble believing: we were raised on space flight and lightyear distances and whirling galaxies. But that the God of all this universe should care for each one of us, down to the smallest details of our lives, we find incredible. It is when this incredible caring reveals itself as the basic power shaping our lives that we are challenged to faith, to personal commitment—trusting that God is "for us." We are then challenged to actions which can convey that same specific caring to those around us.

*Here is wisdom distilled from a great American's half
century of service to mankind. Millions of people have
been helped by this challenge and plan to bring God
into your everyday life.*

Eight Ways God Can Guide Your Life

by Dr. E. Stanley Jones

SO many people say they want, but cannot find the will
of God for their lives. Why is this so hard? Perhaps for
two reasons: we want God's guidance in some things, but not
in all things. But God will not guide us under those circumstances. He cannot be called in for advice in certain things
when our lives are not controlled by Him in all things. God
is God, and not our lackey; He will be Lord of all, or not
Lord at all.

At the very center of guidance then, is self-surrender to
God. Not merely your plans surrendered to God, but *you*
surrendered to God.

I find that God can guide us in eight ways:

I. *Through the life and teaching of Jesus as contained in
the Scriptures.*

This is our general guidance. Jesus was the human life of
God and in Him we see what God is like and what we may
be like.

When in doubt, do the most Christ-like thing, and you will
not go wrong. If any guidance seems to be at variance at any
point with what you see in Christ, then doubt that guidance,
for it cannot be of God, however implemented it may be by
reason or emotion. God does not ask you to do an un-Christ-
like thing—that would be contrary to His own nature.

II. *Through the accumulated wisdom of the centuries, mediated through the Church.*

The Church can and does guide us. We are the inheritors of the accumulated wisdom and experience of the Christian centuries. We can see that history is *His-story* as God guides us through His guidance of others. So we can look into the past and see people's mistakes and the results of those mistakes, and we see their right decisions and the results of those right decisions, and we are guided by them.

III. *Through disciplined group guidance.*

This is one of the greatest lacks in the Church today. Too often our church committees are places where we debate rather than meditate, where we talk to one another rather than listen to God, where decisions are made by majority vote, rather than by the Master's voice heard in the silences. We become competitive instead of cooperative. We go away disgruntled and ruffled instead of leaving with calmness and assurance.

If our group and committee meetings would begin by a long period of silence, then we would let down barriers so that God could speak, and immediately we would come to a group mind under the guidance of the Spirit. It would save endless time spent in clashes and endless mistakes.

IV. *Through the counsel of good people.*

It is safer for God to speak through a group, but often we cannot find a sufficiently disciplined group, so we have to turn to individuals for counsel and help in reaching decisions. This has to be done with great care, for the wrong counsel may send a life off on a wrong tangent. The word of James is to be heeded at this point: *My brothers, do not swell the ranks of the teachers; remember, we teachers will be judged with special strictness.**

God does guide us, however, through trusted friends. The added luminous words of a friend will often clear our minds.

---

* James 3:1 (Moffatt)

But that friend, while listening, should be breathing a prayer for guidance in order to give guidance.

We must not take the word of a friend's counsel as final. Take the counsel, but submit it to God for final decision. In His presence decide the matter.

V. *Through opening providences.*

This means that you must be open and sensitive to human need. God cannot guide you if you are wrapped up in yourself and indifferent to others. If there is a need which you can meet, then there is strong probability that God is guiding you to meet that need.

If we have money we do not really need, for example, and there are people and causes that do need it, then the burden of proof is on us to show why we should not give it. The weight of probability is on the side of giving.

VI. *Through the discoveries of natural law by science.*

The God who revealed Himself supremely in Jesus is the same God who reveals Himself less supremely in the material world and its laws. Obedience to the laws of nature is obedience to God.

A lady asked advice as to whether to depend on prayer alone for recovery, or whether she should have an operation. I saw it was a case for surgery and advised her thus. She came back radiant from the operation, and thanked me for showing that obedience to science was obedience to God.

That doesn't mean that we should blindly obey science, for science can become unscientific and get off the track; but it does mean that when there are true discoveries of science, there is an uncovering of the will of God. The laws of your being are not other than the laws of God; they are the laws of God written into blood and nerve and tissue. God guides through the discovery of natural law.

VII. *Through our heightened moral intelligence.*

This method of guidance is perhaps the most usual and continuous, and perhaps the one most to be cultivated, for to cultivate guidance through heightened moral intelligence is to cultivate ourselves. As we grow in possibility of coming to right decisions, we grow as persons.

Jesus apparently wanted to cultivate this type of person when He said to His disciples, *Can ye not of yourselves judge that which is right?** He had taught them and had shown them by example how to live, and then He turned to them and said, I now expect you to be able to come to right decisions.

This emphasis upon guidance through a heightened moral intelligence calls us away from trying to secure guidance through chance methods which border on the magical. For instance, some would open their Bibles and take the first verse they see as God's guidance. I do not question that this might be God's guidance on a rare occasion. But suppose it were continued? The moral intelligence would dry up and we would try to get guidance through opening the Bible for the first verse our eyes might light upon, instead of a patient study of the Scriptures to get the mind of God.

VIII. *Through the Inner Voice.*

When none of the other methods are available, then I believe God speaks through the Inner Voice. I believe God uses this method sparingly; for if He were always telling us what to do, it would weaken us. The problem for God is to guide us, but not override us.

Where there is a matter which is not right or wrong, but a decision between two good things, then the Inner Voice will speak.

How does the Inner Voice differ from conscience? The subconscious argues; the Inner Voice does not argue—it tells you, and the quality of authority in its words can be distinguished by practice.

These, then, are the ways God guides us. He guides us according to a pattern He has for us, for God has a plan for every life. To find that plan of God, under His guidance, gives meaning, dignity, and worth to life.

* Luke 12:57

Bible

OF course, any program for strengthening faith would not be complete without the Bible. This Book, the all-time best seller, is the greatest source of wisdom and inspiration. God speaks to us through the Bible; if we don't listen we may be passing up the spiritual knowledge and insights necessary for creative living.

Over and over I am fascinated by the countless stories of people—both famous and little known—who tell how some truth from the Bible has enabled them to overcome a weakness or achieve a personal victory: like the story in this section by Jimmy Stewart about the Scripture passage that sustained him as a bomber pilot during World War II; or the articles by Dr. Tom Dooley, Jimmy Dean and Jane Wyman who likewise drew upon the wisdom of this great Book for spiritual sustenance at times of personal need.

Marion Wade built up a million dollar business based on one verse from *Joshua*. A baseball player, a housewife and merchant each found a Scripture promise the turning point in their lives.

There are no set rules for effective Bible study. Each person must work out his own plan. The important thing is to keep a Bible near, refer to it often. I suggest that when you find a passage that speaks to a need inside you, write it on a separate piece of paper, memorize it, and let the words become a part of your subconscious mind.

The Bible—you will discover—provides a great impetus to your spiritual vitality.

NORMAN VINCENT PEALE

Something of the character that James Stewart reveals in his every film performance is a reflection of his father. Their special brand of comradeship extended, through a Bible passage, even into the cockpit of a bomber that James piloted over Europe during World War II.

Thank You, Dad

by JAMES STEWART
as told to FLOYD MILLER

WHEN I was a boy in the town of Indiana, Pennsylvania, Stewart's Hardware Store seemed the center of the universe. It was a three-story structure filled with everything needed to build a house, hunt a deer, plant a garden, repair a car or make a scrapbook.

Even after I moved away and saw larger sights, the store remained with me. But then I realized that what was central to my life was not just the store but the man who presided over it—my father.

Alexander Stewart was a muscular Irishman whose talk was as blunt as his face. The store not only provided his family a living but also was a forum where he pronounced opinions seldom tailored to the popular style. If he ever heard the slogan about the customer always being right, he would have scorned it as toadyism as well as a falsehood. And yet his tone was never harsh, and he was never vindictive. If a man failed to follow his advice, Father merely made allowance for human frailty and felt no ill will.

Dad was a Presbyterian, strong in his religion as he was in all beliefs. He sang in the choir with a true but penetrating tenor voice, and someone once described the hymns as "solos by Mr. Stewart, with accompanying voices."

142

Strangely, Dad never sang very loudly at home. We lived in a rambling house with a large front porch loaded with wicker furniture. The living room, high ceilinged and trimmed with dark woodwork, held a grand piano, around which we gathered for family sings. My sister Virginia played the piano, my other sister Mary played the violin and I played the accordion—after a fashion.

During these sessions, Dad sang very softly, so as not to cover up Mother's clear, sweet voice. Her name was Elizabeth, and he called her Bessie and adored her. Though small and gentle and not given to contention, she frequently had her way over him because she possessed patience and endurance.

Doing things with my father was always fun, for his imagination added a dimension to events. When, at 10, I announced that I was going to Africa to bring back wild animals, my mother and sisters pointed out my age, the problems of transportation and all such mundane and inconsequential facts.

But not Dad. He brought home books about Africa, train and boat schedules for us to study, and even some iron bars which we used to build cages for the animals I was to bring back. When the departure day approached and I was becoming apprehensive, my father brought home a newspaper that told of a wreck on the railroad that was to take me to Baltimore. This postponed my trip and, by the time the train tracks were repaired, he and I were off on a new and more exciting project.

When President Harding died, the funeral train was scheduled to pass through a town about 20 miles from ours. I wanted desperately to go and see this train, but Mother pointed out that there would be school the next day and that it would be a long trip. That ended the discussion.

But Dad did not forget. When the day arrived, he came to me and, in a voice as near a whisper as his nature would allow, said, "Jim, boy, it's time to see the funeral train."

We drove along without talking much, bound together by the comradeship of our adventure. When we came to the railroad station, a half dozen people were talking in hushed tones and looking down the tracks. Suddenly the tracks gave off a low hum—the funeral train was coming!

Dad shoved two pennies into my hand and said, "Run, put them on the rails. Quick!"

I did as directed and jumped back to hold his hand as the engine thundered past, pulling a glass-windowed observation car in which we saw the flag-draped casket, guarded by two Marines, their glistening bayonets at attention. I could hardly breathe, so overwhelming were the sight and sound.

After the train had roared off, I retrieved the two flattened pennies from the track. Dad put one in his pocket and I kept the other.

As we drove home, I examined mine and found that the two feathers of the Indian headdress had become a great plume. On the other side two slender stalks of wheat had grown and burst, as if the seed had ripened and scattered.

For years, Dad and I carried those coins flattened by the weight of history. And the knowledge of what we shared made me feel very close to him.

With his temperament, it was amazing how patient Dad could be, how subtle his discipline. I don't recall a time when he stood across my path; he always walked beside, guiding me with his own steps. When a neighbor's dog killed my dog Bounce, I vowed to kill that dog in revenge. I vowed it day after day in the most bloodthirsty terms, almost making myself ill with my own hate.

"You are determined to kill the dog," my father stated abruptly one evening after dinner. "All right, let's get it done. Come on."

I followed him to the store, to discover that he had tied the dog in the alley. He got a deer rifle out of stock, loaded it, handed it to me, then stepped back for me to do my bloody work. The dog and I looked at each other. He wagged his tail in a tentative offer of friendship and his large brown eyes were innocent and trusting. Suddenly the gun was too heavy for me to hold and it dropped to the ground. The dog came up and licked my hand.

The three of us walked home together, the dog gamboling in front. No word was ever said about what had happened. None was needed.

During World War II, I enlisted in the Air Corps and became part of a bomber squadron. When we were ready to fly overseas, Dad came to the farewell ceremonies in Sioux City, Iowa. We were very self-conscious with each other, talking in generalities, trying to conceal our awareness that, starting tomorrow, he could no longer walk with me. At the time of the greatest crisis in my life, he would have to stand aside. We were both afraid.

At the moment of parting, he studied his shoes a moment, then looked at the sky. I knew he was searching for a final word to sustain me, but he couldn't find it. He opened his mouth, then shut it hard, almost in anger. We embraced, then he turned and walked quickly away. Only after he had gone did I realize that he had put a small envelope in my pocket.

That night alone in my bunk, I opened it and read, "My dear Jim, soon after you read this letter, you will be on your way to the worst sort of danger. I have had this in mind for a long time and I am very concerned. . . . But Jim, I am banking on the enclosed copy of the 91st Psalm. The thing that takes the place of fear and worry is the promise in these words. I am staking my faith in these words. I feel sure that God will lead you through this mad experience . . . I can say no more. I only continue to pray. God bless you and keep you. I love you more than I can tell you. Dad."

Never before had he said he loved me. I always knew he did but he had never said it until now. I wept. In the envelope there was also a small booklet bearing the title *The Secret Place—A Key to the 91st Psalm.* I began to read it. From that day, the little booklet was always with me. Before every bombing raid over Europe, I read some of it, and with each reading the meaning deepened for me.

I will say of the Lord, He is my refuge and my fortress. . . . His truth shall be thy shield and buckler. Thou shalt not be afraid for the terror by night; nor for the arrow that flieth by day. . . . For He shall give His angels charge over thee, to keep thee in all thy ways. They shall bear thee up in their hands, lest thou dash thy foot against a stone.

And I was borne up.

Dad had committed me to God, but I felt the presence of both throughout the war.

When Mother died in 1956, we buried her in the family plot in Indiana, Pennsylvania. With his wife gone, Dad could work up no new enthusiasms. Her quiet strength had sustained him, and with her gone he quickly withered away.

It was a bleak January day when I saw him placed beside his ancestors, men who had lived longer than he had but who were perhaps less demanding of life. Most of the town came to the funeral with respect and grief.

After it was all over, I went to the hardware store and let myself in with a key I hadn't touched for 30 years. The interior smelled of metal, leather, oil and fertilizer, the odors of my childhood.

I sat at his scarred oak desk and idly pulled open the middle drawer. It held a clutter of pencils and paper clips and bolts and paint samples. Something glinted dully among them. I picked up the funeral-train penny with the flattened Indian face and the burst grain.

For a long time I sat there at his desk, fingering the Indian head penny and thinking. Then I put it in my pocket, took a last look at familiar and loved objects, and walked out of the store, locking the door behind me.

This famous American doctor gave his life to the cause of suffering mankind. Behind this giving was the inspiration of one very special verse of Scripture.

Our Search for Inner Peace

by DR. THOMAS A. DOOLEY

I WAS waked this morning by a very angry old man. His wife was dying, he said. My medicine had hurt her very badly. I sat up slowly, trying to get fully awake. I'd been up all night, operating on a child whose eye had been ripped out by a tiger; I'd been in bed less than an hour.

I followed the man groggily to where his wife squatted in the little clinic room. The old woman's face was distorted with pain. I remembered her well. Two weeks ago, I'd removed an immense growth from her neck. I'd kept the incision as clean as I could: sterile instruments, scrubbed hands, antiseptics, a sterile dressing, but even in the pale dawn light I could see, all around the bandage, the livid purple lines that said infection had set in.

Anxiously I peeled off the layers of dressing. Last of all, next to the woman's skin, was a putrid black object. I picked it up between thumb and forefinger.

It was a rotting bat's wing.

I looked inquiringly at the husband. "Yes," he said proudly, "I put it there to keep away the pain. And it's a good thing I did! See how purple the neck is!"

With the aid of penicillin and blood plasma, I believe this old woman will survive her husband's well-meant ministrations. But for me, she was only the first of the nearly 100 suffering people I saw during this one day. As I was rebandaging the old woman's neck, a mother carried in a five-year-old boy who could neither sit up nor see. What was his diet? I wanted

147

to know. Why, rice and water! What else should a child eat?

A man showed me a tiny scratch on his wrist, so long-infected I had to tell him he must lose his hand. A sad-eyed woman timidly asked me if I could make her have live babies. Of course, she knew one out of two babies always died—that was only normal. But she had had 11 babies and all had died. Was there something in my magic bottles to make the next one live?

Why have I come half-way round the world to live with heartbreak? I suppose the best answer would be that I was born with a burning desire to help people—it would be the best answer—but it wouldn't be true.

If people can be born with a desire, I guess mine was to have a good time, and good times came easily in our home. There was plenty of money; I had my own horse, went to school abroad, studied to be a concert pianist.

They weren't just surface good times, either. We were genuinely, deep-down happy. I think my father's religion had a lot to do with that. We were the prayingest family you ever saw. We prayed when we got up in the morning, when we sat down to eat, when we finished eating, when we went to bed, and frequently in between. Among my favorite prayers were the Beatitudes.

I loved them, I think, because they talked about what interested me. "Blessed" means "happy"—and that's just what I wanted to be. Here were the rules for happiness.

But now, in retrospect, it is the second Beatitude, *Blessed are they that mourn . . .* that means something special to me. My father must have explained to me many times that to "mourn" as it's used in the Bible, doesn't mean "to be unhappy." It simply means, he used to say, "to be more aware of the sorrow in the world than of the pleasures."

But I couldn't really follow that explanation. How could you think about sorrow and be happy?

Even when I entered med school, it wasn't because I was stricken with the sorrow of sick people. It was more that I wanted to share my own good times with them.

There were some lonely old people at the hospital where I was a student. So I bought a convertible—a long, sleek one—and, weekends, I'd pile the old folks into it and drive them out to the stable. While I jumped my horse, they enjoyed the fresh air. Have fun and share it—that was my formula for happiness.

I might have gotten away with it, too, if it hadn't been for a sizzling morning in July, 1954. I was fresh out of med school with a brand-new "Doctor" in front of my name and a new Navy lieutenancy as well. My ship was assigned to cruise-duty in the western Pacific, and I passed the slow days trying to decide where, in all Missouri, was the very best place to raise horses. I hardly heard the Captain that morning when he announced we'd been ordered briefly to Haiphong, on the coast of North Vietnam, to transport some refugees of that civil war to Saigon in the South.

In the harbor at Haiphong a small boat approached us from the shore, an open landing-craft, built for less than 100 men. As it came nearer I saw that there were more than 1,000 people on it—and, oh Lord, so many of them were babies!

The waves in the choppy harbor washed over the open boat again and again. In the 115° heat, most of the children fainted. Now they were alongside, and I thought I would be the one to faint. Here were smallpox, terminal tuberculosis, hideous cancers, and some diseases I couldn't even name. It was my first glimpse of Asia.

As they struggled up the ladder to the ship, the stink of long-untended sickness overwhelmed me. I wanted to run, to vomit, to pretend I'd never seen them.

But I was the only doctor on the ship, and so I set out my poor array of bottles and needles and cotton swabs, and blindly, hopelessly attacked the mountain of suffering before me.

But before long, a strange excitement began to grow in me. It was so apparent that a simple plaster cast would take the agony out of this broken arm! A few shots of vitamin C could have this man on his feet! This swollen hand needed only a simple lancing. I was learning that even my inexperienced, fumbling hands could work miracles for people who had never seen even a greenhorn doctor.

Hours later, I stopped for a moment to straighten my shoulders and made another discovery—the biggest of my life. I was happy. Deeply, joyously happy, happier than I had ever been before.

We came back to Haiphong for another boatload of refugees. Now we expected cholera, and whooping cough and leprosy, and rather than simply ferry these highly contagious diseases down to Saigon, I set up a make-shift hospital on shore to treat them before they boarded ship. I volunteered to work ashore for one month. I stayed nine, and processed 610,000 of the most neglected human beings in the world.

Here I was, the guy who loved convertibles and new clothes, working around the clock in sweat-stained khakis and a two-week growth of beard. Scrubbing patients who—some of them—had never had a bath. Cleaning wounds that had festered for years. Glowing with happiness.

When the evacuation was finished, I went home; but only long enough to get out of the Navy and raise enough money to come back to Indo-China on my own. To come here to the disease-haunted jungles of Laos, to build this little shack of a hospital, to show a Lao great-grandmother a cake of soap and teach her how to wash her hands.

Not long ago I had a letter from one of my old professors who knew about my plans for the good life. "What happened, Tom?" he asked. "Why the big change?"

"There wasn't any change," I wrote back. "I'm still the same, egotistical, self-centered guy to whom you tried to teach some medicine. I've never wanted anything except happiness for Tom Dooley—and here I've got it."

You see, when Jesus gave us the Beatitudes, He wasn't describing some dream-world that might someday come to pass.

He was talking, simply and matter-of-factly as He always did, about things as they are. If you're extra-sensitive to sorrow, He said—and you do something, no matter how small, to make it lighter—you can't help but be happy. That's just the way it is.

I know—and I'm a guy who'd do anything to be happy.

What can a housewife do when she has that regular 18-hour "rain-tears-spilt milk and what next" kind of day? Here's a woman who discovered a way to enjoy her days at home and her family—and be a better wife and mother too.

Trapped Housewife

by GRACE ERICKSON

ON the bulletin board in my kitchen, beside the grocery list and the family memos, is a picture of Christ. Nine years ago I might have said that was an undignified place for it, but that was before I became a wife and mother.

In those single days I was well-satisfied with my religious life: church three times a week, daily Bible reading, long periods of prayer—devoted largely to asking for God's plan for my life (first choice: a husband and family).

And then God granted my request. With truly celestial abundance, He gave me Ray, a home in the suburbs and four children in five years. As I chased toddlers and boiled formulas and scrubbed floors, gone was the Bible reading and the tranquil meditation. I scrambled through an 18-hour day feeling miles away from God and wondering if my early faith had been just so much illusion.

It was one of those "rain-tears-spilt milk and what next" days when I found the picture of Jesus that had hung on the wall of my bedroom as a teen-ager. I pinned it on the bulletin board to cheer myself. I never intended to leave it there. But right away I noticed a curious change.

In the mail that day came news that seemed to me to indicate bad judgment on Ray's part. Anxiety and annoyance swelled up inside me. I wanted to shove the letter in his face the minute he got home and demand an explanation.

Then as I started supper, I saw the picture. Suddenly I was thinking about Jesus, who had all human error on His shoulders and remained the most loving of men. I tucked the letter out of sight till after dinner.

When Ray read it, he was as worried as I. The children were in bed, so we had time to sit down and talk it over together and evolve a plan that saved the situation. If I had followed my first angry impulse, there would have been such tension between us that we never could have approached the problem so reasonably.

The picture helped me again a few days later when my oldest boy broke my crystal vase. He was jumping rope with an old necktie. I asked him to stop. He didn't. The necktie hit the flowers in the vase and the whole thing crashed to the floor. Tommy knew he was in trouble and fled crying to his room.

I stormed out to the kitchen for the broom and dustpan. "Lord Jesus," I found myself praying, "help me and Tommy to learn something from this."

After mopping up the mess I went with a much calmer mind to Tommy's room. I pointed out that his disobedience had caused the accident. "I know you didn't mean to break the vase," I said, "but because you disobeyed, you broke something I liked very much. Now I expect an apology." Tommy listened wide-eyed and apologized quickly and nicely, something he always had found very hard to do.

The magic was not in the picture itself, of course. It reminded me I didn't have to run away from my chores or shut the door on the noise to find God but that He had entered with me into the thick of it.

On another occasion I was cleaning the house for guests that were coming that evening. Everything was done except that I thought the living room floor should be freshly waxed and polished. Then the children asked me to read to them. I already had put them off several times—but what about the floor?

And suddenly I was remembering Jesus in the house of Mary and Martha. Martha was a whiz of a housekeeper, but Jesus praised Mary because she put things of the mind and spirit first.

I read to the children. We had such a happy time, and it helped me relax so that I was in better condition to be a gracious hostess.

Jesus put an order of importance on things. He said: *But seek ye first the Kingdom of God . . .* * and *Mary hath chosen that good part . . .* ** and He helps me make distinctions among the endless claims of a home. Sparkling windows are nice, but nothing to compare with light in the eyes of a happy child. The dusting needs to be done, but not necessarily now or even today.

Jesus was a busy man, but never a rushed one. When He looked at someone, He really saw him—saw down to the deep need of which the person himself wasn't aware. I was thinking about this one day recently when it occurred to me that lately Tommy had been saying, "Mommy, look at me." I realized how often I talked to the children—answering questions, issuing orders, settling disputes—without really looking at them.

I've tried to correct this and the results have been amazing. I know much better what my children look like, how they react to what I say, and how much they understand of what I tell them. It helps me to discern between disobedience and times when they just don't understand. I can catch their teasing looks and we can enjoy a laugh together.

And when I really look at each child, I see a priceless treasure, a human life, a personality unique in God's sight. Then I know that being a mother is a truly exalted calling. And if this exaltation includes such things as changing diapers, wiping noses and accepting dandelions as though they were orchids, that's all right with me. You see, on my kitchen memo

* Matthew 6:33
** Luke 10:42

board I keep a reminder that there's a purpose to it all.

A strange place for a picture of Christ? I don't think so. Here I can see Him as I warm a bottle at 3:00 a.m., and as I wash the endless amounts of laundry. Isn't that what the Incarnation was all about? Not that we were miraculously lifted out of daily irritations, but that the Lord of all creation came down to walk with us through them.

Jimmy Dean, a recording and TV star, had to face the bitterness in his heart. He hated his father who had deserted his wife and children. Years passed. Then one day a telephone call came for Jimmy—from his father. It was a moment of truth.

The Day I Learned to Forgive

by JIMMY DEAN

IT'S strange how little, unexpected things can change our lives—like the telephone call I had three years ago. I was at home when the call came. I picked up the phone and heard a voice that made something inside me tighten with anger and resentment. The voice at the other end of the line belonged to my father.

How can a son despise his own father? In my case, it wasn't hard because I felt I had plenty of justification. To explain, let me go back through the years to the time when I was 11, my brother Don was nine, and we lived in Plainview, Texas.

That was a long time ago, but I can still see my mother's drawn face as she tried to explain the grim fact that our father had left us. Had walked out. Had deserted us. I remember the deep hurt in her eyes and the numbness in our hearts as she told us we all would have to work hard just to eat and stay alive.

She was right: it was hard, brutally hard. Mama opened up a one-chair barber shop in our rented house and cut hair for our neighbors at 15 cents a head. Don and I did everything we could about town to earn money. We pulled cotton and cleaned out chicken houses and milked cows and helped build windmills. My mother had a little garden, and we worked it with her. We needed the food we got from it.

I remember Mama tacking paper on the ceiling of the

house we lived in. The ceiling was so thin that if she did not plug up the holes, dirt would fall on us and our food.

The only clothes Don and I had were bib overalls. At school we were kidded cruelly by our classmates. I hated those kids and the school and wondered in pain how my father could walk out, leaving us with this shame and this need.

One day, I finally came home and told my mother how we were being ridiculed and asked her why we couldn't get some other clothes.

"Overalls are nothing to be ashamed of," she said. "They're something to be grateful for. Besides, it's what you wear inside your heart that counts."

If I knew then what I know now I never would have asked her that question. Imagine how much it must have hurt her.

Mama always told us, "Be yourself. If people don't like you the way you are, they're not going to like you when you pretend to be someone else."

Our life was not all despair, though. On Sundays, we would walk the three-quarters of a mile from our house to the Sethward Baptist Church. Then, after Sunday dinner, the neighbors would drop in, and Mama would play our old piano, and we'd sing from the green-backed Boardman Hymnal. Later we'd parch peanuts and eat them. Sundays weren't bad at all.

We never heard Mama complain about being poor. There was never any doubt that we would outlast it. Hope was in all of us; deep hope because it was nourished by a deep faith.

Mama got this faith from her father and Don and I got it from both of them and it became part of our lives and our being.

We called Grandfather "Papa." Maybe because for the brief time we knew him he was all the Papa we had. He was a short man with tall beliefs who held that in times of distress you depended on your prayers. All that happened was God's will, he would tell us, and if you couldn't see the why of it at the time, it all would be clear later on.

Mama told us how a hail storm once destroyed half a section of Grandfather's wheat. A section is 640 acres, and 320 acres supplies a lot of wheat; in fact, it is a year's work. The storm lasted less than 30 minutes. Grandfather stood on the back porch watching it and when the destruction was over he said, "The Lord giveth, the Lord taketh away." *

He went inside to thank God for what he had left—little as it was.

Then there came the day when the bitterness in me came out and I angrily criticized my father. Grandfather started to reprimand me, changed his mind, and picked up his Bible. He leafed through the pages quickly, and read this:

*It is a very small thing that I should be judged of you, or of man's judgment: yea, I judge not mine own Self . . . but he that judgeth Me is the Lord. Therefore, judge nothing before the time, until the Lord come, who both will bring to light the hidden things of darkness, and will make manifest the counsels of the hearts.** *

But I was 16 then, and words from the old black leather-bound Book didn't help the heartache I felt. Besides, for most of my years I had been trying to live down my father's name. It seemed that he had borrowed money from many people and never paid them back. They didn't let me forget it. I felt I couldn't ever forgive him for that. Or for leaving Mama to do his work and fight his fight. Or for the bib overalls.

After the 11th grade, I left Plainview, enlisted in the Air Force and was stationed in Washington, D. C. A quartet of GI's who sang at night just for tips asked me to come along with my accordion when their fiddler took sick. By the time I was out of uniform I was a solo singer and soon was making a nice living from personal appearances and records. I'd made about a dozen single records and three albums of prayers and hymns before I wrote and recorded *Big Bad John,* which became a surprising hit.

* Job 1:21
** I Corinthians 4:3-5

Suddenly, after a silence of 17 years, my father called me one day and asked for money to finance some crazy scheme. I turned him down cold. He called several more times with various requests. The conversations were quick and brief— a flat no. I'm sure he could tell how bitter I was; after awhile the calls stopped.

My career moved along nicely, and one day I was surprised to receive an invitation to appear at a dedication of a new school in my home town of Plainview. Remembering all the taunts about our bib overalls, I was tempted to say no. But my mother reminded me gently of the fine neighbors we had had. She said we owed them something.

When we arrived at the school, Mama was given a front row seat and she looked very proud and pretty sitting there waiting for the program to begin.

When I walked out on stage, everyone was standing and applauding. I was so moved that I couldn't talk or sing or anything. Looking down I saw that Mama was crying, but they were tears of joy. At that moment I felt that all the years of poverty and the humiliation she suffered because of my father were wiped away.

The memory of this experience was still in my mind three years ago when my father called again. I began to harden myself against the usual request.

But this time his voice was different. There was an urgency in it.

"All I want from you this time is your forgiveness, Jimmy. I haven't been much of a father, and I'm sorry. Please, will you forgive me?" There was a pause. "I have cancer. My time is nearly all gone now."

For a moment everything came to a stop. Scenes from the past flashed before me in a matter of seconds. Suddenly I felt small and tongue-tied, because a man I hardly knew—my father—was dying and we had to bridge the long years of resentment and anger and hate quickly.

The silence was probably no longer than 10 seconds. Yet it

was long enough for me to look back through time and see the futility and senselessness of any man trying to judge another. For a moment I felt set apart from life's struggle; it was almost as though I was given some new insight into the mind of God.

I forgave my father, and I asked to be forgiven, too, for ever trying to judge him.

"Thank you for that, Jimmy," he replied. A few days later he was dead.

I'm sure his last phone call to me helped my father leave this world with a peaceful mind. And I feel that it did something for me. For today whenever I read of bad conduct in the newspaper, or see a drunk reeling about the sidewalk, or feel criticism rising inside me toward any human being, I try to stop myself at that very moment. And my memory returns quickly to the words of St. Paul:

Judge nothing before the time, until the Lord come, who both will bring to light the hidden things of darkness, and will make manifest the counsels of the hearts.

*A senseless murder of an innocent youth stirred an
entire city to cries for vengeance. Then, into the midst
of this whirlwind of hate came a letter from the dead
boy's father. The letter came from half-way around
the world—and it had an unexpected message.*

Act of Mercy

by GLENN D. KITTLER

AT nine o'clock on the night of Friday, April 25, 1958, a
young Korean exchange student left his Philadelphia
apartment and went to the corner to mail a letter. His name
was In Ho Oh. In a few hours, everyone in Philadelphia knew
it.

It was a warm night. The 26-year-old University of Pennsylvania student had gone out in his shirt sleeves. The letter
he carried was addressed to his parents in Pusan. He dropped
it into the mail box, and when he turned around he stepped
into the path of 11 teen-age boys.

Without a word, they attacked him, beating him with a
blackjack, a lead pipe, and with their shoes and fists. Neighbors later said there were no shouts, no screams, only the
steady sound of thudding.

Then one boy cried: "I've got his wallet. There's no money
in it." And they all ran away.

When the police arrived minutes later, they found that In
Ho Oh had rolled off the curb and slipped under a parked
car. He died before an ambulance arrived. His face had been
beaten beyond recognition, and at first none of the neighbors
could tell who he was. But from his smooth black hair, the
color of his skin and his small body, they deduced he was an
Oriental; there was a family of Orientals in the building
across the street.

The police went to the apartment of Ki Song Oh and his wife Za Young, the dead youth's uncle and aunt, both also students, and they asked about the young man.

"He has gone out," said Za Young. "To his work, I think."

An officer held up a ballpoint pen. "Does this belong to your nephew?"

"Yes," said Ki Song Oh. "He has just bought several like it."

The detective nervously cleared his throat. "I have bad news for you," he said. "Your nephew has been attacked on the street. He is dead."

Ki Song Oh and his wife could not speak, they could not move, they did not hear the neighbors come and answer the detective's questions. Their hearts dark with sorrow, they could not believe what had happened.

The first hours of Saturday, April 26, were cruel for Ki Song Oh. He had to identify the body of his nephew; there were the piercing questions of the police and reporters, and there was a cable to be sent to Korea. Late that afternoon the telephone call came from Pusan.

From 10,000 miles away, the stunned voice asked: "My brother, is it true what I have heard about my son?"

"It is true."

Silence. Then: "Why did it happen?"

"I do not know," said Ki Song Oh. "I cannot understand it."

By their own intensive methods, the Philadelphia police rounded up all 11 boys within 42 hours. At first there were denials and alibis, then a few of the boys broke down.

They said that early Friday evening they had been refused admission to a dance, some because they were improperly dressed, some because they lacked the 35-cent fee. They had stalked the streets in ugly anger, then decided to rob the next person they saw. Their victim was the young Korean who had turned from the mail box, intending to go home and dress for his part-time job at the Provident Tradesman Bank.

All Philadelphia cried out for vengeance. The Philadelphia *Bulletin* declared: "A soft policy toward the owners of hands dripping with blood is a frightful mistake." District Attorney Victor Blanc acquired legal authority to try the boys as adults so that those found guilty could receive the death penalty.

Only the Oh family seemed calm. Ki Song Oh said: "We cannot understand the hatred. Why should others be so distressed? They have lost nothing."

In view of the brutal murder, this was a strange attitude, one not easily grasped. A fine young man had been killed savagely, a young man whose entire life had been moulded to the service of the new republic his homeland had become. Didn't justice require the death of his killers? The outraged city felt it did.

Then a letter arrived from Korea that made everyone stop and think. It was from the parents of In Ho Oh, and it was also signed by 20 other relatives. It said, in part:

"Our family has met together and we have decided to petition that the most generous treatment possible within the laws of your government be given to those who have committed this criminal action. . . . In order to give evidence of our sincere hope contained in this petition, our whole family has decided to save money to start a fund to be used for the religious, educational, vocational and social guidance of the boys when they are released. . . .

"We vitally sense an obligation for the better guidance of juvenile delinquents whose souls are unsaved and whose human natures are paralyzed. . . . Please interpret our hope and idea with Christian spirit and in the light of democratic principles. We have dared to express our hope with a spirit received from the Gospel of our Savior Jesus Christ who died for our sins."

In the city which had clamored for justice, this distant whisper for mercy came like thunder. The people who had been most directly pained by the killing had refused the salve of vengeance. Why had they not demanded retribution? The answer lay hidden in the lives of those who had experienced so little of mercy.

Sixty-six years ago, the Oh family became Christians, and ever since they have taken active leadership in church affairs. During the 35-year Japanese occupation of Korea, family members were imprisoned because the precepts of justice and equality implicit in the religion had made them fight against dictatorship. In prison, they taught religion to other prisoners, and they planned a project to evangelize Japan. Three times they were forced to give up their homes, their business, all they possessed in order to move elsewhere where they would be free to practice their faith.

This was the environment in which In Ho Oh had grown up. Daily religious exercises were practiced in the home; all famliy decisions were based on Christian doctrine, a doctrine which did not promise comfort and fortune, but nevertheless provided dignity and private peace.

There was dignity and peace in their plea for mercy and suddenly Philadelphians realized that though the law prescribed a trial and punishment, there was a separate act of mercy that each one could perform. Dr. Eugene Carson Blake, the Presbyterian leader, cabled Pusan:

"All of us feel a deep sense of responsibility for our failures as Christians to deal adequately with the evils that beset our society. We are humbled by the Christian spirit you have demonstrated in asking that leniency be granted your son's slayers. Your willingness to go the second mile has made its impact upon millions of Americans."

Funds were created to provide a scholarship for a Korean student, to send milk to Korean children, to help Ki Song Oh devote his full time to study so that he could hurry home to help his country. And in Korea, the Oh family set aside part of its annual income for guidance which could change a teen-age gang into decent human beings. Philadelphians have asked to be allowed to share in this.

Ki Song Oh said: "My brother has often said that Christianity affords its followers the opportunity to let God love through them. This is surely his guide. My family believes in the Christian spirit, and it is from this that our personal pain has been mercifully lessened."

That this was true was evident in the man's actions throughout. In His Fifth Beatitude Jesus said: *Blessed are the merciful: for they shall obtain mercy,* and so in the death of In Ho Oh, perhaps there are other pains that shall be lessened—the pains of the failures which Dr. Blake expressed.

The slow roots of goodness, planted in the actions of people, could well produce the same dignity and private peace among the young in the City of Brotherly Love that exist in the small house in Pusan. When this happens, then In Ho Oh will have fulfilled a unique destiny: for in the Korean language, the name his father gave to him means He Who Does Good.

Who are the shy people? Certainly not this Academy Award-winning actress, you would say. Here's a heart-warming story with an answer to a common problem.

A Case of Shyness

by JANE WYMAN

HOW annoyed I get today when I hear someone teased for being shy! "Come on!" they shout, dragging him into a crowded room. "Don't be shy!" As though not being shy were a matter of will power. Or, "You're just shy!" as though that were the most minor of problems.

Shyness is not a small problem: it can cripple the whole personality. It crippled mine, for many years.

As a child my only solution to the problem of shyness was to hide, to make myself as small and insignificant as possible. All through grade school I was a well-mannered little shadow who never spoke above a whisper. In ballet class I haunted the corners of the room, hoping the dancing master would not see me.

The very thought of performing in front of someone made me wilt with fear, quite literally.

The saddest part of it was that I idolized Dad Prinz, the dancing master. He was the most understanding man I had ever met and I longed to tell him so. I never did.

Then my parents left St. Joseph, Missouri, and moved to Los Angeles. And now a new and more threatening dimension had been added to life outside the big city high school walls. Dating. It seemed to me that on some prearranged signal, every boy and girl in school paired off.

Every girl, that is, except me. I don't know whether I could have had dates or not; it simply never occurred to me to try.

166

Hadn't I been told many times that I was not pretty? I lugged home piles of books every night and disappeared into them.

And then the Depression came. In California it seemed to hit older people like my father especially hard. Overnight I was thrust from my safe little book-world into the world of job hunting.

In all that vast, bewildering city, I knew only one person who might give me a job: LeRoy Prinz, the famous Hollywood dance coach, Dad Prinz' son. He gave me a tryout and discovered I had a sense of rhythm. "As long as you've got that," he said, "I can teach you the rest."

Under LeRoy Prinz' coaching I began to get chorus parts in the movies, those lavish, glittery, extravagant movies we loved in the hungry '30s.

It was work when the family badly needed the money, but for a girl who had grown up in terror of being looked at, it was also agony. Then I made a discovery: a good shield for shyness is a bold exterior. Did my heart turn over when the man with the megaphone bellowed out my name? Were all the other dancers prettier? Never mind. I covered up by becoming the cockiest of all, by talking the loudest, laughing the longest, and wearing the curliest, most blatantly false eyelashes in Hollywood.

And then one day a fellow chorus girl gave me a piece of advice:

"Jane, you'd improve your looks about a thousand percent if you'd peel off those trimmings and wash your face."

I was crushed. I wept. I hated her. But the next day, feeling completely bald, I showed up on the set without my disguise. We hadn't been rehearsing half an hour before a comparative stranger stopped and stared at me.

"Gee, Jane," he said. "You look great."

For me it was the heavens parting. Could he have meant that *I* looked great? It was the first hint I had that I could be myself without the sky falling in.

But the insight went only skin deep. I shed the eyelashes, but I wasn't about ready to shed the tough, smart little shell. I had begun to get a few minor acting parts and they were just the kind you would expect. I was the brash blonde girl reporter rushing into the newspaper office to shout "Stop the presses!"

Then one day on the set someone else said something that shone another bit of light through the defense I'd set up.

"When I first came out to Hollywood," he said, "I discovered there are two kinds of people here. There are the 'closed people,' the careful ones who don't take risks and don't get hurt. And there are the 'open people,' the ones who give life all they've got. They make mistakes, they get hurt, but they also get back a lot of joy."

I recognized myself right there as one of the closed people and my bright personality as the shell for a clam. I began to want very much to open the shell. I began to loathe the brassy blonde I played in the movies. Suddenly I longed to play real people, to move the hearts of real people. Today I would call this quality of deep yearning, "prayer," and what happened next, a small miracle. Then, I only knew that no sooner had I set my heart on changing than I was offered two roles about unmistakably real people: first in *Lost Weekend* and then in *The Yearling.*

I worked on those parts as I'd never worked before, sat up nights with my lines, studied them for hidden meanings over my meals. When those films were finished, the studio decided I was ready for the role of the deaf-mute in *Johnny Belinda.* With that part came the Academy Award, and surely, I thought, surely now I will stop hiding. Surely I will feel some kind of self-esteem and confidence.

But the months passed, my Oscar collected dust on a shelf, and I made a dismal discovery. External achievements change nothing: inside I was the same tormentingly shy person I always had been. My real self still was hiding in the shadows, sending someone else out front to greet the world.

It was an exhausting way to live.

Then, 11 years ago, I went to England to do a picture for the Royal Academy. It was a lonely time: I knew no one outside the cast and I did a lot of walking, and thinking. During my solitary rambles I found myself wandering into Westminster Abbey, first as a sightseer—then over and over again to try to grasp something I felt there. Something that felt like approval. Like acceptance. Like love.

I tried to dismiss the experience. It was, I rationalized, only the reaction of a homesick woman in a foreign land. I almost had convinced myself when I met the man who at last threw a searchlight on the girl in the shadows. I was back in Hollywood and he was a kindly old priest with a manner so gentle, so uncritical, that suddenly I found myself talking to him about things I'd never told anyone. I found myself telling him about the little girl who was too shy to speak above a whisper, about my lifelong struggle with the same feelings. "I thought if I only could succeed at something, then I wouldn't be shy. But I have had success, of a kind, and I feel just the same."

"Of course you do." The priest smiled at me. "Shyness isn't a matter of doing well, or not doing well. It isn't a matter of whether you're handsome or plain."

Over his cluttered desk, he looked at me. "Shyness, Miss Wyman, is a little matter of self-centeredness."

I blinked. The words were harsh but he said them so mildly, that I resisted a familiar impulse to flee into a protective shell.

"That's all," he continued cheerfully. "Just a little tendency to think of the whole world as terribly interested in oneself. You know, the feeling that every eye in the room is focused on one—whereas actually most of the other people there are pretty much involved with their own problems.

"Now fortunately," he went on as he rummaged for something in the maelstrom on his desk, "the Bible gives us some very specific instructions for dealing with self-centeredness."

He located his Bible, found the passage he wanted, and handed it to me.

I looked at the Bible passage. It was the Ten Commandments.

"The first four," he said, "deal with our relationship to God. They get our attention out where it belongs: on Him and His majesty. And the last six tell us how we ought to conduct ourselves toward other people. They keep our attention out there, away from ourselves and onto our neighbors."

I looked down at the Commandments again. I had read them a hundred times, of course, but something in the old priest's voice filled them with an unspeakable promise.

It was the first of many interviews with this priest who became my spiritual mentor. And I have never forgotten what he told me the first time we met, about the cause of shyness, and its cure. Not that I have succeeded in following all the Commandments in all their fullness, but the act of trying to has worked a big change in my life.

For when I looked away from myself I discovered a whole world full of other people. Fascinating people, people with woes and joys I had never imagined. I didn't have much time left to worry about the impression I was making, once I really began seeing them.

But best of all, out there, I am finding God. Not much of Him, yet. At first it was just a shadow, a glimmering. But getting to know Him better, listening for Him, contemplating Him, loving Him, is a 24-hour-a-day assignment. Shy? I just haven't got time.

Discouragement nearly defeated this All-Star second baseman for the New York Yankees at one point in his career. Then came a letter from his junior high school coach.

The Thin Line Between Success and Failure

by BOBBY RICHARDSON

MINE has been an unusual baseball career of ups-and-downs . . . from defeat to victory, from periods when I could do nothing wrong to periods when I could do nothing right. This covers 20 years of baseball—beginning at age ten when I was a catcher for a Salvation Army team in Sumter, South Carolina, and up to my present career with the New York Yankees.

I have discovered that the difference between winning and losing can be a matter of inches. Perhaps you have heard the expression "baseball is a game of inches?"

Here is an illustration of what I mean:

During a game with Baltimore several years ago we were behind by one run. It was the last inning; I was at bat with one man on base. I hit one high and deep into the left field stands. The crowd roared, thinking we had won.

"Foul!" cried the umpire. My hit had just missed being a home run. On the next pitch, I flied out. So we lost—by inches.

My ups-and-downs in baseball have taught me how important it is to have a balanced mental approach to the game. For me, this means having a solid religious philosophy. Let me tell you of three experiences in which I was given a spiritual lift at important times.

When I was 14, I was playing in the American Legion

League and our team from Sumter was competing with a team from Richmond for the Sectional championship. The winner was to go on to the National Tournament.

There were some 5,000 people in the stands . . . mothers, fathers, brothers, sisters . . . and the excitement was intense. Before the game, our coach, H. N. Hutchinson, called us together for a pep talk. He read us the League's rules of conduct.

Now boys are always having regulations read to them, and often their inclination is to only half listen. Yet these rules were well thought out:

- Keep faith with your teammates.
- Keep a stout heart in defeat.
- Keep your pride under in victory.
- Keep a sound soul, a clean mind and a healthy body.

On this particular day, one of these rules was to become especially pertinent to me. For we lost the game by one run. What was worse, the winning run scored when the umpire ruled that I did not touch second base while pivoting on a double play. I was sick at heart. And the next day when I read the newspaper, I felt even worse.

"Bobby Richardson was the goat of the game," said the story.

At 14, it is pretty devastating to be a "goat" before 5,000 people—and to over 100,000 newspaper readers. My parents tried to have me take a philosophic point of view. I would have none of this.

Yet after brooding for a while, I knew that my dream was still to be a Major League player. *Keep a stout heart in defeat . . . keep a sound soul, a clean mind . . .* I began growing up the hard way.

Today, I find that I still repeat these rules subconsciously before each Yankee game.

A second turning point came after I signed a contract with the Yankees. Just out of high school, I was assigned to play with their farm club at Norfolk, Virginia, in a "B" league. Nervous, in competition with older players, I did miserably . . . booted easy grounders . . . struck out time after time.

After a month of this, the Yankee organization reassigned me to a team in a slower league. And so I faced a decision. Did I belong in baseball?

Several years previous to this, I had given myself to the Lord. At the time I considered going into the ministry. But then, it was pointed out to me that perhaps the Lord wanted me to serve Him in baseball. The offer from the New York Yankees seemed to be my answer.

But now I was in doubt again. I wrestled with the problem during lonely nights in hotel rooms and while taking long walks in unfamiliar cities. My playing continued poor.

Then came a letter from my first coach in junior high school, Conley Alexander. It was an encouraging letter. "Just remember, Bobby, that Jesus gave us the only real answer to discouragement when He said *Seek ye first the kingdom of God, and His righteousness and all these things shall be added unto you.*" *

This was great advice just when I needed it. *Seek ye first the kingdom.* As long as I made God first in my life, kept in touch with Him through prayer, and didn't violate His laws, then somehow my questions would be answered.

Thus, freed from confusion, I gave myself completely to baseball. And at once there was an improvement. Within a few years I made it to the Big Leagues.

And, of course, my wife Betsy is wonderful at helping me ride out depressing periods. When I get home after a game in which I'd missed a homer by inches, we talk for a while, drink some coffee, then meet this whole matter of defeat through the devotions which Betsy and I have whenever we can before bed.

In the prayer we tell God how grateful we are for our love, for our healthy children, and for all the friends and experiences that have come through baseball.

* Matthew 6:33

Finally, I repeat the words of a verse that has come to mean a great deal to us. It was sent to us by Betsy's aunt, Jenny Alderman, who is a missionary to Formosa. Somehow this verse always helps us to see difficulties in proper perspective and to realize again that our goal is always to *seek ye first the kingdom:*

He giveth more Grace when the burdens grow greater,
He sendeth more strength when the labors increase.
To added affliction He addeth His mercies;
To multiplied trials—His multiplied peace.
When we have exhausted our store of endurance;
When our strength has failed ere the day is half done;
When we reach the end of our hoarded resources;
Our Father's full giving is only begun.
His love has no limit,
His power no boundary known unto men,
For out of His infinite riches in Jesus
He giveth and giveth and giveth again.

*To conserve money for her round-the-world trip,
Helen Klaben hitched a ride in a light plane for half-
price. Her journey ended two hours later in mangled
wreckage on a Yukon mountainside in the dead of
winter. Now, another journey began—a voyage
through the interior of her soul.*

Stranded in the Wilderness

by HELEN KLABEN

THE needle on the gas gauge of the plane bounced nervously off EMPTY as if it were reacting to something hot.
Yet each gyration brought it closer to the inevitable flame.

My eyes moved in a triangle: from the gauge to the face of
the pilot to the snow-covered mountains just 250 feet below.
Then back again to the wildly jumping needle. We were
going to crash. I knew it; Ralph Flores, the pilot, knew it. Yet
neither of us spoke.

Squinting through the clouds and falling snow, Ralph
searched the rugged Yukon countryside below for some iden-
tifiable landmark; for an open stretch to set the small craft
down. He was lost. Lost, two hours out of Whitehorse over
the Canadian Yukon enroute to San Francisco. There was no
hint as to our whereabouts. No radio contact to tell the outside world we were falling, falling, falling. . . .

We must have blacked out for about half an hour from the
impact of the crash. The next thing I remember is rubbing my
left arm. The pain and knot above my wrist told me immediately that it was broken. My right foot was wedged between the seat and the side of the plane; I couldn't move it
and it hurt. Then I realized my chin was split, and the right
side of my face was bruised.

Suddenly, I remembered Ralph. His seat had broken loose

and he was crumpled against the front of the plane. There was blood all over his face from deep cuts on his head, lips and chin.

"Ralph," I called. He lay there motionless. I was afraid to shake him, afraid of broken bones. "Ralph, do you hear me?"

Night was coming. We would need protection from the cold to survive. Finally, he opened his eyes. When he was fully awake, he moved to the back of the plane and returned with some coats and sweaters.

I struggled to get my foot free and finally succeeded. It was badly swollen and felt as if it had been crushed. My feet were like ice.

Cold and sleep are poor partners. We covered ourselves with all the clothing we could find, but it was impossible to sleep much. Occasionally, we talked. Ralph, a devout Mormon, told me not to worry; that we wouldn't die.

"God has placed us in this mess for a reason," he said matter-of-factly. "They will be out searching for us tomorrow, but it may take several days to find us. Meanwhile, there's something I want you to do: read this Bible. Especially the New Testament. Will you?"

I agreed because of the urgency in his voice. Since I'm Jewish, I think he expected an argument. Really, I had intended to read the entire Bible some day because I wanted to learn more about Christianity.

Learning—that had been my reason for leaving Brooklyn in the first place. I wanted to go out into the world and see the truth for myself. Though my mother understood, she wanted me to stay home, finish my schooling, get married and raise a family—like other girls. I reasoned that to make any meaningful contribution to the world one must live life—explore, participate, grow.

After I was graduated from high school, I worked in many jobs to save money for college. In each one I found something new, so I have found work an education in itself.

Anyway—shortly after my 20th birthday—I heard of a girl

who was driving to Alaska. She wanted a companion to share expenses. We struck a bargain and September 12, 1962, I arrived in Fairbanks—the first leg of my round-the-world trip. For the next five months I lived there—really lived. I studied at the University of Alaska, did drafting in the Bureau of Land Management, skied, hunted, painted, camped, danced. I enjoyed it. But I decided to get on with my trip in January, 1963, and made plans to head toward Hong Kong by way of California. Through an advertisement, I was led to Ralph Flores, a man of 42 who was flying south in his light plane. A mechanic on the DEW line (Defense Early Warning system), he was flying home to see his wife and six children. As his price was about half regular air fare, I accepted. Accepted an invitation to see life by coming face-to-face with death.

After that first horrendous night, daylight came about eight o'clock. Our thermometer registered 48 below. Ralph crawled out of the plane through the broken windshield to build a fire.

Meanwhile, I checked our food supply. It consisted of four small cans of sardines, two cans of tuna fish, two cans of fruit salad, a box of saltine crackers, one-half bottle of protein pills, one-half bottle of vitamin pills, five pieces of chocolate, two tablespoons of orange crystals to make a drink. Our water supply was the snow around us. We had to melt it over fire.

In the afternoon of the first day, we heard a plane. Neither Ralph's shouting nor waving caught the pilot's attention. Dejectedly, Ralph crawled back into our shelter. In the days that immediately followed, we heard other planes, but all our frantic efforts failed.

We marked our first week in the wilderness by inventorying our food. It was nearly gone. I told Ralph this was a good way to diet. Surprisingly to me, my hunger was not very severe. We had water which we imagined was all sorts of hot and cold beverages.

I think I worried more about my right foot than I did food. The toes were blackened and they throbbed constantly. The thought of my toes dying preyed on my mind. I repeatedly asked Ralph if they were dying.

"Don't give up, Helen," he said in a fatherly tone. "Keep praying. Christ will not let us down."

At first Ralph's religious zealousness bothered me, but I came to realize that his strong faith was what kept him going. Even though our food supply ran out on the 10th day, he continued to pray. Instead of thanking God for our food, Ralph now prayed for strength to carry on.

The days crept by. We passed our 15th day, then 20th, 25th and finally we reached the one-month mark. About this time we realized that the search had been given up.

Ralph decided he should go looking for help. Maybe he could find a highway or a lumber camp. While he was gone I read the Bible most every hour of daylight.

My first reaction to Ralph's going for help was, "I don't think we should separate." I was afraid—afraid to face the darkness, the cold and the wild animals alone. But when I was alone for the first time a strange calmness swept over me.

As I read the Bible, prayed and meditated about God, I felt His nearness. He had never before been this real to me. I felt love for Him and love for my mother and family as I never had had before. Fear of dying was completely absent. Instead of complaining, I was able to thank God for His goodness, for Mother, for life. My big worry was that Mother didn't know I was alive. I wanted so much to tell her. Then I realized that for one of the first times in my life I was deeply concerned about someone beside myself.

Ralph returned after eight days, but two days later—our 45th in the wilderness—he left again, hoping to find the source of a buzzing noise. It was ever so faint, but he thought it might be a lumber camp.

That was Thursday. I completed reading the New Testament on Friday. The next day was a beauty, and I was warming in the sun when I thought I heard the sound of a plane. Sunday the noise returned.

This time, however, the plane was clearly visible. First, I

threw an armload of boughs on the fire to raise smoke. Then I signalled with a mirror. The pain in my feet was so intense that I fell to the ground, crying. The plane moved away, but then it happened. Banking sharply, the pilot brought the light craft around and circled back. He had spotted me. My heart was in my mouth, tears of joy streamed down my cheeks. *Thank you, God.*

The next morning men came in on foot and carried me piggyback three miles to the rescue plane. Another party had found Ralph and we rendezvoused in an Indian trapper's cabin. After the best cup of tea I ever have had, they flew us to the hospital at Whitehorse. There I called Mom in Brooklyn and we took turns crying.

Two days later I went to Ralph's room to say goodby. He had lost 58 pounds—down to 120. (I dropped from 140 to 100). When I left the room, he called after me, "Keep reading your Bible."

"Okay, Daddy-O," I promised. He smiled. One week later he flew home.

Upon arriving in New York, I was taken by stretcher to a hospital where the toes of my right foot were amputated. Doctors told me it wouldn't be much of a handicap, and they were right.

While recovering in the hospital, I had time to think about my 49 days away from civilization.

One thing I see is that God was able to use this time to speak to me, because for once I had time to listen. The distractions were minimized. True, I was cold, hungry and in pain, yet I believe even these maladies were helpful in turning my complete attention to God. There was something beautiful and exhilarating about facing death and yet feeling His comfort and presence so strongly.

Now that I am back in college, I think a lot about my Alaskan adventure. From it came one overwhelming truth: God is Love. This truth is mine, not because someone else told me, but because I experienced it myself.

Does religion and business mix? Here is a man who would answer, "Yes," because he built a flourishing business based on one Bible passage.

What Success Means to Me

by Marion Wade

ONE day in 1944, I was moth-proofing a closet in a Wheaton, Illinois home when the chemicals exploded in my face. Most of the next year I spent in hospitals, and that year gave me time to think.

Looking back, my career seemed to be a series of near misses. My boyhood ambition was to be a professional baseball player; I was signed by the St. Louis Browns and sent to the minors for seasoning. While grabbing at a foul tip, I split a finger and that ended my career.

I sold life insurance during the Roaring Twenties—a giddy period when most people believed they were going to live forever. I set up my own moth-proofing business in October, 1929—the week of the stockmarket crash.

Even the most critical experience of my life lost its full impact because I failed to carry it through. One evening in 1930, I accompanied my mother to services at Moody Church in Chicago. It was purely a filial gesture—no more than that.

For a half-hour, the preacher's words were wasted on me because my mind was on my business problems, but gradually some of his phrases penetrated my own thoughts. His text emphasized the Divine inspiration of the Bible. Religion had never made a deep impression on me. Questioning the Divine authority of the Bible never occurred to me because I had never given the Bible that much thought. But now, listening to the preacher, I realized there was something to what he was saying. My experiences in a bitterly competitive business world were evidence enough that mere men could not have written the Bible because mere men were incapable of the selfless and noble ideas in it. God simply had to be the inspiration of it.

For the first time in my life I felt as if God were talking directly to me. When the preacher issued an altar call I went forward calmly. Mother was delighted, of course, but my only feeling was that I was doing the sensible thing. My mistake was in not realizing that I should have done more.

After the altar call, I took a more active part in the church and Bible classes. I subsequently taught a Bible class of boys and coached the baseball team they formed. But I realized that I still had not derived the full personal benefits of the Bible. It was not until the accident and my hospital confinement in 1944 that I made a life changing discovery. I remember turning to the Book of Joshua which I had never seriously studied before.

In Chapter I, I came upon this:

This book of the law shall not depart out of thy mouth; but thou shalt meditate therein day and night, that thou mayest observe to do according to all that is written therein: for then thou shalt make thy way prosperous, and then thou shalt have good success.

I learned later that this was the only appearance of the word "success" in the Bible, but even at the moment I was struck by the clear statement; only when a man lived according to the Bible could he hope to obtain success—success with God, success with his fellow men, success with himself. I read on in Joshua. In Chapter 24, I found:

Choose you this day whom ye will serve . . . as for me and my house, we will serve the Lord.

The thought struck me that although I was serving God more in His house, I was not serving Him enough in my house, particularly my house of business.

What had happened was that in expanding my business to include rug cleaning, I soon saw that the available cleansing substances were either too weak to do good jobs or so strong that they damaged fabrics. To protect myself, I did not offer any guarantee of my work. Then, one night while working in an office building I came upon a magazine advertisement about a new substance and ordered it. I found it wasn't precisely what I needed, but by adding other substances I concocted a really fine cleanser. But still playing it safe, I did not guarantee the results to my customers. While recuperating in the hospital, however, I discovered the real meaning of "responsibility." I was answerable for my business acts as well as for my personal deeds. If I distrusted my product to the extent that I would not stand behind it, whatever the cost, then it was dishonest to expect a customer to take the unprotected risk. I adopted a new policy guaranteeing my services.

Up to this time, I had kept the product to myself, soliciting for my own customers and doing my own work. I now decided to offer the product to others. The only prerequisite I made was that those who sold my product should be dedicated men who practiced fair and honest business policies.

I had a hard time finding the right men. Some I finally located among my former Bible students. Others responded when I placed an ad in the alumni magazine of Wheaton College, "If you believe the Lord has called you into business and would like to work with those of like mind, contact Marion Wade."

Eventually, we acquired a group of men of all denominations who practiced in business what was being preached at them on Sundays. We called our group ServiceMaster—not implying that we felt we were giving masterful service but rather testifying that we were in the service of the Master. Today, I can report our business has been blessed beyond my fondest hopes.

I am aware that many businessmen flourish on immoral tactics and eventually become the richest men in the cemetery. But I believe there is a world beyond the cemetery, and that God will hold men just as eternally responsible for their conduct in business affairs as in all other areas of human relations.

One of the most important tasks facing American business-men today, I feel, is preparing the young people who will take our places in the business world. They will inherit our morals as well as our jobs. The Bible taught me the meaning of "good success." Our youngsters need to know that success won't stand alone.

If we leave them a heritage of cut-throat ethics in which success means more than spirituality, we will be guilty of the most outrageous evil against them, against our country, and, above all, against God, and never in all eternity will we es-cape the responsibility for it.

It seems clear that American businessmen face a decision. In making it, they need have no fears about the future. Joshua assured that God will provide "success" to those who conduct their affairs according to the principles defined in His Book. Joshua also quite plainly puts forth the challenge which no American businessman can ignore.

Whom shall *ye* serve?

"I could not look him straight in the face. It wasn't only his disfigured appearance but there was something furtive about the way he followed me about the warehouse." A dramatic story with an unexpected ending.

Look on the Heart

by Victor W. Wheeler

HE was the first customer to come through the door of my new lumberyard. But the moment he crossed the threshold, his strangely twisted, scarred face and fixed blue-eyed stare repelled me.

In his late twenties, he was slight of build and held his head low. He spoke in monosyllables throughout the transaction. I wanted his patronage but there was something about his ill-at-ease manner that aroused my suspicion: was he honest? Was he heavily in debt?

In checking his credit rating, I found that Frank Dandridge was a cement finisher and concrete contractor. There was no doubt about his qualifications; he had served his apprenticeship under one of the city's most highly respected general contractors. Nor was his financial reliability subject to question. Married, he had one child.

And yet, underneath it all, I didn't like his looks and hated to do business with him, much as I needed the money. My attitude distressed me so much that I prayed about it.

Then I remembered what the Lord had said to Samuel, "Look not on his countenance, or outward appearance, or on the height of his stature . . . for . . . the Lord looketh on the heart." *

This passage really spoke to me. I simply would have to

* I Samuel 16:7

184

overcome my human feelings by asking God to help me with this relationship.

The frequency of Frank's trips to the lumberyard increased. Invariably he sought me out personally to serve him, but I could not look him straight in the face for fear of revealing my feelings toward him. It wasn't only his disfigured appearance but there was something furtive about the way he followed me about the warehouse. Sometimes I had the feeling that he was watching me; other times I could have sworn he wanted to talk to me on a personal basis but was hesitant to do so.

I continued to pray for him and for a change in my own attitude. I reminded myself that "there but for the grace of God, go I."

Weeks followed weeks and a gradual change in Frank began to take place. His conversation was more natural; he seemed less tense.

Yet I still had my original feelings of aversion and could not completely dispel my suspicions.

Then one morning Frank Dandridge came in to make a purchase. When his order was completed and put into his red pickup truck, he scanned his load with more than usual thoroughness, suddenly turned on his heels and headed back into the office!

Naturally I guessed something was wrong, and his abrupt manner seemed to confirm my fears. As I followed him into the office, it flashed to my mind that the common brick I had in stock was not of the best color and hardness and that a few of the bags of cement were packed very hard, though it was all fresh merchandise. I bristled, ready to defend the quality of my merchandise.

Neither of us spoke for a long minute, as my customer stared at me. A trace of a smile played on his lips, as at last he said, "You don't know who I am, do you?"

"Well," I haltingly replied, "I know you are Frank Dandridge, a cement contractor, and a good customer. Other than that, I'm afraid I don't know much about you."

There was another uncomfortable pause.

"I'm *Frankie*. Does that mean anything to you?" The young contractor stood expectant.

Frankie? I sifted through my memories but could find no answer. My consternation apparent, young Dandridge asked, "Do you remember a Mrs. Standish who once worked for you as a bookkeeper?"

"I do, indeed. But that was years ago."

"And do you remember her son and how he accidentally shot himself in the face while hunting?"

Of course, I remembered the little boy: an uncomplaining, courageous and, yes, handsome child—about eight years old. His father was dead and his mother had remarried.

"Well, then," Dandridge continued, "you must remember how you used to visit the boy after the accident and bring him toys and ice cream and draw funny animal pictures to make him laugh?"

My unattractive customer faced me motionless as sculptured granite. "That was 18 years ago but I've never forgotten," he said.

A prickly sensation traveled up and down my spine. That small boy, bravely returning to school, stoically enduring the taunting of his thoughtless classmates about his artificial eye and scarred face, had not only stirred my sympathy but my admiration. I often had wondered what had become of the boy.

Frank Dandridge was obviously that boy. All manner of feelings swam around inside me.

"But, Frankie," I protested, "why didn't you tell me who you were that first day?"

"Well, from the moment I read the advertisement in the paper announcing the opening of your new business, I decided to be your first customer."

"I wanted to say 'thank you' in this way for the help you gave me so long ago," he continued. "I started to tell you who I was—I realized you wouldn't know the name Dandridge—but I thought you'd recognize me."

I felt ashamed. All the time I had been trying so hard to find the good in this man, to overcome my feelings of aversion, to see behind his unattractiveness, it had been his very goodness that had brought him into my lumberyard.

Suddenly from deep inside me came the words I had thought of the day I first met Frank Dandridge: *look on the heart.*

I looked at him now and for the first time I did not see scars. I saw his kindness, his desire to be friendly and I recognized a brighter radiance in his personality.

I put my arm on his shoulder as we walked back to his truck. "Frankie," I said, "do you remember the day when you asked me to help you build a wren house to put up in the old cherry tree. . . ."

Love

WHAT is love? The Bible states that "God is love." A famous author declared that "love is an act of faith." A Harvard professor describes love as "the most effective force in the world."

Regardless of your definition, I am convinced that no search for God and a deeper faith can succeed if the seeker does not have love in his own heart. As Paul said in his famous speech to the Corinthians: *Love is patient and kind; love is not jealous or boastful; it is not arrogant or rude. Love does not insist on its own way; it is not irritable or resentful; it does not rejoice at wrong but rejoices in the right. Love bears all things, believes all things, hopes all things, endures all things.*

The kinds of love I know about make demands on you: love of work, love of friends, love of country, love of family, love of God. The 10 stories which follow will not only give you a deeper understanding of what real love can be, but they also contain practical help for every person who sincerely wants to increase his capacity to love.

NORMAN VINCENT PEALE

Why are so many people frozen when it comes to ex-pressing how much they care for members of their own family? Here's how one woman unfroze.

I Dared to Say "I Love You"

by BECKY BURRIS

ONE day, reading the newspapers, and feeling utterly gloomy about the dark headlines, I asked myself: "But what can one woman do?"

The question gnawed at me all day, until I had to tell myself: "I must do something—even if it's only a little something—to make the world a better place."

My heart spoke first: "The only weapon powerful enough to destroy the hate in the world is love."

My head spoke next: "Before you can make the world better, you must be better yourself; clean everything alien to love out of your heart."

But I was rusty at loving, loving others, anyway. I loved myself. I was self-centered, grabby, given to whining and finding fault. I had to study love, how to get it . . . more, how to give it. I couldn't do it alone, so I asked God for help.

"Take everything unworthy out of me, dear God, and fill me with love," I prayed.

I had to help, of course. I dug and hacked away at malice and envy and greed. After a while I began to feel a joy instead of the stomach knots these evil feelings always left inside.

"Take your home next," my head advised me. "Make things a little nicer for those you live with."

I started next morning. Up early, I told my drowsing husband: "Let me bring you some coffee, honey."

Formerly, I stayed in bed and begged him to bring me coffee.

He was puzzled, but pleased when he got his coffee. I kissed him, and said: "I love you." I had never said that so boldly. "What would you like for breakfast?" I asked him, and there was real pleasure in his eyes, for I'd made him feel important. In a better world everybody will be made to feel important.

Then I woke up my son, and called him: "Darling."

He came out of his room, tugging his shirt into his jeans, grinning: "Did you call me, 'darling', Mom?"

"Yes I did. Why not? I'll call you darling every day, and tell you I love you every day."

He laughed and blushed, but he liked it too.

We'd never been a demonstrative family. But affection should be freely shown, so why not let people know we love them?

My family has a regular ritual now. My husband tells me he loves me, every day I tell him I love him. And we both tell our son we love him. Corny? Maybe. But we live different lives since we began this. We think up ideas to make one another happy. We laugh easier, and surprise one another with novel schemes for laughing. We praise each other a lot, so the little world of our home is a better world.

The next step was to move outside my home. My neighbor was a little lady of 84, all alone. I'd been nice to her in a skittish way. Skittish because I dreaded being regaled with her ailments. "I'm so rushed," I'd gasp, when she caught me, "I can't stop for a moment to talk."

Well, I took some cakes to her. She was sick. And she was happy that anyone thought of her. She said shyly: "Do you mind if I give you a little kiss?" Then she brushed my cheek with lips as soft as rose petals.

The next day she lapsed into a coma, and a week later she left for good—with a smile on her face. I'll never forget her rose petal kiss. It sent me on to others like her, lonely old ladies who live in a row of remodeled apartments in our block, for whom nobody gives parties. I decided to invite them all to tea.

I went to each house, issuing invitations, and with each one, making friends. One lady had just sprained her ankle, but she exclaimed happily: "I'll be well by next Wednesday." She was. They all came, and we had a lovely time.

The world is full of lonely people, old, middle-aged, even young. All of them should be invited to parties; they need to be noticed and made to feel important.

From people alone, I went to people together. At a meeting to study mental health, when given the chance to talk, I said a little hesitantly: "Forgive me for getting off the subject a bit, but I was just wondering what are we doing to make this a better world?"

For a while, they looked at one another in puzzled silence.

Then one lady said: "I'm working with people who give free concerts two nights a week all summer, I'm sure such things make the world a better place."

Another little lady, whose face glowed, said quietly: "I put cookies out for the garbage man."

Everybody laughed. I did too, but I was touched and curious. "How do you do it?"

"I put them in a box, on top of the can," she said. "The first time I put them out, I tacked on a little note saying, 'These are for you, with thanks.'"

Another woman took courage from this and said: "Sometimes I call people on the telephone and tell them I like them."

We looked at her with sudden interest.

"People don't always know that," she said, blushing a little. "I'd be very happy, sometimes, if somebody called me up and told me."

Many of us, I'm sure, told ourselves that from now on we would.

At home, after the meeting, my friend Ruth called. Ruth is a self-sufficient divorcee. She had hooted at the very idea of improving the world.

"You'll howl," she said exultantly, over the phone. "Honest, it's a scream. Here I am running a nursery school."

"You mean, you've got a job?"

"Young mothers, servicemen's wives," Ruth bubbled, "all do their wash in the community laundry on my street, and their babies stumble around under their feet. I asked one mother if she'd like me to watch her kids while she did her laundry. She fell on my neck. And now, honey, I've a regular nursery school; it's the first baby tending I ever did in my life and I love it!"

There was a new note in Ruth's voice. She had put others before herself, and had learned what it means to serve.

That's the only way to show love. Jesus showed us how when He was everybody's servant. We can do no less—if we want a better world.

Is real love of work disappearing in this age of feather-bedding, automation and increasing leisure time? Here's a story by the Art Director of Guideposts which dramatizes one of man's greatest needs.

Love of Work

by SAL LAZZAROTTI

TO this day I don't think my mother has forgotten the loud cry that Pop let loose from the basement.

"Teresina!"

Teresina is my mother's name and whenever Pop calls her suddenly and loudly like that, it means he's in trouble. Mama dropped her sewing basket and rushed to the basement. There, standing dejectedly in the middle of his saws, tools, glue pots and clamps, was Pop.

"What's the matter?" Mama asked.

Pop spread his hands outward toward a pile of kindling in the middle of the floor; and then Mama saw. My father had been refinishing an antique chair for a friend. Somehow it had slipped from the work bench. It had fallen to the floor and the brittle, old wood had shattered into hundreds of pieces as if it were glass.

"What are you going to do?" Mama asked. And in answer my father shrugged, knelt down and began to pick up the little fragments of wood.

"I'll just have to put it together again," he said.

Pop must have spent literally a hundred tedious hours fitting those bits of wood together like a puzzle; glueing, clamping, sanding, varnishing. Today, 15 years later, this beautiful antique still stands firm and solid and Pop's friend, to our knowledge, still doesn't know of this happening. The chair represented my father's craftsmanship. He simply couldn't return it, damaged, without lowering his respect for his own work; to Pop that would be a sacrilege.

This story sums up my father's personality better than anything I know about him. I'm a bit prejudiced, but I think my father is the best example I have ever known of a person who uses work as a quiet, everyday form of worship.

Six days shalt thou labour, and do all thy work: says the Third Commandment. *But the seventh day is the sabbath of the Lord. . . .* Most people read this Commandment with the emphasis on the Sabbath. But my father points out that it is a dual command, and that the first part tells us to work. To Pop, work is a way to get close to God because it is creative, and through it we can better appreciate Divine Creation. It's as simple as that, but this attitude has affected his whole life and the lives of a dozen other people.

My father learned his love of work back in Sicily when he was apprenticed to a master cabinetmaker. Pop remembers so clearly the way this old cabinetmaker would say to him, "Do it right, son: *con amore.*" Pop learned that he'd either have to do a job *con amore*—with love—or do it over. If he failed, the old cabinetmaker would pull him gently by the ear back to his bench and make him stay there until the job passed muster. After a while Pop got so he insisted on a fine piece of work too. He learned how to admire beauty, and how to identify with it, as if it were a thing he had created out of his love . . . which it was.

Pop brought this idea with him when he came to this country. He wanted to see some kind of beauty created in every piece of work he did. A while after he landed here, he got a carpentering job where his foreman wanted the work done "the quick way." One day on an office remodeling job, the foreman told Pop to put up a frame for a heavy glass door. Pop set to work, whistling. Carefully he measured his angles and prepared to brace and counter-brace the frame so it

* Exodus 20:9,10

would carry the door properly. Apparently all this fussing around got under the foreman's skin.

"You're taking too long, Pete," he said, and came over to show my father how to do the job the quicker way, which consisted of little more than driving a couple of nails into a couple of two-by-fours.

This really hurt my father. "Won't you let me do it my way?" he asked, but the foreman pointed out that he was still the boss and that Pop would have to do things his way. Well, my father didn't argue, but he certainly wasn't happy. He kept looking up at that door frame and thinking about how a heavy door just wouldn't hang right in it. And it was too much for him. He couldn't take it. He waited all day for a time when the foreman was out of the building and then, at the risk of losing his job, he slipped back and did the job right!

I love that story about my father. That's the kind of guy he is. The office manager later tested the work and came up to congratulate the foreman on having done such a good job. "That's the way a door should be hung," he said. "No one ever got it right before. Congratulations."

The foreman looked at the frame and he looked at Pop, but Pop looked the other way and nothing was ever said.

My father believes that money should never be the incentive for doing a job well. And this is a remarkable thing because there were times during the Depression when Pop didn't have a regular job and money was mighty scarce. I can remember more than once asking for a dime to go to the movies. He'd give it to me, but he'd say: "Think, now. This could buy enough bread for us all to sit down and have a party ... bread and jam. Wouldn't you rather have the party?" So I'd get the bread. The five of us boys would sit down with Mama and Pop and have ourselves a wonderful ten-cent "party" that would also serve as a meal-reinforcement.

During those days my father supported his family with odd jobs and yet I never knew him to do a piece of work sloppily so he could finish it and get on to another one. He loved his work too much for that. And he felt there were rewards other than money, such as satisfaction, for instance, and a kind of manly confidence. "Confidence comes when you love your work and do it well," he says. "And when you don't, something goes out of you. I remember working with one fellow who held his hammer up near the head . . . with just three fingers. He was no man at all!"

Pop's confidence isn't just a matter of driving a nail straight and planing a true edge; it spreads over into his personal life as well. During those Depression days he often had to work from five in the morning until midnight and many was the day he came home with only $1.50 to his profit; yet I never knew the feeling of insecurity. Pop was as confident that he could raise a happy, healthy family as he was that he could create a strong, beautiful piece of cabinetwork. And this confidence he laid to the fact that he put love into both jobs, and he *knew* what the result was going to be.

Nonetheless, the day Pop got a regular job was a big one for us. He found work as a civilian carpenter in the furniture shop at Fort Wadsworth on Staten Island, New York, where he is still employed. Almost from the day he took the job, Pop was a strong influence on the men around him. Within two years he was made foreman. He spent half his time encouraging his men to do ever better work. If he saw a fellow get impatient when something went wrong, he'd walk over to him and start talking, softly.

"Sit down," he'd say. "Right now you can do a better job sitting than you can working. Take it easy. In a minute things will go well again."

Or occasionally a man would get angry at his work. "You got troubles at home?" Pop would ask, and get the man to talking. Somewhere along the line he'd gently slip in the idea that it wasn't good for a person to take out the troubles of the night before on the work in the shop.

And Pop was always telling his men that if you don't love

your work you can't have much fun in life. He couldn't stand to see a fellow unhappy in what he was doing. Once the Army assigned to him a man who simply didn't like working with wood. "You put a piece of sandpaper in this fellow's hand," says Pop, "and tell him to finish off a table top and he won't do any more than give it a good dusting. As long as he had to work in wood he was a gloomy and slow guy. No man should live this way. But I found out that if you give this same fellow some metal to work with, he's a different man. So he became our specialist in wall lockers. When he's working on the metal lockers, you can hear him all over Fort Wadsworth, singing and hammering and banging away."

But I think the one thing that means the most to Pop about work is the fact that there is a special spirit of dignity that takes hold of a person when he does his job *con amore*. And the job doesn't have to be glamorous, either. A man's job might seem insignificant, but he can still do it with dignity.

"He adds something special to his job," Pop says, "and that something special is himself."

There is the thing. My father thinks that a man should put a little of himself into all his work, because this is what creation is all about. Work is a form of worship for my father because with it, each day, he can see *beauty created out of love,* and to Pop's way of thinking this is about the closest any of us can come to understanding the Force that created us all in the first place.

How many "love" decisions do you make daily? And how many are "self" decisions. Knowing the difference between the two can make an all-important difference in life. An eminent businessman has found a way to distinguish one from the other.

The Right Decision

by ARTHUR LANGLIE

WHEN I was the Mayor of Seattle 26 years ago, I belonged to a group of men that met once a week at an early breakfast for prayer, Bible reading and discussion. We were of many denominations and therefore of many opinions. But we all believed in God, that Jesus Christ is our Saviour, that the irresistible force of God in the world is love.

I soon noticed that after each morning meeting my day went better than normal. The other men admitted the same thing. Our work seemed easier to accomplish, our relations with others were more harmonious, the day seemed richer. Many of us felt that merely having gained more Bible knowledge was not the answer; it was deeper than just knowledge, it was the spiritual impact from this love-filled book and the challenge to try out the eternal truths that it expressed.

In our studies and discussing God's word, I had been particularly impressed by Paul's letter to the Corinthians on the subject of love and Henry Drummond's book entitled "The Greatest Thing in the World." This book explains the spectrum of love and helps break it down to practical and understandable dimensions.

As an awareness of God's willingness to help in problem solving became more apparent to me, more and more I turned to Him in prayer followed by meditation. I found that all decisions made in love brought excellent results.

Since then, deterred from time to time only by my own limitations, I have tried to follow this same procedure before making decisions. That is, I ask God what I should do. There are occasions when I am puzzled for a time as to whether the answer I seem to be getting is actually God's will, or my own thoughts and self-will. But it is my conviction that I know an infallible way by which to test the answers I get: if it is indeed God's answer, my action will be rooted in love.

What happens then is that one manages to get the emphasis away from self. One begins to think of actions to produce the most spiritual opportunity for the most people.

You do not have to be told when you decide against love. Usually the most deadened conscience knows when its attitudes are rooted in resentment, prejudice, envy, pride, when its motivations are self-profit, self-protection, self-importance.

Several years ago came a very difficult decision involving my career. After serving two terms as Mayor of Seattle and three terms as Governor of Washington, national leaders of my party urged me to run for the United States Senate. I did not wish to do this; administrative not legislative work was more interesting to me and seemed a greater field of service. Besides, I wanted more time now with my family. However, my wife and I made the decision together on the basis of the love principle. We agreed that my political experience should not be put aside because I preferred a more private life. I became a candidate for the Senate and worked harder in that campaign than I had in any other. But I lost.

Friends told me that it was a shame my public career should end in the darkness of defeat, but I did not feel defeated. In fact, I felt great. I trusted in the love decision that I had made. Soon after this experience a new career opened up in the business world where I have been busier and happier than ever.

I have never been involved in a "love" decision which, whatever the immediate effects, did not eventually prove abundantly rewarding in some way or another. I have never been involved in a "self" decision which, sooner or later, did not boomerang, causing embarrassment, frustration and a loss of some kind.

It is my conviction that the responsibility for making "love" or "self" decisions is one of the most dignifying traits of human beings. No other creatures, animal or plant, face that responsibility. They merely respond to the forces of nature.

Only human beings have the free will to accept or reject God's will, to use faith-talents positively or to bury them in the ground. Only human beings have the alternative of living within the orbit of God's love or outside it.

A famous comedian tells how he came to separate love from smotherlove. He speaks here as a parent but what he has to say can be wisely applied to any especially close relationship.

The Gift of Giving Love

by DANNY KAYE

HAVE you ever, as a parent, felt guilty about your children? Have you ever worried for fear you weren't giving them enough time, enough love, enough of yourself? If you have (and you're an unusual parent if you haven't), I'd like to pass along something I learned some years ago when our daughter Dena was quite small.

Dena is an only child, and like most very young children she could never understand why occasionally her parents had to leave her. My work required me to travel a lot, but this is hard to explain to a three-year-old. Dena just didn't understand why I had to go away.

When she was about six, I used to fumble around, trying to prepare her for my departure so she wouldn't be quite so hurt when I did leave. I would be extra nice, or talk about plans for all kinds of new fun. Whenever I did such things, Dena would say, "You're going away again, aren't you?"

And each time I returned home I rushed to her, and overwhelmed her with kisses and presents and promises of picnics and parties. All expressions of the guilt I felt at leaving her. I wanted her to overwhelm me too, and make up in one burst of love all that had accumulated during our separation.

I wanted very much to hear her say, "I missed you." But she never said it. Each time I left and each time I returned I sensed a greater withdrawal by Dena.

While I was struggling to find some answer to this dilemma I had to go off on a long trip.

The World Health Organization and the United Nations Children's Fund had told me that millions of children in Asia and Africa could be saved by modern medicine from the scourges of TB, leprosy, malaria, malnutrition, and the like, if the world could be made aware of their plight. They asked me to help make the world aware of them by visiting the WHO's centers to make a film called *Assignment Children*. I couldn't refuse.

At one point on the trip, I found myself in a hospital in New Delhi, India, in a room where a mother and father sat quietly watching their little son who had just been brought in from the operating room.

When the boy awoke I expected them to rush toward him. They continued to sit quietly in their corner. The boy looked around and saw them, but said nothing. After a while he called to them, and they came. They touched him gently, never losing the restraint they had on themselves, never showing any fear or concern, though they must have felt both deeply. They attended to his need, and when done returned to sit quietly. When he wanted something they saw to it. The boy determined when he needed them and how much he needed them. The parents did not smother him with their love or their fears but were pillars of strength and security.

The lesson was vividly in my mind and heart when I returned home, and Dena and her mother met me at the airport. This time I didn't bring the usual ton of gifts, nor did I lavish on Dena kisses and promises.

I greeted them both with a warm hug and kiss, and on the way home talked easily and casually about ordinary things. My wife, Sylvia, sensed what I was trying to do and, bless her, helped right along. I let Dena set the pace and ask the questions. For once I was trying to find out what she wanted, not satisfy what I wanted.

When we got home Dena squeezed my hand and said what I had wanted to hear her say for a long time, "I missed you, Daddy."

I learned a lot that day—that day and the day I spent in a New Delhi hospital room watching a mother and father who knew how to give love, not smother it.

He began his career as a country teacher, not in a log cabin but on one log! What began as a "one log" school is now an educational complex of 25 buildings. Here is how it came about.

Love of Knowledge

by Laurence C. Jones

FIFTY-SEVEN years ago, while working in Braxton, Mississippi, I dreamed of starting a school. Often I'd wander through the piney woods to pray and think, or sit on a log and read.

One day a boy, about 16, came upon me; I showed him my book, but he couldn't read. I offered to teach him. Next day he came by with two other boys.

That was the beginning of Piney Woods School. A pine log and three illiterate students in their teens. But I stood before my tiny class with a deep sense of fulfillment, and announced: "We shall begin by singing 'Praise God from Whom All Blessings Flow.'"

Before the first class was over, 12 students, ranging in age from seven to 60, were on that log. The next day a country woman marched up, head high, shoeless, leading two live geese on a rope. "Professor," she said, "I'm a widow woman and these geese are all I can give, but I have eight children and I sure want you to have a school."

They came in a steady stream, bringing what little they had: a sack of corn, a few potatoes. They were wide-eyed with hope, hungering for knowledge. Most of them could neither read nor write. Among them were the lame, the halt, the blind.

Since that first day, more than 5,000 students have been graduated from Piney Woods. Today they are teachers, doctors, engineers, editors, scientists, skilled farmers and artisans.

They, and the 500 here now, have made Piney Woods 52 years of adventure. During that time I have witnessed what love of knowledge can do to and through people.

When the log became too crowded, we cleaned out a sheepshed nearby, making two classrooms. I slept in the airway between, cooking my meals over an open fire. A sawmill owner in the area, John Webster, gave us 10,000 feet of lumber and Ed Taylor, owner of the sheepshed, gave us the 40 acres around it. We built our first building and planted the acres to corn and garden truck. Others sent us furniture which we repaired and used, and clothes, which we made over to fit us.

One day, a husky boy of 14 walked into the classroom and deposited a sack on my desk.

"Sweet potatoes," he explained. "My papa says I can't come here without money. But Preacher says you'd take me anyway; I'll work hard to learn things."

His name was R. P. McGhee. His family was pitiably poor. But every day, barefooted, in the summer dust and on the winter's icy ground, he walked two and a half miles to the school—after he finished his labors on the patch of land his father share cropped.

Without education he would have spent his days in backbreaking toil, tilling the barren land. R. P. McGhee is now the head of the vocational training department in a high school and has sent his three children through college.

At first my pupils' thirst for knowledge was simply an effort to better their lot. At the time this was not only a land of starvation and ignorance, it was also a land of superstition. But as our students learned modern farming, masonry, mechanics, plumbing, sewing, stenography, bookkeeping, along with their regular subjects, a new awareness filled them; it was awareness of God and the wonders of His creation.

Sometimes we took in whole families. When the bookkeeper at the school told me about the troubles of his distant cousins, we decided to move all of them to Piney Woods. The mother had just died; there were nine children. One by one they were graduated and attended higher colleges. Today one is a postal clerk, another, a skilled carpenter, the third, an expert mechanic, the fourth a social worker, and the other five are all teachers.

When our hopes for the future of the school were at their height, a sudden tornado twisted our building and littered our fields. For three days not one student appeared. I was angry at their ingratitude. On the fourth day, one came, and said cheerfully: "It wasn't too bad, was it Professor? Not a man, woman, or child was lost."

I felt shamed. Worrying about the school, I had forgotten about its heart—the people.

Others soon arrived. They studied the wreckage, and one said, "Nothing we can't fix quick." All agreed.

I came to teach them, and nothing I ever learned or could tell them could equal the lesson they gave me that day.

How did it all begin? My father, head porter in a hotel in St. Joseph, Missouri, where I was born, and my mother, fragile and fiercely devout, both held that doing one's job was nothing more than one's daily duty to God, and beyond that lay the infinite possibilities of him who dared.

"To him who hath it shall be given," they said, and they explained the saying: "To him who hath *faith* it shall be given, not the goods of this world, but a fire to build a better world for other men."

While at the University of Iowa, working as a waiter, bellhop, and firing furnaces, I wondered what I would do with my degree. A friend invited me home for Christmas in Braxton, Mississippi. It was a glorious holiday, but I also saw the pitiful plight of the people there. I knew then what I had to do. Any knowledge I had acquired would be useless unless it were used to help others. Was that not why we were born with this hunger to know, that we might learn in order to help others, and by helping others, grow closer to God?

On graduation, I refused a number of jobs and the security

that went with them, pawned the watch given to me by
friends at the fraternity house where I waited on table, and
went to Braxton. . . .

Today Piney Woods is a large school of farms, gardens,
dairies, with 20 frame and five brick buildings. Everything
was built by the students. They even made the bricks. They
run their own dry cleaning shop, shoe and auto repair shops,
and printing plants. From the beginning each student was
taught two trades, so if work was scarce in one, he could find
it in the other; he learned academic subjects to feed his mind
and nourish his curiosity; and above everything he was taught
the simple direction of Christ's way to free his soul from
hatred and ignorance and fear.

On that very first day, as I stood before my three teen-age
students singing the hymn on the log, our voices seemed to
touch the woods around us, calling for others to come. Suddenly I felt a pair of eyes fixed on me. As I turned to find
them, a twisted old figure hobbled into the clearing, tapping
his way with a cane. He sat down on the log. One of the boys
said, "Professor, this is Uncle Tom Brown," and pointing beyond the woods, added, "He lives back there."

"Do you live alone?" I asked, thinking of the remote cabin.

"Oh, no," the old man said. "Me and the Lord live there."

My heart surged. From that first moment I felt that the
Lord would always be at Piney Woods. The gift He gave us
here was a hunger for knowledge. All He asks in return is for
us to build His Kingdom. Did He not say, *Thou shalt love the
Lord thy God with all thy heart, and with all thy soul, and
with all thy* mind . . .?*

* Mark 12:30

At eight, Kenny was teased by school mates because he couldn't talk properly. His mother, loving her son too much to see him suffer, found an answer that took all her strength, courage and patience.

Love Has a Voice

by Edna Dillon

THE waiting room was full and I was trying to be calm. "The doctor wants to see you, Mrs. Dillon," the nurse said. She had brought my eight-year-old son, Kenny, out of the examining room.

Kenny was almost in tears. I told him to wait, and I followed the nurse in. I looked at the doctor and somehow knew what was coming.

"Mrs. Dillon," he said, "I am going to be frank. If anyone can help your boy to talk it will be a Higher Power than me."

I left quickly. I didn't want to hear about the mustard seed or the mysterious way God works, His miracles to perform. I just wanted my boy to be able to talk.

That night, I picked up my Bible and tried to read, but my mind was in no shape to receive the Word. I kept seeing our unpaid bills, the unfinished chores and always the look of hurt bewilderment on Kenny's face. I laid the Bible down and began to talk to God. You really couldn't call it praying. Some of the things I said were not appropriate to say to God. I hope He has forgiven me.

I just told Him that if Kenny had only fallen down and hurt himself, I, as his mother, could have taken care of him. But Kenny somehow had been hurt in a way that left me helpless. He could not speak right, hardly at all. I told God I knew He had made the world and I said that if He could do that He could certainly help Kenny.

I sat there for a long time. I don't know when the feeling came, but from then on I knew our boy would talk.

Time passed. It was May and school was almost over when my sister in Portland, Oregon, wrote that she had seen a boy in Kenny's condition helped. She had talked to the doctor and she felt sure he could help Kenny. Could I come down?

My husband Elmer said no. "We have five other children besides Kenny to feed and clothe and educate," he said. "If the doctors here had told us to take him to Portland, okay, but I can't see doing it on what your sister says."

That night I sent a letter to my sister asking if there was any work there I could do to cover the expense of the trip. My sister wrote back that I could work at a big berry farm near Portland. The kids and I could live there too. They furnished a one-room cabin with lights and water, rent free, starting the middle of June.

Elmer was surprised when I brought up Portland again.

"Good grief!" he exclaimed. "It's 400 miles from here. Even if you and the kids could make your living which I doubt, it would take $80 to get you there and settled. I can make a car and house payment with that." He stomped out.

I was fixing supper the next evening when I looked up and saw my husband leaning against the door frame staring at me. He looked beat and helpless. Then he told me what had happened. A bunch of boys had teased Kenny, mocking the jumble of sounds he made. Kenny had lit into them, fists swinging. When Elmer heard about the fight and found Kenny, his tormentors were gone. But Kenny, though tough as whit leather, was a tattered and torn little boy.

Elmer suddenly had come up against something he couldn't swear out of his system, or whip with his hands. His kid was getting hurt and there was not a thing he could do about it.

"Mama," he told me, "you get ready and we will get him to Portland somehow."

We decided to go later that week. I stuffed our station wagon like a suitcase. When we were finally loaded, I put the two oldest children and Oakie, our cat, in the back on top of the bedding. The four younger ones sat in front with me. We started out fresh and clean, but by the time we arrived at Sandy Farm outside of Portland that night we were a mess. It was raining and very cold. I waded across two acres of mud to the office of the camp boss.

He had not been sure I was coming so he had given out all the cabins. I'd have to take a tent. It was a big wooden frame with a canvas over it. Inside were two wooden bunks with a bale of straw on each. He loosened the wire and scattered the straw out and I began to make our beds.

At last the children were able to get into their beds and I crawled in myself. I was chilled to the bone. I missed my home and my husband. Turning over I buried my head in my pillow and cried myself to sleep.

Next morning at the hospital, the doctor carefully explained to me that there was a long waiting list ahead of us and it might be six months before he could accept Kenny into the clinic—perhaps longer. My heart sank.

The doctor's examination of Kenny took over two hours. I tried to pray but couldn't. Finally, the doctor called me back into his office. "We don't know what causes this trouble in the vocal chords," he explained. "Sometimes the condition can be helped, sometimes not. It depends a great deal on the child." I asked if Kenny had a chance.

"Yes," he replied. "His I.Q. is very high. We feel he should start treatment at once." He smiled at me. "You are to bring him to the clinic three times a week starting tomorrow."

I started to cry. If I ever believed in a Guardian Angel, I did at that moment.

At the farm we started picking berries at four in the morning. I found that by working till 11 A.M. I could earn enough to help keep us and still be able to take Kenny to his appointments.

Kenny responded well from the start, they told me at the clinic. They wanted me to watch Kenny and his teacher. They put me in a room where I could see him but he couldn't see me.

He and his instructor sat facing each other. The instructor took Kenny's hand and put it on her throat, then looking in a mirror, said a word. He felt how her throat worked and then tried to make his do the same. The muscles on his neck stood out as he tried to bring out the word. His face paled with the effort. Then his face relaxed. I couldn't hear them but I knew he had said "Mama."

Kenny practiced hard at the clinic and at the camp. We would go down the strawberry row picking berries and repeating the words—Mama, Papa, potato, tomato—day after day, week after week.

It rained a lot that season, but we pickers had to work rain or shine. Big Tom, the boss, would drive through the muddy roads of the camp blowing his car horn. If we didn't get out to work, he would come back hollering, "Pick or pack." With us it was pick to eat.

Elmer came down about the Fourth of July. The children all ran out to meet him. Then it was that Kenny said carefully, "Hello, Daddy."

Elmer squatted down on the hard dirt, startled, in awe.

"Hello, Son," he said.

He and his son then had their first conversation.

Soon it was school time again. Kenny was so much improved we decided to go home for the winter. But we returned the following June for more clinic visits—and berry picking.

Meanwhile, I found I was to have another baby. If the farm boss knew I was pregnant, I would lose my job. What to do?

My husband had some striped bib overalls. I dug them out and shortened them, and patched some of his old shirts. As the summer wore on, more and more I fell back on the long-tailed shirts and my "Oakie" pants. I looked like an odd ball, and felt worse, but they kept my secret well.

That fall the doctor called me in and told me Kenny could finish his course in November. I sent the rest of the children home to go to school and settled down to stick it out till November. The berries were finished and the only work was picking up potatoes. It was rainy now and cold and I don't think I could have held out without this Scripture verse to live by: *I can do all things through Christ which strengtheneth me.**

Finally, Kenny was finished at the clinic and we returned home. In February my baby—a boy—was born.

As the days passed, Kenny continued to improve. By eighth grade he was doing above average in school. They gave him a large part in the school play. Everyone said he was good.

Junior high school graduation night came and our whole family was there for the presentation of awards. The last award was to the outstanding speaker of the year. I heard them call Kenny's name. For a minute he seemed stunned. When he arose to accept it, I screamed right out. Both of my girls grabbed me and told me to be quiet. They were ashamed of the scene I made, but everybody else laughed.

My son walked over to me and gave me the award. He wasn't laughing. I felt very close to him. He seemed to be saying, "They forget, Mother, but we never will, will we?"

I went out and sat in the car and watched the graduates go by. I was laughing and crying. I looked down at the award. It was a small clown's face and I was holding it so tight it had cut into my hand.

Someone whistled and I looked up and saw my son go by with a group of happy young people. I tooted the horn and started the car. I felt a sweet kinship with him and with God. We had kept the faith and fought a good fight, and God had given us the victory. I drove home to lay a funny-faced clown among my sacred memories.

* Philippians 4:13

The Ku Klux Klan was out to stop this crusading newspaper publisher, first by threats then by violence if necessary. But Klan members were up against a quality of caring that baffled them.

Love of Country

by W. Horace Carter

THE sound of the car wakened me. It stopped opposite my house, its motor still running. I took a revolver from my night table and sat at the window, watching.

My wife whispered: "Who is it, Horace?"

"I'm not sure," I said. "Are the kids all right?"

Cile listened. "I think so."

I sat at the window for an hour, waiting. Then the car drove away. I went back to bed and was just about to doze off when I heard another car. I returned to the window with my revolver. Two men stepped from the car. I aimed. . . .

Then I heard: "Horace, this is Sheriff Nance."

I called: "It's a good thing you hollered, Sheriff."

"I got a tip they were coming for you tonight," Nance said.

"They were here, but they decided not to get out of the car."

"They probably know you've got a gun," said the Sheriff. "They're not so brave when they suspect you're ready for them, but be careful, they might come back."

For months I had been waiting for the Ku Klux Klan to come for me. Already there had been many threats—by telephone, by mail, even pasted to my office door. Friends in town warned that I was making a serious mistake by fighting the Klan; others showed their feelings by removing their ads from my weekly newspaper, The Tabor City *Tribune*.

But I knew I never could give up.

Today, once more, racial tension and bitterness in the South are rising. Boycotts, sit-downs, mass meetings—the problems go deep, and will not be solved in a moment. But they will be solved in God's good time, I am sure of that. I am sure because of what happened in our little North Carolina town that tense and uneasy summer 15 years ago.

The trouble had started on Saturday night, July 22, 1950, when a 32-car Klan caravan drove slowly through Tabor City. In each car were hooded, white-robed men; on the lead car glowed a four-foot electric cross. For weeks there had been rumors that the Klan was organized across the line in South Carolina. Now we knew they were coming to our town, too.

Monday morning I received a telephone call from Willard Cole, editor of the Whiteville *News Reporter,* a friendly competitor, 18 miles away. We talked about the Klan. "What do you plan to do?" Willard asked.

"I'm going to fight them," I said.

"Swell," he said. "We'll fight together."

For both of us, a fight would have a special meaning. We were both Southerners. I was born and raised in North Carolina and attended the state university. If it had not been for World War II, I probably would have gone right into the newspaper business, but the Navy had other plans for me. Willard had worked on many papers across the country, but finally gave up his wanderings and settled back in the South for the sake of his teen-age children.

We had both learned that people—any kind of people—could live peacefully together as long as they respected one another's rights and freedoms under the protection of mutually beneficial laws. In this nation that protection is provided by the Constitution. I have always had a great love for my country and for what such rights could mean for better living. To us, the mere existence of the Klan was a violation of those laws, and a danger to them. The laws, reflecting so clearly the laws of God, had a moral implication for us. The Klan, we felt, was immoral as well as illegal.

A few weeks after joining forces to fight the Klan, Willard and I decided to attend a Klan rally to observe their tactics at close range. It was held in an open field between our two towns. We heard speeches damning Catholics, Jews, Northerners, Negroes, unions, the United Nations, foreigners, Wall Street and the Federal Government.

These outrages against human dignity and the basic spiritual freedom which our United States Constitution guarantees to every citizen, infuriated us. Immediately, both our papers began an all-out attack. We asked the Klan, so proud of its following, why its membership was kept secret. We asked why the Klan, so falsely American, had no respect for American laws. We asked the Klan, which boasted a fiery cross as its symbol, how they reconciled their actions with the teachings of Him who died upon a Cross.

Then the real trouble started. The Klan attacked a Negro dance hall. Klan bullets flew, and one of them hit a Klansman who turned out to be a Conway, South Carolina, policeman. Then the Klan went to the home of a Negro farmer whom they accused of annoying white women, a charge most people knew was false. The man wasn't home. The Klan took his wife and beat her savagely. Later the Klan whipped a white man, charged with being unkind to his mother. A white man and woman were taken across the state line and flogged. The Klan accused them of having an affair. This was the case that brought the FBI to the scene: having kidnapped persons across a state line, a Federal offense had been committed. Quietly and discreetly, the FBI worked for weeks, preparing its evidence.

At the same time a strange thing had been happening. In South Carolina, several arrests were made for Klan activities, but each time the complaints were submitted to the Grand Jury, the cases were dismissed for lack of evidence. This was shameful, for in some cases the evidence couldn't have been more substantial.

"They're afraid," Willard said. "The Grand Jury members

are afraid that if they return an indictment, a true bill, the Klan will get after them."

There was little doubt of that. Knowing that with the FBI at work there would inevitably be a similar situation in our county, we wondered how our Grand Jury would react.

I knew that I would understand if people were afraid—for months my own life had been full of fear. Threats to me and my family arrived by mail and telephone; warnings were pasted to my office window, and others slipped under the door. The terror was in not knowing whom to trust, in realizing that any number of men who claimed to be friends could secretly be Klansmen, and be used as bait to lead me or my wife or my children, to a darkened place for the Klan's kind of punishment. I always had the feeling that I was being watched, yet I knew I could not give in to the fear.

Klansmen stalked Willard at his office, and once tried to enter his house, but in their confusion they went to a neighbor's home. After that, Willard never answered his door without being armed.

At last came rumors that the FBI was ready to make arrests. At the same time there was talk that, because of the fears that existed, the case should be submitted to a Grand Jury in a distant county. I knew that if this were done the case would be lost in a special way, even before it started.

I talked to Willard. Together we talked to Sheriff H. Hugh Nance, and found that we all felt the same way.

We agreed that laws were useless when the people were afraid to enforce them. Without brave people to make the laws work, our country would become a vacuum where freedom was helpless, justice meaningless. Without courage, the United States and all it stood for would soon become a great hoax. I did not want that to happen to this land which thousands of brave men, some of them my dearest friends, had loved enough to die for in the war. I felt I must not let this happen to the land I loved, the country which my children would one day inherit.

Willard and I talked among our friends and in our papers against the change of venue. Sheriff Nance declared publicly: "The Klan will continue to function in Columbus County until our own people punish the Klansmen with our own laws. I mean to give them that chance." It was a risk, but it had to be taken.

On the day of the Grand Jury hearing, hundreds of cars lined the circle around the courthouse in Whiteville. We knew that some of them contained Klansmen; others contained policemen. To protect the witnesses, Nance had other people, not associated with the case, stroll in and out of the courthouse several times to confuse the watching Klansmen.

All day the jury listened, and all the next day. So important was their decision that I could not think of anything else, nor could Willard. Even in war, neither of us had ever been in greater personal danger than we were in the past few months. A wrong decision would have meant we had struggled for nothing. Worse, it would have meant that our communities had permitted a disgrace.

Then the verdict came: 89 men were indicted, including Grand Dragon Hamilton. At the trial, 74 were fined, many receiving suspended jail sentences; others were imprisoned on terms ranging from 18 months to seven years, and Hamilton was sent to prison for four years. The Klan's hold on the community was broken. The people had triumphed over lawlessness and bigotry.

Looking back over the terror-filled weeks, Willard and I both wish that there could be some special medal provided for people like those who served on the Grand Jury—people who could put aside their justified fears in order to enforce the laws of honor and dignity in this land which God has given us.

Twenty years after German aviators destroyed a famous English church, another group of Germans invaded England with a completely different mission. A story of contrast from Aktion Blitzkrieg *to* Aktion Sühnezeichen.

They Build With Love

by RAYMOND CRIPPS

ON a well-remembered night of horror in October, 1941, the people of Coventry, England, awoke to hear the familiar throb of German bombers overhead. When dawn came the next day a great part of the city, including the famous Coventry Cathedral, lay in charred and smoking ruins.

Twenty years later, an exciting series of events began taking place as a direct result of that October, 1941, bombing. The results could be far-reaching.

In November of 1961, a group of 16 young German workers landed in England to offer their services, skill and labor to the city of Coventry. They were part of a movement called *Aktion Sühnezeichen.*

The name is virtually untranslatable, a mixture of atonement, reconciliation and restitution.

Aktion was founded by East German Lutheran Provost Walter Kreissig, who felt moved to call for a demonstration of reconciliation and friendship from the young people of Germany toward their country's former enemies. Kreissig was convinced that many young German workers and students would be willing to give up their jobs for six months, and work for practically no pay on group projects in former Nazi-ravaged countries.

Friends told him he was crazy—that many young Germans still believed in the former brown-shirt terrorism—but, despite the danger from East German authorities and Communist secret police, Walter Kreissig went ahead with his plans for *Aktion* just the same. Schools, youth clubs and churches all over the country promised to contribute three to six dollars per month to support the working groups. In the end over 200 volunteer workers came forward.

When the 16 Germans who volunteered for England arrived in Coventry, they found a new cathedral nearly completed, that of Saint Michael, a magnificent, modern architectural structure. But alongside, with its bomb-shattered walls and jagged pillars reaching gauntly to the sky, the bombed-out Gothic cathedral was to remain, a permanent reminder of man's potential for destruction.

It was beneath the old cathedral, in what were formerly the vestries, that the young German Christians began the task of constructing the International Centre planned by the cathedral authorities.

Group leader was 43-year-old Ludwig Schmidt, a woodwork teacher in a West Berlin Technical College. Ludwig Schmidt spent the years from 1945-50 as a prisoner-of-war in Russia. Youngest in the group was Bernd Radtke—an 18-year-old bricklayer from West Berlin. Two girls also came with the men to do the sewing and cooking. Ellie Greitschus, 21, and Helgard Eichel, 19, who heard of *Aktion Sühnezeichen's* appeal over the radio.

When they arrived in Coventry, the group did not really know what to expect from a city which their fathers had tried to wipe off the map. To their surprise they were welcomed warmly and showered with invitations. The first job on hand for the group was to clear out the rubble in the old vestries. They also put in windows, erected a roof and plastered the thick stone walls.

By December the roof was on the new structure within the ruined walls of the old cathedral.

By Palm Sunday, 1962, the International Centre, comprising a chapel, library, lounge and coffee bar, was finished. The

Centre has been decorated and furnished in modern German style, funds coming once more from West German churches. Konrad Adenauer personally gave $10,000 to the building fund. Students and tourists meet here and encouragement is given to gatherings for informal discussion of Christian work and ideas.

The *Aktion* group has now returned to Germany and the members are making plans for additional projects in Asia, Africa and Latin American countries.

Meanwhile, the great new Cathedral of Saint Michael, like the old, ruined Gothic predecessor beside it, will bring man closer to God for generations to come. But no activity within the new walls will surpass the quiet love-action of the 16 young Germans, two of whom have seen the inside of Russian prison camps, and most of whom have seen a wall divide their city of Berlin and its people from one another. These dedicated Christians have demonstrated that forgiveness and love are not mere words, but a healing, unifying power.

He sweet-talked her, then left her with child. It is the age-old story of a compromised woman. But what is new and different is the reaction of friends and neighbors in this particular community.

Love of Friends

by HEATHER HUME

I CANNOT give the names of the people involved, nor shall I identify the place where this story was lived out. Yet I feel that it is a story about the love of friends which ought to be shared.

Our neighbor Joan was a woman of sincere faith. She took her four children to church. She contributed her share of time and effort to all the school and community projects. None of this was easy. When her last baby was born, her husband had deserted her. She had come home from the hospital to an empty house.

Her husband never returned. He had periodic breakdowns and was in and out of hospitals so that he never could give her any financial support. There were no close relatives to help. Because of a car accident she had suffered just before the birth of the last baby, her health was such that she could not seek a job. She had no choice but to accept welfare help. This was not easy for her, but it meant that she could stay at home and care for the children, and for this she was grateful.

She had little recreation, and never had anyone to share the responsibility of the children. They were four lively boys, yet she dressed them neatly, disciplined them fairly, and made them behave as well as any other children on the block. They had none of the pleasures of the other children, no luxuries at all.

Oh, the rest of us were "good" neighbors, I suppose. When

our children outgrew clothes we passed them on to her. Sometimes we remembered to ask if she'd like a ride when we went shopping, but usually we forgot. Most of the time she had to drag a wagon nearly two miles to the shopping center with her boys helping to get her groceries home this way.

Sometimes we dropped over to chat. Sometimes we thought to bring a cake or a pie. But usually we just forgot her. Our lives were busy. Our lives were pleasant. Or if there were problems that made us tearful or frightened, there was a husband to take us in his arms, to say the right things, to comfort us.

It was no special heartache to Joan when she received divorce papers from her husband. But it didn't change her life. There was still no money for a baby sitter; no opportunity to get out anywhere to meet anybody; no chance to extend her circle of friends, let alone meet a man. And what man would want to take on a family of four boys?

This feeling that there was never any hope, that each day would be the weary repetition of caring for the children, keeping the house clean, making the small welfare money stretch farther than seemed humanly possible, was, perhaps, the worst of all problems for Joan. For escape there was the radio, there was T.V.—nothing more.

When Joan's roof had to be reshingled, we were all mildly interested and pleased to observe that the shingler was a pleasant looking, middle-aged man with a nice new car. Moreover, he took an unusually long time doing the job. All this was to the good, we thought, because each weekend he took Joan and the children off for some of the good times they'd never had before. She said very little about it to any of us, but her step was lighter. She looked younger. She looked happy. Each week, now, he came and took her shopping in his car, and her children were saying: "Maybe we're going to have a new Daddy. He's asked us and Mom may be going to say yes—that is, if he keeps on liking all us boys."

The roof was finished, but we saw the car there often in

the next few months. Sometimes we asked jokingly, "When are we going to have to give a bridal shower for you, Joan?"

She smiled. "I'm not certain but I'll sure let you know."

And then, one day, the car wasn't there anymore. Someone asked the boys about this. They said, "Well, he had to go out of town. When he gets back, he and Mom will get married."

But more weeks passed and the car didn't come back, and Joan looked old and tired, and her face was so sad it made you want to cry. She stayed in the house now. She didn't accept rides to get groceries. We noticed she found a store where prices were too high for her to pay, but which delivered groceries.

When one of us discovered she was hanging out clothes at night, and never answering the door anymore, but sending the boys to say she was lying down, we exchanged opinions. Somehow most of us women were together in a group when these facts were mentioned. Someone said, "She must be all broken up because he doesn't come any more. It was so nice for her and the kids when he did."

And then someone else: "Well, I think it's worse than that—I think the man has walked out on her because she's going to have a baby!"

There were ten of us sitting there on the lawn. We all gasped. *That* was why no one ever saw Joan outside anymore. *That* was why the groceries were delivered. *That* was why the clothes were hung out at night!

Nobody said anything. We, the women who had comfort and love from kind and protecting husbands—what had we done to keep her from the kind of loneliness that had brought her to such an unhappy end?

"She's ashamed," someone said finally, "and she's afraid we will shame her too. Well, we'll have to show her different. It's terrible he's done this, and left her—just as her husband did. Left her!"

There were some bitter remarks about "that kind of man," and then decisions. "All right, girls, we've got to do something about this. It's our problem now. She can't carry it alone."

And Joan didn't have to carry her problem alone. The closest neighbor simply walked in and gently let her know that her problem was understood. More than that, that everyone would help.

She was too bewildered to do anything but cry. She's been about ready to commit suicide trying to face things alone.

We left nothing more to chance. We took turns seeing she got her groceries. We took turns seeing she got to the clinic. Every Sunday one family on the block made it their job to see she was invited with her children to their house for dinner.

Her children blossomed at all this wonder. But there was the problem of our own children. It would not be long before the situation would be apparent to them.

The ladies talked it over one day. "We've got to tell them," we decided, "tell them the exact truth."

And so in each home the parents explained to their own children in this way: "Joan is going to have a baby. You need a father and a husband for this, but the man who said he wanted to be her husband lied and left her all alone. This makes it very hard for Joan. Very often people laugh and say cruel things when this happens to a woman. People expect her to be wise and never let this happen. But sometimes people are so lonely they let mistakes happen. Often people say cruel things about the little baby who does not have a father to love it. We *never* want to hurt Joan, or her children, or the little baby she is going to have. It's up to all of us to give them some of our love to make up for all they don't have."

The children listened—and they understood.

Joan was given a shower, just like any other prospective mother on the block. Our husbands kept her lawns mowed, her small house repaired. When she was in the hospital, different families kept her boys. The men on our block painted her house outside, we painted it inside. Among us we all provided the clothes and the baby equipment she needed.

No woman was ever more watched over and prayed over

than she. The day she left for the hospital, every man, woman, and child on the whole block was kept informed on how she was doing, and the whole block woke up happily at midnight as doorbell after doorbell was rung to say she was safe and had—at last—a little girl. No one minded being wakened. Everyone wanted to know the minute it had happened. A whole neighborhood was "standing in" as family for this event.

Each of us learned something from this, something unforgettable, something profound. We learned that the "first stone" is not the one flung by a cruel and self-righteous hand. The first real stone is the one we don't take the trouble to remove from the road where others, less strong than ourselves, may fall over it.

None of us *before* our neighbor's tragedy had cared enough to bring her close to our busy, happy lives. Some of the sinning had been our own.

We will be more careful now. We have drawn closer, all of us, since we learned the importance—the supreme importance—of loving our neighbors as ourselves.

*"How can I love a God who allows so much suffering
and tragedy to happen in the world?" You have heard
this question raised many times, but have you heard
it answered? This author gives an answer out of her
own experience.*

Love of God

by Laura Margaret Evans

WHEN one of our daughters was five, she saw a picture
of a house that had burned to the ground. She studied
it silently for a few moments, then said, "If God let *our* house
burn down, I wouldn't love Him any more!"

I looked across at the brimming eyes and her trembling
mouth—and I remembered. I remembered the time in my
own life when I had experienced the same rebellion and bewilderment. There was a time when I had looked at people in
the midst of tragedy and thought, "How can they still love
God after this?"

I can barely remember those days now—not because they
were so long ago but because my whole conception of God,
my love for Him, has deepened so tremendously that my life
has taken on new dimension.

This new dimension in loving God began quite late for me
—much later than it does for some people. For I had graduated
from college and had gone into training as a physical therapist.
It was my first real face to face encounter with physical, human tragedy and, for once, I could not turn my back in youth-
ful escape. I *had* to look because I was there to help.

My first day in the out-patient clinic started well. I worked
in occupational therapy with the Cerebral Palsy children,
helping them with the peg games and the blocks. As I watched
their infinite patience, their dogged attempts to master the

art of co-ordination, I felt a deep affection for these extraordinary children, and, with it, a tremendous urge to do all I could to help them succeed.

The first week wasn't bad. I was so full of hope and high expectation. But as the weeks wore on, a gradual change began to take place in me. I found myself straining as hard as they over the smallest task; I felt the same tearful dismay at each tiny failure. I tried to smile. I tried to remain optimistic and gay but I was becoming so fully identified with them, that this attitude was impossible.

I found that when lunch-time came, my stomach was knotted and my throat so tight I simply couldn't eat. At night, I was so exhausted and discouraged, I pushed my dinner aside. Then I began to be aware of a coldness within me—a hard, unyielding "something." Yet, strangely, it seemed to give me strength against despair, and so I kept it.

I thought no one noticed it. In fact, I myself was unaware of its real nature. But one of our supervisors—a wise and compassionate woman—knew. She walked through the cafeteria one day where I was toying with a lukewarm milkshake. She stopped by my table and put her warm, capable hand on my shoulder. "My dear," she said, "don't try to bear their sorrow. They are given strength as they need it. All we can do is to help as much as we can. You must not allow yourself to become so involved."

I remember clenching my teeth and thinking: "Not get involved! *I* care what happens to these children even if God has forgotten them!"

Then in a flash—in an ugly, sickening flash—I knew what was the matter. I hadn't been able to blame the parents, I couldn't blame the doctors, so I had turned to the only available object at which to shake my fist—God. And I was a minister's daughter and a Christian, as well, by my own personal choice. Yet I was angry with God! Why?

Well, why not? Had I ever known anything but the warm, reassuring life of health and well-being? Why then should these children have to struggle so hard just to run and talk and jump rope like other children? Where was this benevolent God and His compassionate Son I had worshiped for years? Why didn't God answer my prayers for the children?

Because I did pray for them every night, but He never seemed to hear. It was as though, suddenly, for no reason, He had ceased to care. And so I started to resist and draw away, like a bewildered, petulant child.

That noon, as I walked back to the clinic, I was more aware than ever of the coldness in my heart and I wondered if I had ever really loved God.

At one o'clock, I gave treatment to a twelve-year-old post-polio patient. She was a lovely, redhaired girl with a wistful smile and beautiful hands. She wanted to be a concert violinist but polio had left her trunk and legs nearly useless.

That particular day, I did my best to be cheerful and amusing and I worked especially hard with those legs, giving vent to this rebellion inside me. For it was rebellion, of course, and I even found myself savoring it, as though by its mere presence, I could hurt God and thus retaliate in some way against His "abandonment" of these children.

When we had finished the treatment, she said, "Sometimes after you've 'done' me, I feel as though maybe I will walk again!" And her eyes almost sparkled. When she had gone, I turned, I remember, and pressed my head against the wall as hard as I could because the tears were coming and I was so angry I didn't want to cry!

Those months were difficult months for me. They were months of real spiritual seeking. I listened intensely to each sermon, to every Bible lesson with the hope that I would find the answer to this struggle I was having.

Then, one Wednesday night, I heard a young chaplain fresh from a tour of duty in the South Pacific and what he said that night opened a whole new world for me.

He said, "I have seen two kinds of men in this war: men whose love for God is no more than a parasitic vine, supported only by what life can bring to them. When anything in their life goes wrong they blame God and their love for Him crumbles and dies and they are destitute.

"Then there are those whose love for God is like an oak tree. You sense their stability—their lives are strong and confident. These men have a taproot that goes deep into God Himself; they are rooted in Him rather than superficially supported by their own desires."

There were over a hundred people in the room that night, but I felt he was talking directly to me when he finally ended by saying: "Our love for God must be strong and unwavering, unconditional, dependent on nothing but God's love for us. *We love Him, because He first loved us.** "

Suddenly, I was ashamed of myself. How many, many ways God had been showing His love to me through the years, proving His presence over and over. Yet, at the first touch of dismay, I had turned from Him, disregarding all I had learned. Now, I realized, I had to change my attitude from one of resentment to one that was open and receptive to Him. I knew somehow that if I trusted Him, someday I would be given wisdom and understanding.

It was hard for me at first, very hard. But as I continued praying in this new way, I found my entire outlook changing. Instead of my being drawn down to the sorrow and grief around me, I was being sustained on a higher level than I had been. I realized that what I had thought was concern for others, had really been a selfish feeling of frustration, of uselessness that stemmed from pride. My love had been selfish—certainly not the oak-tree type the chaplain had described!

Now all this was being changed! In place of resentment, I found a buoyancy growing within me.

It was *this*, then, that sustained the children—not just the medicines and therapy. It was this quiet strength and assurance, this love that comes only from God, that they sense and from which they in turn draw strength . . . a long, un-

* 1 John 4:19

ending channel of love that starts with God and runs like a cable through hundreds of dedicated people to those who need it most.

How good God was to have shown me this, how patient! Only He could have known how much I was to need it, for not many years later—a marriage and three children later— it was I who was in the hospital bed and who had just heard the doctor tell me as gently as he could: "Laurie, you must stop fretting about getting back to your family and face the fact that it may be a long time before you can return to them as a wife and mother."

Looking back on it now, I think that my bout with polio and the long convalescence that followed might have been a bitter experience if I had not already learned to love God with real confidence. I don't think I could have learned to love Him during my illness. I have watched too many struggle to find Him during such times, but because they were so spent, physically and emotionally, it was a hard, lonely struggle.

For me, that struggle had been resolved before and though I was not immune to times of discouragement, the bitterness never again crept back. For with my love for God, came a complete trust, a giving over of anxiety.

It is a knowledge that your life is fully held in God's hand, that though situations may seem impossible, even hopeless, the worry and the despair are replaced by the presence of God and the realization that each one of us is an essential part of His plan.

Now, in our home, our girls are learning the truth of this. They are learning that when we turn from God, *we* are the losers—bitterness takes all beauty from life; separation from God takes away all purpose from living and, year by year, they will know that the man or woman who loves God, is never alone, is never defeated.

Courage

HAVE you ever noticed how the words faith and courage so often go together? When you think about it awhile, one is a part of the other. So, any faith-strengthening program needs a section on courage.

The word, courage, means "mental or moral strength to venture, persevere, and withstand danger, fear and difficulty." Too many people, however, think of courage as the risk of one's life solely in a physical way. The truth is that almost everyone shows courage, or the lack of it, in the small everyday situations of life.

How do you get courage? And, having it, how do you keep it from slipping away? There are answers and help in the following stories—stories that concern both types of courage: like the bravery of FBI agent Sam Cowley; the moral strength of a teen-age girl faced with a decision on a date; a businessman who encountered pressure to pad his expense accounts; a father who was tempted to lie for his son; a mother threatened by social boycott and violence if she didn't follow the crowd regarding a racial situation.

All of the people in these stories show great courage, the kind of courage that bears out the Scriptural promise: *Be not afraid . . . the Lord thy God is with thee whithersoever thou goest.*

NORMAN VINCENT PEALE

The Director of the F.B.I. tells a story of an intrepid Special Agent who was instrumental in bringing to justice such murderous thugs as John Dillinger and "Baby Face" Nelson.

Courage Takes Time

by J. Edgar Hoover

I HAVE known some very brave men in my time.

But there is a difference between physical bravery and moral courage. Bravery is a temporary manifestation. It flashes forth to meet a sudden challenge. Moral courage, however, has the dimension of *duration*.

The latter may be less spectacular than the sudden type of heroism, but it is more important because it endures. It's the month-to-month, year-to-year, steady, sustained devotion to duty and principle as opposed to self-interest that may never make any headlines, but without which the world would be a dark and dangerous place indeed.

What I am saying, I suppose, is that the greatest adventure in moral courage is a moral life. I truly believe this. Every life—yours, mine, everyone's—is an endless series of choices between right and wrong, good and evil. No one makes *all* the right choices. But the struggle to make as many right choices as possible goes on ceaselessly, and this is what makes life the great adventure that it is.

Now, what is the quality in a person that makes a moral life possible? It's discipline, isn't it? Self-discipline is precisely the quality that the criminal lacks. He can never say no to himself. He can never deny a selfish impulse. He steals, he robs, he cheats, he kills because that seems to him the easiest way to get what he wants. The undisciplined person is always wondering what he can take from life with the least possible effort. It takes a controlled and disciplined person to wonder what he can give.

It is also a theory of mine that physical courage, in its highest form, rests squarely on a moral base. Let me tell you about a man whose life was a shining example of this.

His name was Samuel P. Cowley. He was not quite 30 years old when he entered the FBI as a Special Agent back in 1929—a big, young fellow, as solid and dependable as he looked.

At that time, when the Bureau was smaller, I made a point of knowing all my men personally, and so I knew all about Sam Cowley. I knew that he was deeply religious, that from 1916 to 1920 he had done missionary work in the Hawaiian Islands for the Church of Jesus Christ of the Latter Day Saints. I knew that he had attended the Utah Agricultural College, working as a salesman during the summer months to pay his tuition. I knew that later he took a law degree at the George Washington University. I knew that he was a Sunday school teacher, that he lived a clean, honest, hard-working life. *I knew, in other words, that Sam Cowley was already trying to make his life an adventure in moral courage —and I knew that this was the kind of man we needed.*

To come into the FBI in those days, you had to be an ideal-ist. Sam Cowley's starting pay was $2,900 a year. The FBI had made no great reputation at that time. Except in special cases, its agents were not even allowed to carry guns. With his edu-cation and character, Sam Cowley could have earned far more money in a far less difficult and dangerous job. He chose not to consider these things.

Did this choice involve moral courage? I think it did. The Depression had not yet struck the country. There was easy money to be made almost anywhere. Like most young men, Sam Cowley wanted to raise a family, to give his wife and children a few luxuries. But he chose the FBI because he felt that the most important thing to do with his life was to fight against evil. His personal comfort and safety meant less to him than being on the side of good.

We brought Sam Cowley along as fast as we could because we needed him. We were fighting a crime wave that was a grim hang-over from the Prohibition Era. Bootlegging had put vast amounts of money into gangster pockets and had bred in them a chilling contempt for the law.

Perhaps the most vicious of all was John Herbert Dillinger, bank-robber, jail-breaker, police-hater. His gang included a trigger-happy murderer known as "Baby Face" Nelson. Between September, 1933, and July, 1934, members of this gang killed ten men, wounded seven more, robbed four banks, and broke out of three jails.

In June I called Sam Cowley into my office. By this time I knew that he was one of our most determined and capable men, but I think my choice was based on something more than that. To me, Dillinger and his gang were the personification of evil. Sam was one of the finest characters I had ever known. I think that, unconsciously perhaps, I was trying to oppose this vile personification of evil with the highest example of good it had been my pleasure to know, because religion teaches us that good is stronger than evil.

I remember quite clearly the orders I gave to Sam. "Stay on Dillinger. Go anywhere the trail takes you. Try to take him alive, but protect yourself."

It was a tough assignment, grim and dangerous. The hunted man was constantly on the move. In his dogged pursuit, Sam Cowley crossed the country from coast to coast, from southern Florida to northern Michigan. He was almost never at home. He and his wife were planning to buy a house where their two small children could have their own play yard. Their plans had to be postponed.

The days lengthened into weeks. And if Sam Cowley was displaying moral courage, what about his wife? What were her thoughts every night as she tucked her two small boys into bed and waited for the phone call that might, or might not, come? It would have been very easy for her to show her fear, and by showing it to distract her husband, or even sway him from his hazardous task. But she never complained. Love can make you courageous—very courageous.

Everyone knows how Cowley and his men cornered Dillinger as he left the Biograph Theatre in Chicago. When the gangster clawed a gun from his pocket and started to run, three of our men fired five shots . . . and Dillinger fell dead.

Next day I wrote a letter of commendation to Sam, praising him for his persistence, patience and energy. As a reward, he was promoted to the rank of Inspector.

Some men might have been content to rest on their laurels, but Sam Cowley was not that kind of man. He considered his job unfinished so long as any members of the Dillinger gang were at large. In particular, he wanted to capture "Baby Face" Nelson . . . and four months after Dillinger's death Sam got his chance. In a gun-battle near Barrington, Illinois, one of our agents was killed and Sam Cowley was mortally wounded. He died early the next morning. But their mission had been completed, as that same day the body of "Baby Face" Nelson was found in a roadside ditch not far from Chicago.

So in one murderous moment, the FBI lost two of its finest men. And what is my point? My point is that this sacrifice was not just a magnificent demonstration of momentary heroism. It was the culmination of that greatest of all adventures in moral courage—a truly moral life. As a friend of Sam's said at his funeral, "I have thought that his name should have been Peter. He was a veritable rock to those who knew, who loved and trusted him. His was the calm of a man who did his best and left the final decision to a Higher Power."

There, it seems to me, is the key, the answer to those who wonder what the secret of a moral life really is: do the best you can and leave the rest to God.

Religion points the way. I honestly believe that if every child in this land went to Sunday school every week, if every adult went to church with the love of God and his fellow man in his heart, if each of us would make a conscious and sustained effort to live by the Golden Rule, a moral revolution would come not only to America, but eventually to the whole world.

This may seem visionary, but we can all hope for it and work for it and pray for it. I know I do. Every single day.

"How will my daughter act?" is a question all parents ask themselves when they see two teenagers leave the house on a date. Here's a story of how one teenager faced a small crisis.

The Girl Who Said "No"

by Nora S. Houghton

THE excitement of the preparations for Donna's big night left me exhausted. How could one dance entail so much planning, so many dreams? Sometimes I felt as if I were the 16-year-old, not Donna.

"I honestly believe, Dear," Mike had said to me one evening, "that you mothers get more fun out of these parties than the kids."

"Fun?" I almost shouted. "You mean agony."

And it was true. When Donna met Bobby Cameron she had known at once that she liked him and she had known too, even though nothing was said about it, that he would ask her to the dance.

But time grew short and Bobby did not call. I, myself, began to jump when the telephone rang and was as disappointed as Donna when it was only the upholsterer or Elsie, Donna's best friend.

But finally Bobby phoned. Donna spent the money she had earned baby-sitting to buy a party dress. It was beautiful— blue organza, short and very full. Mike and I treated her to a white fur jacket and Bobby brought a gardenia corsage when he called for her.

It was only after they had left the house that I realized that Mike had been right, that we mothers do live our children's experiences with them. I was exhausted. It was a relief just to sit in blessed quiet. Mike had taken his Boy Scout troop on a week-end hike and I was alone.

I must have dozed off for, suddenly, I was startled by the opening of the front door. I looked at my watch—11 o'clock—too early for Donna. Cautiously I hurried to the hall.

But it was Donna, holding her white fur jacket at arm's length, carelessly dragging it on the floor. I almost scolded her but I stopped myself in time. She looked so woebegone.

"Donna, you're home?" I said tentatively. "So early?"

Donna shrugged her shoulders and threw her jacket onto a chair. "I had a terrible time, Mother. I just want to go to bed." She pushed her lower lip out as she always did when she was unhappy, a habit she'd had since babyhood.

Then I watched her slowly climb the stairs. I asked no more questions because I felt her hurt without knowing what it was. More, I felt my own hurt at being shut out.

Later, as I lay awake, I wondered what could have happened. Was it just a minor adolescent mishap or was it something more serious? Bobby had seemed like a nice boy, yet. . . .

Pictures came to my mind of situations in which Donna might have found herself. Some of them brought an ache to my heart and I was afraid.

Mike and I had tried to teach Donna spiritual and moral values so she would have inner resources for emergency use. Rather than merely giving arbitrary rules and specified do's and don'ts to obey, we had tried to instill in Donna the will to behave because she, herself, wanted to be good.

When she studied the Ten Commandments in Sunday school, we had tried to identify each Commandment with a situation in everyday life so she would know it wasn't just history she was studying but some really practical, modern-day guides.

But were these things really enough? Had we really given Donna adequate preparation to meet the problems of growing up?

I remembered, then, something we had laughed at only the year before. Donna had begged to go to a beach party with the boys and girls from school. I gave in, reluctantly, after a lecture on behavior, stressing that people are more relaxed at the beach. "A girl has to be very careful," I warned. "There are so many things that could happen."

"Oh, you don't have to worry, Mother," Donna had reassured me. "We're going with *boys*."

But now she was 16 and a high school senior even though she'd gone to bed looking like a tearful little girl.

Suddenly, I heard a very quiet knock on my door and Donna stuck her head in. "Mother, are you asleep?" she asked softly.

Before I'd even said "No, Dear," she had rushed in and sat at the foot of my bed.

"Oh, Mother, the dance was awful," she began. Then slowly, painfully, she told me what had happened that evening.

The party had started out pleasantly enough. There was chatter and laughter and the girls stood in groups, admiring new dresses and corsages. Then, gradually, the boys and girls paired off and began to dance and the parents who were chaperoning went off to watch TV.

"We'll be back in a little while to see if you need anything," they said as they left. This was to let the youngsters know they were being chaperoned, though unobtrusively.

Donna and Bobby danced. The only trouble was that now and again Bobby would leave her for a few minutes to pay a rather mysterious visit to some of the boys clustered in one corner of the room. Finally, curious, she followed him over. The boys were passing around a bottle of whiskey.

When Bobby saw Donna and the disapproval on her face, he said, "Oh, don't be a baby. After all, I'm old enough to join the Army."

Donna didn't say anything but she didn't like it. Soon Bobby's face became flushed; he danced too fast and laughed too loudly.

"The other boys, too, were acting silly and every time they

did something goofy, the girls would laugh at them. This made them even worse," Donna told me. "But they all quieted down whenever the parents came in."

After a while one of the older boys said, "Let's drive over to my house: we can have a real ball. No one's home and we won't have to be so quiet." Bobby was the first to agree to go. Some of the other boys went with him to get the girls' wraps.

Donna was worried. She didn't think she should go but she was suddenly facing a decision. Should she refuse to go? Should she risk ruining her very first date with Bobby? And the girls? What would their reaction be if she backed out?

Bobby returned with her jacket. She looked at him a long while.

"I'm not going." Donna was almost as surprised as the others when the words popped out.

"What do you mean?" Bobby asked.

"I mean I'm just not going."

But it was Elsie, not Bobby, who became angry. "If you don't go with us, it makes the rest of us look bad." Then she threatened, "You've been my best friend, Donna—but if you leave, you won't even be in our crowd."

"Come on, be a good sport," someone else urged.

"It's O.K. They're nice kids," Bobby coaxed. "Nothing will happen."

Donna didn't know what to do. She wanted her friends to like her but. . . .

She grew silent now, telling me about it. But it didn't matter. I could see how it had been: the boys flushed from the unaccustomed drink, the girls lovely in their party dresses and Donna standing before them, unsure of herself and puzzled. Her friends didn't believe they were in the wrong. How could she be sure she was right? What if they did stop being friends with her?

I remembered how Donna had waited for the phone call from Bobby, how she'd planned for the new dress. I remembered the excitement, the happiness, only a few hours before.

Did she have to learn so soon that it's easy to be disappointed in people—that the choice between right and wrong is not always easy?

"Donna, what did you do then?" I asked at last.

"I came home by myself. I called a cab and waited until it came for me." It sounded so simple the way she said it, until she started to cry, "Oh, Mother, I really liked Bobby, I really did. . . ."

The next morning we had breakfast—just the two of us— in near silence. I could do nothing to ease her distress.

Then, shortly after we returned from church, the doorbell rang. It was Bobby.

"Did Donna tell you?" he asked sheepishly.

I nodded, then asked him in, breathing a prayer that I could handle this episode correctly. Donna turned off the radio and stood up. She didn't say a word.

"I came to tell you I'm sorry," the boy blurted out. "I thought you were a square for making such a fuss but I've been thinking it over and, well, I guess I'm the square."

"You're not angry?" Donna asked.

"Angry? With you? Heck no," he smiled and then asked hesitantly, "Will you go to the movies with me Saturday?"

Donna looked at me but I gave no sign of either permission or disapproval. I felt she had earned the right to decide for herself. But I hoped she would go with him, because I liked a boy who could admit he was wrong.

"Sure," Donna said.

The old glow was back in Donna's face—and in my heart. A real challenge in the process of growing up had been met. I realized now that the seeds of morality, if planted early and firmly, do take root and flower. I had a great sense of relief and pride that my daughter had not followed the crowd, had had the courage to say "no." I don't know how Donna will make big decisions in her life, yet I am grateful that she had been able to make a small but important one with true moral courage.

A Cuban editor refused to knuckle under to Castro. Here's what happened to him.

The Night Our Paper Died

by José I. Rivero

HAVANA was filled with an excitement which you could see in the brightness of men's eyes and hear in the pitch of their voices. The hated dictator Batista had fled. Rumors flew from lip to lip that Fidel Castro was on his way to Havana, coming from the mountains where he had fought Batista for five years. Already the city was filled with Barbudos, the bearded, war-dirty Revolutionaries, carrying carbines, waving to the crowds that lined the Prado.

And then Castro himself did come, bearded, smiling; yet if you looked closely you'd see that his eyes did not pick up the smile on his lips.

At first I was happy to throw the support of our newspaper behind this man. I am sure that Castro was happy, too, about that support. *Diario de la Marina* was the oldest and most influential paper in Cuba, with a reputation for speaking out against tyranny. My grandfather had been stoned because of his editorials. My own earliest memories are of exiles: my three brothers and I were taken often to the United States "to visit relatives" while my father stayed on to fight the dictator Machado.

When it was my turn, I, too, printed the truth as I knew it about Batista, and rejoiced to see his regime topple. None of us was aware that the biggest fight was still ahead.

I was full of hope as Fidel Castro came into Havana. Within a week, however, I began to suspect that something was wrong. For Castro was bringing Cuba not freedom, but hatred. He spent long hours on TV spitting out promises of revenge. He showed us how he dealt with his enemies: he executed them before TV cameras. On home sets children were watching the death throes of men who were shot before the paredon, the firing wall.

Castro's reforms? He seemed bent on coupling them with vengeance. New schools were rising, but with this went a harsh proclamation: any academic degree earned during Batista's regime was invalid.

Economic aid? He had promised cheaper housing: arbitrarily he cut all rents in half, whether the landlord was a millionaire speculator or a widow whose only income was the rental of a spare room. Under another law, hundreds of farms were seized. Farm workers had their wages cut almost in half. Of this, only 50 cents a day was paid in cash, the rest in script usable only in "People's Stores."

A suspicion was growing that Fidel Castro was a Communist. In my mind, I began to review: his use of hate to gain support; his People's Courts; his division of society into two classes, one the hero, the other the villain. But most disturbing of all were the advisers he called to sit with him in the Palace; many came from Communist countries.

What should I do about it, I asked myself? I had watched Castro handling his enemies before the paredon. There was no doubt in my mind that if I crossed him, mobs would appear outside our windows shouting "Paredon! Paredon! . . ."

What should I do? I was proud of the new buildings which housed *Diario* now: the rotogravures, gleaming behind glass doors; the thump and whir of our new presses. Here was a powerful, ready-made medium, but it could speak only if I told it to.

Then one day, early in February, 1959, I sat down at my desk, and suddenly, I was aware of the crucifix. It was a simple ivory crucifix which my mother had given me. I had mounted it on velvet and hung it over my desk to remind me always to use the power of the paper in a Christian manner. Now it seemed almost as if Jesus were looking down at me with sadness in His eyes, saying:

"You will lose the paper. You may lose your life. But do you have any choice?"

I knew in that moment that I did *not* have any choice. From that day on I began to write editorials about the things I did not think correct in Fidel Castro's regime.

Castro reacted as I knew he would. After my first editorial he berated me on TV, shouting that I was the newest "enemy of the people."

But I did not stop the editorials.

A month passed. And another. Castro broadened his barrage: not only on TV but also on radio and through the controlled newspapers he urged the public not to buy *Diario*. When our circulation doubled under his attack, he turned to the brute strength of the mob.

"I cannot take responsibility for the actions of fired up Fidelista," he shouted over TV.

And the Fidelistas took the hint. They burned bundles of *Diario* on the street. Crowds of hundreds appeared outside my office. I began to hear the cry I had been awaiting: "Paredon! Paredon!"

And they began to harass my family. One evening my home was surrounded by 12 secret police. The next day I sent my wife and part of our family to Miami "to visit relatives." I never went back to our home. From then on I spent each night in the house of a different friend, and drove to the office in a different car. I felt the end was near.

I cleared the office of all valuables. Almost all, that is. I didn't know what to do about the crucifix. I didn't want to lose it when the paper was seized, yet I didn't want to be without it. I do not mean, of course, that an ivory crucifix had any power of its own. But it did remind me of my need to be especially close to Him. I left the crucifix on the wall. It gave me the sense of Christ's participation in our paper's martyrdom, and this gave me the strength to carry through the next few days.

It happened just as I had expected. A group of Fidelistas arrived at the paper, walked through the plant, urged our employees to strike. After the Fidelistas left, however, our men passed a petition supporting the paper. I wrote an editorial about that petition and sent it to press. Later that day, while I was away from the paper, the Fidelistas came again—this time with machine guns. They broke through the glass doors into the rotogravure room and smashed the plates. Then they left.

I returned as quickly as possible, and my three brothers and I went through the rotogravure section picking up fragments of the plates. As we stood there amid the debris, I heard a stir and a gasp of surprise from the employees behind us.

I turned around. There stood Mother! She was supposed to be in Miami, safe. "If my sons are going to die," she said, "I am going to die with them."

"Now, Mother," we answered, "no one is going to die. But you can't stay here in Havana."

Mother stood firm. "The *paper* is going to die," she said. "I am not going to watch it happen from Miami. I fought beside your father and I'll fight beside you."

We literally had to pick her up and carry her from the building.

Mother's visit had stirred us with still greater determination.

We prepared another engraving of the petition, then started the presses. I waited at the plant until nearly 11 o'clock, then went to the home of friends for dinner. We had barely seated ourselves when the telephone rang.

"They have stopped the presses. Do not come down, José. They are after you now. . . ."

On that night the *Diario* died, after opposing Castro for a year and a half. It was the last independent journalistic voice in Cuba.

I hid in a friend's home. I cannot identify the person who

later took me to asylum in the Peruvian Embassy, but this much I can say: it was not easy to arrange. The Fidelistas had guessed my plan. Before dawn they lined up at the Embassy, carrying their machine guns. I hid beneath a shroud-like sheet in the back of an automobile and was driven up to the Embassy door. Minutes later I slipped into a private entrance.

I was safe. A few hours later I escaped by plane to Peru.

Looking at it one way, I have lost my fight. Our family home is gone. I sneaked out of my own country. Our newspaper is dead there.

But I wonder if the battle is really lost? A few days after I reached Peru, I boarded a plane for the United States. We landed at Miami where, to my amazement, a crowd was waiting, shouting and waving placards saying "Hurrah for *Diario de la Marina!* Viva Rivero!"

It wasn't really "Viva Rivero!" that they were shouting. It was "Viva!"—that power which each of us is given to stand for what he believes. It was "Viva!"—the spirit in each of us which can stand up to injustice. As long as this spirit lives, is the battle lost?

I am sure, quite sure, that it is not.

"Everybody lies. You will, too, someday," said the defiant boy. "Never!" replied his father. Then came an agonizing test of his stand.

I Saw My Son Running Away

by HAROLD R———
as told to SIDNEY FIELDS

STEVE," I asked, "where are you going?"

He scowled. "To see Betta," he said. "I'll be back soon."

Betta was his girl friend. She lived a few blocks away, near the park. A nice girl. Good parents.

Steve is my son. Tall, with a broad back, and thick, dark hair. When I held him in my arms, proud of our only son I told my wife: "He is a gift to the world." And his mother shared my pride with her soft lovely smile.

For 17 years he is our son—and a mystery. We do not know him. Strong and headstrong—and maybe a gifted artist. He works at it in spurts of fury. He will draw a laughing bunch of boys and girls, trees in bloom, kids playing in the snow. Gentle things like that. He has promise.

"Come home early," his mother said. "Tomorrow is a school day."

"I said I'd be back soon, Mom. You worry too much."

"Before ten-thirty," I called.

"Okay," he said and left. It was nine-thirty.

"He'll be all right," I assured my wife. "He's just growing up."

"I don't like those new friends he has," she said.

We had tried to talk to him about his new friends, but we were in two different worlds. The boys a few blocks away were tough. Steve seemed to want to prove that he was just as tough, that he could hold his own. We tried to talk to him about those friends, about living with purpose. But it didn't help at all.

How do the walls get so high between parents and a child? Steve used to share the music we loved. We all would go to the park and to the concerts together to hear it. Two years ago he got his own record player, money he saved from a summer job helping commercial artists. He liked his own kind of music, and laughed at ours.

He used to share our faith. A year ago he stopped going to church with us. Maybe we didn't know how to make it a real living thing for him. He just stopped going. It didn't seem good trying to force him. Every Sunday we asked him:

"Coming with us, Steve?" And he would shake his head.

"You have to be at least thankful."

"Sure, Pop, I'm very thankful."

And he began lying—first little lies, then bigger ones.

"Steve, you can't lie and live with yourself," I said. "You can't lie no matter how the truth hurts. It's against God and it's against man. Lying is stealing with your mind."

"You're making a big thing out of nothing," he said. "If you don't lie now, you will one day."

"Never," I told him. "No matter how it hurts. I couldn't live with myself."

My own son, and I don't know him. What could I do or say to show him the meaning of God and truth? How many parents are there like us?

We went on worrying, and hoping, and praying.

At ten-thirty my wife said, "I won't phone Betta's house. He'll tell me I'm treating him like a baby."

"You lean over backwards not to treat him like a baby," I said.

I went out to find him.

Betta was standing in front of her house. "Where's Steve?" I asked.

"He went into the park with the other boys a few minutes ago," she said. "He told me he'd be back soon to say good night. He'd better hurry. My mother called me twice already."

"I'll find him," I said.

I took the first entrance into the park. Why would they go into the park? It was almost eleven. I hurried, searching the darkness for a movement, a sound.

A few seconds later, a man's voice suddenly shattered the silence: "Help! Help!" I rushed toward the noise. Just beyond the glare of a street light four figures bent over a fifth figure on the ground. Racing footsteps were coming down the walk. A flashlight swept the darkness. A cop's whistle shrilled. The four figures leaped up, ran in my direction. As they rushed into the lamp light I saw their faces clearly and my blood froze—one of them was Steve.

Someone came sprinting from behind me, another policeman. He tripped one boy, thudded his foot down hard on his back, grabbed Steve with one hand.

"Stay right here, mister!" he ordered me. The first policeman moved towards us, holding the two other boys. They forced all four to a bench. With guns drawn they made them sit down. One policeman stood behind the bench, the second in front.

I was standing at one end of the bench, Steve sat at the other end.

We did not look at each other.

The man who had been on the ground hobbled over to us, cursing. "They mugged me!" he yelled. "One of them has my watch."

The policeman in front of the bench quickly searched all the boys. He found the watch in one boy's pocket. He found a switchblade in another boy's pocket.

The man who had been mugged looked at them one by one, in a blind, cursing rage. He stared at me.

"Who's this guy?" he asked.

The second policeman pointed to the spot under the light where I had been standing. "He was there."

They asked me questions: My name, address, what I did for a living, and finally the question that drained the blood from my heart.

"Did you see them?"

I tried to speak. No words came out. My mouth was dry with the taste of ashes. I was trembling. I shut my eyes to shut out the ugliness before me. I couldn't. I was there. My son was there. Three other boys were there. A man who might have been killed was there. I had seen it all.

To myself I said, "No, officer. I live just a few blocks away. I was just taking a walk. I heard a man yell, help. But I saw nothing. Nothing."

"Steve, you can't lie, and live with yourself. . . . It's against God and against man. . . . Lying is stealing with your mind. . . . You can't. . . ."

"Did you see them?" the first policeman asked again.

"Look, mister," the second policeman said, "this is important. You let a few punks get away with this and they laugh at the law and go on mugging, and worse. Tomorrow it might be your wife, or your kid."

My wife! What would I say to her? Where were the words for that? My mind was an agony, my words came out hoarse:

"I saw them."

The policeman behind the bench pointed his ungunned hand at the first. "Was this one?"

I nodded. He pointed to the second boy, then the third. I nodded. He reached the end of the bench. I looked away.

"Was this one, too?"

I couldn't turn my head toward Steve. I nodded.

"You're not looking at him," the second policeman said. "Look at him. Look at him good."

"Steve, you can't lie and live with. . . ."

My heart was weeping. I was numb with pain.

"Come on over here!" the second policeman ordered Steve. He waved him in front of me with the gun. The policeman behind the bench flashed his light full in Steve's face.

I looked up slowly. Steve's eyes were filled with dread.
"Steve," I said. "Steve. . . ."
"Steve!" the second policeman said. "You know him!"
"He's my son."
They were the most painful words I would ever utter.
Both policemen stared. The mugged man's mouth opened in disbelief. Steve glared at me, hate and tears filling his eyes.
"Steve," I said, "one day you'll know you can't lie. . . . Steve!"
He turned his back on me.

•   •   •

EPILOGUE

Steve and the other three boys have now served out a three-year sentence. Here is part of a letter Steve sent his father from jail:

"Dear Dad, I thought about what you did for the thousandth time and hated you for it. But what I see here in prison made a lot of that hatred go. All of the guys here are full of hate—and I don't want to hate. . . .

"I know now that life has to have truth. Without it, it's no life, here or hereafter. . . .

"You asked me to forgive you for saying those words that terrible night in the park, 'He is my son.' You wrote me that those words were not your last words, that your last words would have to come from me, from what I make of myself. I ask you and Mother to forgive me. I pray God that He will, too, so the final words will be good words, and you can say, not with pain and shame, but with pride and love, 'He is my son.'"

"No one but God knows the struggle I had," wrote the Senator who determined the fate of a President. "I almost literally looked down into my open grave. Friendships, position, everything . . . were about to be swept away. . . ." A dramatic and crucial moment in American history.

This Was a Man

by Starr West Jones

IS there moral courage in politics today? How many really big men are there among our elected officials?

Some people say we've never had so few good men in politics—or so much corruption. I don't agree. I think there is a trend toward more sacrifice, moral courage and personal integrity among elected officials. The trouble is the bad ones get publicity and the good are too seldom known.

But one remarkable example of moral courage by a U.S. Senator stands out in my mind. It is a story that I feel should be told and retold.

Senator Edmund G. Ross of Kansas experienced an incredible ordeal in 1868 during the impeachment proceedings against the 17th President of the United States—Andrew Johnson. Perhaps never has there been so public a testing of the fiber and character of a man.

President Johnson, lacking in tact and powers of persuasion, had not been able to further the postwar reconciliation plans of the assassinated Abraham Lincoln. He had made enemies by refusing to follow the demands of the Radicals in Congress who wanted to hold the defeated South in subjugation.

Then, convinced that his Secretary of War, Edward M. Stanton, was the pawn of the radical Republicans, President

Johnson asked for Stanton's resignation. Stanton refused to resign.* The President suspended him. Stanton barricaded himself in his office and thus touched off a violent struggle between the executive and legislative branches of the government. Passions became so heated that Congress determined to impeach the President.

The trial continued through nine weeks of political debate and personal vilification with the anti-Johnson forces having a clear edge in numbers.

In the Senate of 54 members, the Republicans held a majority of 42 to 12. All Democratic Senators would vote against impeachment and six Republicans had indicated that they believed the evidence was not sufficient for conviction. That left 35 Republicans who would say "guilty." They needed only one more for the necessary two-thirds majority. The one uncommitted Senator was Edmund G. Ross.

Ross, appointed to fill the unexpired term of one of Johnson's strongest supporters who had died in office, was a Kansas newspaper editor. He had opposed the policies of his predecessor; the radical Republicans felt sure he was the needed 36th vote.

Shortly after the impeachment proceedings had begun, Senator Ross quite casually exploded a bombshell. One day, in conversation with a fellow Senator, Ross said:

"So far as I am concerned, though a Republican and opposed to Mr. Johnson and his policy, he shall have as fair a trial as an accused man ever had on this earth."

From that moment on, Ross was subjected to unbelievable pressure. He was hounded and spied upon. His entire background was carefully scrutinized and analyzed. His every move, and all his companions were recorded in special notebooks.

Finally, the night before the Senate voting was to begin, Ross received this telegram from home: "Kansas has heard the evidence and demands the conviction of the President.

* Basing his action on the Tenure of Office Act.

Signed D. R. Anthony and 1,000 others."

Ross telegraphed back to Kansas:

"To D. R. Anthony and 1,000 others: I do not recognize your right to demand that I vote either for or against conviction. I have taken an oath to do impartial justice according to the Constitution and laws, and trust that I shall have the courage to vote according to the dictates of my judgment and for the highest good of the country. Signed E. G. Ross."

What background made Ross act as he did? Who was Ross, really? That he had been the editor and publisher of Topeka's *Kansas Tribune* was generally known, but little else.

Edmund Gibson Ross was born on December 7, 1826, on an Ohio farm, the third of 14 children. In an ox-drawn covered wagon he had emigrated to Kansas Territory from Milwaukee, the head of a group of settlers determined to keep Kansas from becoming slave territory.

Ross settled in 1856 near Lawrence, Kansas. He and his brother William established newspapers there and later in Topeka. In 1859, Ross had a prominent part in shaping the constitution under which Kansas was admitted to statehood.

In July, 1862, Ross organized and captained a company which distinguished itself in the Battle of Prairie Grove— "The Gettysburg of the West." A year after he was mustered out as a major, Ross was called to Topeka by his former regimental commander, now Governor of Kansas. Without preliminaries, Governor Crawford told him:

"We need a man with backbone in the Senate. I saw what you did at Prairie Grove, and I want *you* for Senator."

Edmund Ross went to Washington. With his ability and background, an illustrious future was predicted. Yet very soon he faced a decision which could cost him his career before it was hardly begun. "No one but God knew the struggle I had," he wrote later.

The day arrived for the impeachment vote. When the Chief Justice called his name, Senator Ross rose to his feet. As he later described it:

"Every individual in that great audience seemed distinctly visible, bending forward in anxious expectancy. . . . Hope and fear seemed blended on every face. . . . I almost literally looked down into my open grave. Friendships, position, everything . . . were about to be swept away. . . ."

But Senator Ross' answer to the roll call came in a voice that was firm and final: "Not guilty."

The President had been upheld by Senator Ross' single vote.

Ross paid for his action. In the years that followed, neither he or any other Republican who had voted for acquittal was ever re-elected to the Senate. Even back in Kansas, Ross and his family became social outcasts.

Why did Ross vote as he did? Years later, he wrote:

"In a large sense, the independence of the executive office as a coordinate branch of the government was on trial. . . . If . . . the President must step down . . . a disgraced man and a political outcast . . . upon insufficient proofs and from partisan considerations, the office of the President would be degraded. . . ."

As more years passed, the clamor against Ross waned and shortly before he died in 1907, even the once hostile press praised his moral courage. Said one editorial of the time:

"By the firmness and courage of Senator Ross the country was saved from calamity greater than war. . . . He did his duty knowing that it meant his political death. . . . He acted for his conscience and with a lofty patriotism, regardless of what he knew must be the ruinous consequences to himself. He acted right."

This was a man.

The pressure to conform can be almost irresistible, especially when it affects one's job and home. Here's the unforgettable story of two parents who refused to go along with the crowd.

Hold My Hand, Look Straight Ahead

by JAMES O. GABRIELLE

NO one in New Orleans was especially concerned about the date November 14, 1960. It was, we all knew, the date set by the Federal Court for the integration of Negroes into the public school system. Some integration had already taken place—on the buses, in parks, at Louisiana State University—and all this had come about with very little ugliness.

There was one sign though, if we had known how to read it, that pointed to the trouble ahead. It was the petition that had gone around pledging those who signed to withdraw their children from any integrated school. My wife, Daisy, encountered the first hint of trouble one bright afternoon early in November.

She had built up a little business selling costume jewelry and was showing the new catalog to a neighbor when the subject of the petition came up.

"No," said Daisy, "I haven't signed. I don't think it's right."

The woman slammed the catalog shut. "I'm afraid," she said, "that you had better leave." The friendship of one neighbor, or maybe a two-dollar sale, Daisy thought, was all that her convictions were to cost her.

Monday morning, November 14, Daisy and little Lola stood in the doorway as our five older children set out for school. One of them, Yolanda, our next-to-youngest, was on her way to William Frantz School, three blocks away. As Daisy watched her skip down the street she didn't know that another six-year-old, Ruby Bridges, was also on her way to Frantz. Ruby was a Negro.

I was out on my job as a meter helper when I heard the news. The trouble, it seemed, was mostly fear of trouble. As soon as they had heard about Ruby, mothers—hundreds of mothers—descended on Frantz School and took their children home.

The next morning my wife stood at our door as usual, inspecting Yolanda before school.

We didn't say much.

We had said everything there was to say the night before, over coffee in the kitchen. Daisy had become a serious student of religion in recent years. "If you don't put your beliefs into practice, what good are they?" she had asked. By the time the pot was drained she had my backing.

Daisy walked to school with Yondi, that day. But along the curb of the block opposite the school was a line of women. "Yondi," Daisy said, "those women may say things. If they do, you must not answer. Just hold my hand and look straight ahead."

Already the women were calling. "Hey, Daisy!" someone yelled. "Where you going?"

A few of the women crossed the street and came close. One of them let out a piercing catcall. "Yaaaa! Look at the nigger lover!"

Daisy and Yondi turned into the schoolyard and the women fell back. Inside, the empty halls echoed as they walked to Miss Kay's room. "Well!" said the teacher. "Hello, Yondi. I'm glad to see you. Come over here, dear, away from the window. . . ."

When Daisy left the building, the mob was waiting. All the way home they shouted vulgar words and threats and once Daisy was safe in the apartment, she collapsed into a chair. How was she going to keep up her courage?

Yet Daisy did, for three long weeks. She did it through a very powerful, very simple technique. She never looked around.

This is a most amazing thing about my wife. When Daisy becomes convinced that something is right, she fixes her eyes straight ahead as though they're fixed on Christ; she never looks around. She keeps her eye on the Light, and does not look at evil.

I used to believe this was just ivory-tower thinking. Not with Daisy. She brought it right down into the street, into the long three blocks between our home and William Frantz School!

"How can you stand it?" I asked her one night.

"I couldn't, Jimmy, if I looked at their faces. I'd freeze in my tracks the moment I saw anger and meanness. But those are surface things. I know some of these women. Deep down they are good people. If I look straight ahead I can remember the good things."

What a strange power there is to this idea. It kept Daisy walking the day the rotten egg broke on her dress. It kept her going when the rock crashed through our living room window and when a woman rushed up and struck her.

It worked so well that one day a neighbor called Daisy to say she wanted to join her. "Fine," said Daisy, and a few minutes later the two mothers and two children were walking down the street together between rows of hooting women.

They got to school with no trouble. But on the way home that afternoon, our neighbor forgot. She turned. She froze in her tracks. Like Lot's wife turning toward evil, she saw the hatred and the anger in the faces of 40 fist-clenched, stick-waving women. She didn't join Daisy again.

As the second week passed, the pressures continued to build. Daisy began to be afraid, not only for herself but for her family. So many rocks had come crashing into our home that we hung heavy blankets over the windows and lived in a perpetual twilight. Both Daisy and I had been threatened;

all of us had lost friends. One of the older children spent her time in the kitchen listening to the radio. When you're a teenager, it is hard to lose every friend. . . . "*Every friend,* Dad! No one will talk to me."

The pressure was telling on me too. When I came to work in the morning, everyone—except one man, God bless him—moved to the other side of the room. I was demoted. One day I was called into the head office. "Just had two phone calls, Gabrielle. Your little girl's been shot."

I ran out the door, tipped a taxi driver to speed, yet found Yondi playing in her room. It was a trick. I don't know how much longer I could have stuck it out, but the matter was taken out of my hands.

It was Wednesday of the third week. When Daisy and Yolanda left school, they faced another mob. Daisy's pulse beat faster. There was a new, deeper note in the voices around her. She warned Yondi again to look straight ahead.

And little Yondi forgot. Halfway home, she turned. Her mother felt her grip tighten. "Don't be afraid, honey," her mother said.

But Yolanda had seen the hate. At home she cried, remembering the faces. She hung on to her mother and she followed her everywhere. That night she could not sleep.

That settled it. We adults could stand for our principles in the face of hate, but couldn't force our children to do so. We were glad that there were 10 children in school now for we had to leave. We did, in the middle of the night, moving from the town where Daisy had lived for 35 years. We left our furniture in the apartment.

Today, we live in the little town of Centerdale, Rhode Island. We're starting all over again, from new cups and saucers to new friends. Was it worth it, Daisy's stand?

Recently there have been encouraging signs. We have heard that in the last New Orleans school board election the man who won was an outspoken foe of rule-by-the-mob. And then there are the letters from people who represent the real

South, thanking Daisy for what she did.

But the most important event of all, perhaps, was the action of one single neighbor. This man taught us that an act done for God is never done alone. Where one act fails, another is begun.

This man lives in the same apartment building where we used to live. We didn't know him well. But on the day after we fled New Orleans, he changed his mind about integration. He walked through the same door as had Daisy and Yolanda. He took his son by the hand and started down the street between rows of hooting, jeering women. And as he walked, he looked straight ahead.

This business executive was torn between the fear of losing his job and the conviction that cheating has no place in the business world. "Am I crazy not to play along with my salesman?" he asked.

A Little Matter of Expenses

by NORMAN VINCENT PEALE

IT was nearly midnight when I arrived home, but my daughter Elizabeth was still up studying.

"Mr. Roger Wilcox * phoned," she said. "He says he has to see you tonight."

"It's late," I objected.

"I know," she admitted, "but he insists. He's only in New York for a few days."

Roger Wilcox is a department head in a large company. When I called him, his voice was fuzzy and strained.

"I hate to bother you, Norman," he said, "but this is urgent."

Within a few minutes he had arrived. When we shook hands, his first words were, "I've had a couple of drinks, but I'm sober now." Then he added, "You don't find the answer in a drink do you?"

He sat on the couch and buried his head in his hands. Silently, I prayed that God would reach into this man's heart and mind so that he could unburden himself.

Finally Roger said, painfully, "I'm afraid for my job, Norman. And the thought is pretty devastating." Roger was in his 50s. Perhaps his age had something to do with his fear. Or were there other factors?

"The problem seems so complicated," he said. "Perhaps I'm crazy not to play along with my salesman."

* Names have been changed.

263

"Is one of your salesmen giving you trouble?" I asked.

"It's the padding of expense accounts," he said. "Maybe I'm too old-fashioned."

His top salesman had submitted a convention expense account which showed $100.00 for cab fares. But Roger knew that a friend had provided all his transportation free.

So Roger called the salesman into his office. "My expense accounts are no different from anyone else's," the salesman said angrily. "If I go to the trouble to get a friend to drive me, so what! That's ingenuity on my part. Besides, since my salary isn't enough, I have to find other ways to make ends meet."

Roger then quietly explained that if one salesman got away with padding expenses, every salesman would try to do so. A little dishonesty soon can lead to a lot. The company had to have a firm policy.

The salesman became coldly hostile. "If you refuse to approve my expenses, I'll take the matter to the president. He won't back you; he pads his expenses, too. If you stick to this principle," he warned, "you'll lose your job—just you wait and see."

After the salesman stormed out, Roger slumped back in his chair. An icy feeling of fear crept up his back. Was he making a mountain out of a molehill?

And then Roger tried to face up to the salesman's threat. Would he take the matter to the top brass? Would the president back him? Roger wasn't sure. If, indeed, the president did pad his own expenses, how could he condemn it?

Roger decided that he would go to the president and lay the situation before him. But before he could, the president called him into his office and, in the course of general discussion, made a statement that went something like this: "Roger, we've got to give our salesmen greater incentives. After all, they are the lifeblood of our company. Let's do everything to keep them happy."

Roger went home that night, distraught with inner doubts.

Had the salesman gone to the president? Were the president's words to him a sly warning?

That night Roger tossed and turned. He became convinced that his job was in great jeopardy. If he stuck to his convictions, the salesmen would surely gang up on him. He had no confidence now that the president would back him.

The next day Roger flew to New York on business. But he couldn't get away from the problem. Finally, that evening he sought out the nearest bar. The drinks didn't help. Then he called me.

I felt my friend's problem very keenly. It is one of those extremely slippery dilemmas because nearly every employee has indulged in some petty dishonesty. It could be in reporting one's income tax, or using a few office stamps for personal use, or taking a small item of office equipment home.

Together we prayed about the situation. We prayed for the company president; we prayed that the salesman might see the immorality of his position, and then we prayed for God's guidance.

When Roger left that night, he was calm and relaxed. "God can handle these situations if we let Him," he said. "The trouble is that too often we think our meager brains can solve everything."

When Roger, back home, arrived at his office several mornings later, he still wasn't sure how he should handle the problem. He took out a Bible from his desk and read a few passages. Then he prayed again for God's guidance.

"What happened then was definite and specific," he told me later. "It came to me how utterly ridiculous it was to fear losing my job. If the company couldn't take a firm moral stand on the matter of expenses, then I didn't belong there anyway.

"What I really should fear," Roger continued, "was what would happen to me if I violated my personal morality and gave in to expediency under pressure. Being estranged from God was certainly more to fear than losing a job."

Bolstered by this, Roger called in his top salesman for another conference. The man entered, hostile, confident. Roger was relaxed, his manner friendly.

Roger talked about the company and what it stood for. He talked about the fine group of men in the organization and what a worthwhile product they were selling.

"I've thought a great deal about the question of expenses, too," Roger went on. "And it has occurred to me that this isn't the real problem. The real problem is the relationship we have with each other here—and with our customers. We need a program for our salesmen that will cover compensation if it isn't adequate, that will create more enthusiasm. Will you help me work this out?"

"Then you feel the same about expenses?" the salesman asked.

"Yes, I do," said Roger, "stronger than before. I feel so strongly that I'll stick to this policy even if it costs me my job."

The salesman seemed uncertain. A new policy for salesmen had a strong appeal. He asked for time to think it over. Not only had Roger taken a strong moral stand, he had also presented a positive program for improvement. Later, the salesman was completely won over.

Roger has not told me how his new policy has affected company profits. He doesn't seem to consider this of first importance. But I do know that he is very excited about the new spiritual quality in the organization. He feels closer to his men. He has come to know more about them as individuals, about their families and about their personal problems.

It may be that this spirit has reached up to the president— then maybe not. I have a strong feeling, however, that even if the president disapproved of Roger Wilcox and his new policy that it wouldn't make a great deal of difference to Roger. Once you have been through the crucible of taking a moral but unpopular stand, you develop the kind of inner spiritual braces that enable you to cope with any obstacle that may block your way.

When a person is made to feel inferior for reasons that have nothing whatsoever to do with his true personal worth, he must fight a three-front battle—against those who hold him in contempt, against devastating inner bitterness, and against loss of courage.

When I Met Prejudice

by Anthony DiPaola

I DROPPED the letter into the pile with the rest of the morning's mail. But it wouldn't drop from my mind.

It was much the same letter that came to me as City Clerk every year announcing the annual State Conference of Mayors and Other Municipal Officials, yet my eyes kept straying back to it: ". . . meeting this year at the Lakeshore Club *. . . ."

I knew the place; I'd gone to a Knights of Columbus convention there. Whenever I thought of it, I remembered a scene in the lobby when a Lakeshore member sitting next to me had said suddenly, "We're going to have to cut out these conventions!" Then he winked. "Not you fellows, of course! No doubts about the Knights of Columbus! But some of these other groups—." His you-and-I-are-in-this-together tone increased. "The Jew-boys'll use every trick to get in where they're not wanted. When they come with a convention, how're you to keep 'em out?"

If I'd spoken up, I think I could have forgotten the incident. But, in a sense, I was his guest. I said nothing and the Lakeshore Club sat like an undigested pickle inside me.

Later I read about a series of suits against the Lakeshore; plaintiffs charged that it was a "club" only to get around anti-discrimination laws. The suits failed even though judges ad-

* The club's name here is fictitious.

mitted that the club gambit was transparent.

Now, as I laid the Conference letter down for the second time, I wondered if the Arrangements Committee knew the Lakeshore's reputation. Well, it was too late now. To bring it up would just cause embarrassment. And in public office, next to dipping your hand in the till, causing embarrassment is the most unforgivable sin.

It's funny how much arguing you have to do with yourself to maintain a wrong attitude. Fifty times that day I told myself there was nothing I could do. "It's not my problem," I said to my wife at dinner, though she had only asked if the coffee were hot enough.

"Furthermore," I said as I put on my slippers that night, "it could be risky politically."

I go to church every morning in the year, to ask the Blessed Virgin's help in the day ahead. "Holy Mother," I prayed the next morning, "today I ask you to help me make a decision."

And then, strangely enough, I began to get an answer. The answer seemed to be: "Remember. It is what you remember that determines how you will act."

Remember. How could this help me make a decision about the Lakeshore Club? For as I tried thinking back, I saw only my father, smiling, singing, calling *"Buon Giorno!"* as he wheeled his pushcart down the street.

Papa never learned English but he loved this country with the passion special to new citizens. When I was little he worked a fruit cart on New York City's Lower East Side. He would come home at night, his face bright with sweat, eyes brighter still with the joy of being in America. In the old country there had been a ceiling on every man's dreams that was born with you and that you passed on to your children. But here in America, all men could be equally high.

Papa worked a 14-hour day, seven days a week. In a few years he was able to buy a little fruit stand on Avenue A. When it did well he bought a small store in Brooklyn. Still he worked long hours at the heaviest chores. Then he became a wholesaler, and eventually, a wealthy man.

Papa wanted his children to get the education he never had. I was the eldest. When I graduated from business school with a certificate in accounting, his quiet pride was far more eloquent than the flowery graduation address.

In those days it was the goal of every young accountant to get a job on the Foreign Stock Exchange. I applied at one of the large firms. The application form was pages long but all the way through it my pen shook with the thrill of being able to answer every question. "Languages?" Four. "Math?" I'd worked hard; I was well qualified.

The hour's wait seemed like 20. At last the heavy oak door to the president's office swung open and a stern-looking male secretary motioned me to enter. Behind an enormous desk, the president seemed altogether formidable. At first he appeared not to notice me and then his brown eyes, through heavy horn-rimmed glasses, fastened upon me. There was not a sound in the room until he lowered those brown eyes and turned to some papers.

"Mr. DiPaola," he said, "this firm does not hire Italians."

When I stepped from the building that day it was not into the same world that I had left. Papa had raised me on the idea that here, all men are the same. Now all around me I saw differences. Tall men. Short men. Gray eyes. Brown eyes. As street conversations drifted past me I thought for the first time: Polish. Irish. Chinese. German. The word "American" never sounded so sweet again.

I applied once more, this time to a bank in Brooklyn. The bank manager was kinder. He thought he was sparing my feelings when he murmured something about gangsters—in the public mind—no reflection on you personally of course—still our depositors are understandably. . . .

The bank did not hire Italians.

I never told Papa, it was not something you could say to him, but I blurted it out one day to my cousin, Elena Montrella.

"You're Italian!" I said. "You found a good job in a big firm!"

"I didn't," she said. "Helen Montrell found that job."

She saw my look. "A lot of Italians have done it, Tony, to get a decent job."

So I didn't get a "decent" job. After that I looked for work among "my own kind." I wasn't unhappy about it. Far from it. I found good-paying jobs, I married the girl I loved, life was wonderful.

Then came the Depression. For my wife and me it meant hard times as it did for everyone. For my father it meant disaster. Within a few months he had lost the stores, the stock, the savings. When I went to see him one evening he was sitting behind a tiny fruit stand, trying to catch the eyes of the neighborhood housewives with a little pile of oranges.

"Well, Papa," I said, "once you could have gone back to Italy and been a rich man. Are you still glad you stayed in America?"

"Tony," he said, after a long bewildered pause, "when I came to America my pockets were empty. They are empty again. Has America taken anything away? It is not what is in our pockets that gives us joy; it is to be a man among equals. Here I am still that man. I thank God every day that I am in America."

For the rest of his life Papa tended that little stand. He was very happy.

These are some of the things I remembered that morning in church. And gradually I began to see how my memory of an immigrant fruit vendor could have a very direct bearing on me and the Lakeshore Club.

I went to my office, rolled a fresh sheet of paper into my typewriter. "I am very sorry that I will not be able to attend the Conference," I wrote, "because it is being held at the Lakeshore Club. . . ."

The consequences were more violent than anything I had expected. Overnight, it seemed, every city official in the state had heard about that note of mine. Furthermore, many felt similarly but had hesitated, as I had, to butt in. There were long distance calls, hurried meetings. The papers picked up the story. From that little note, the Conference ended by choosing another hotel.

And here was the surprising thing: I began to hear that I had done a courageous thing. I was cited by civic groups, honored at a dinner—and through it all ran this theme of courage.

Only I knew that I had been most uncourageous, that I had been hesitant beforehand and fearful afterward. I had simply learned this truth: when we remember certain things we must act a certain way, whether we have the courage or not. For some, that thing is a beloved friend, or a passage from the Bible, or the words of some great hero. For me it was a little man with a dream shining in his eyes.

Yellow Fever! *The news raced through the seaport town back in 1876, spreading fear and panic. A man who had much to live for knew that he faced the toughest decision of his life.*

The Man Who Didn't Run

by ARTHUR GORDON

ON that breathless day in July, 1876, the seaport town of Savannah, Georgia, drowsed on its bluff high above the yellow river. On an iron balcony overlooking the river stood a compact, wiry man in a white linen suit. His name: W. W. Gordon. His occupation: cotton merchant.

A stir of activity on a schooner anchored downstream caught the watcher's eye. A stretcher was being lowered into a small boat. Oars flashed as the Negro boatman pulled away. A white man sat beside the sick or injured sailor, shielding his eyes from the sun.

Somewhere a clock chimed twice. Gordon went back into the office, picked up his hat and cane, and started home for dinner.

He walked slowly through the tree-shaded streets, at peace with the world. He had come through the Civil War with only one wound. His family had grown to six children—four girls and two boys. His cotton business was doing well, too.

He came to his house, opened the door, whistled for his wife Nellie and the children, and stood there waiting—a happy man.

Meanwhile, the litter bearers were carrying Able Seaman J. W. Schull into Mrs. Hearn's boarding house on Indian Street. The young man had a raging fever, his eyes and lips were swollen, he ached horribly.

Able Seaman Schull, age 27, grew worse. His skin turned

yellow. He began to vomit blood. On July 28 they took him to the Marine Hospital. On July 30, he died.

Several nights later, Willie Gordon sat at home reading his newspaper. The news was interesting enough. In New York, the hand and arm of the new Statue of Liberty had arrived from France. But Gordon's mind was not on the news.

There was sickness in the city. There were rumors—frightening rumors. It was said that yellow fever was epidemic in Cuba. Some of the children's playmates were reported feverish. A close friend of Nellie's—Belle Lewis—was very ill with . . . something. The doctor had refused to let Nellie see her.

Soon after midnight there was a violent knocking on the Gordons' door. A man looked up at the window. "Captain, it's me, Johnny Lewis. Sister Belle just died—of yellow fever. Mother wants Miss Nellie to come right away."

Yellow fever. The man at the window felt the leaden impact of the words at the pit of his stomach. In the war he had known fear, the honest, controllable fear of bullet or exploding shell. But this loathsome disease, with its yellowed, wasted victims, its sickening smell, its stealthy, treacherous leap in the dark. . . .

He said, "You mustn't go, Nellie. It's too dangerous. I'll go and do what I can."

But his wife was already dressing, the tears running down her face. "They wouldn't let me go to Belle when she was alive. Nothing is going to keep me from her now!"

In the end, they both went, although they knew that once it started, the pestilence could sweep through a house, a district, a whole city. They knew there was no cure. Once stricken, the victim either recovered spontaneously after days of misery—or died horribly.

They walked home at last through the silent streets where the mosquitoes whined their high-pitched song. They did not dream—for years no one would suspect—that it was the mosquito that carried the plague.

Back in their own house, Willie told Nellie that she must take the children to the mountains of north Georgia. There was going to be an epidemic, and a panic.

"What about you?" demanded Nellie fiercely. "I'm not going anywhere without you!"

"The doctors will be swamped," her husband told her. "They will need volunteers to care for the sick and the dying."

"Think of the children," Nellie cried. "Think of your mother!"

Her husband bit his lip. "Don't make it any harder, Nellie," he said. "Someone will have to stay."

Some did stay. But most of those who were able, fled from the city. By train, by horse, by ship they fled—18,000 fugitives from a town of 28,000.

Nellie took her children and her mother-in-law to the hills. Then she came back to be as near her husband as possible. She found a room at Guyton, 30 miles away.

Every morning he would take a quinine pill and a drink of whiskey—these being considered preventive measures—and would set out to visit the sick and dying, give them baths, bring them food. It was like walking through a nightmare: whole families were being swept away. Once he found a single room with a mother dead in one bed, the father dead in another, and the children on the floor, crying with hunger.

At night, the carts rumbled through the deserted streets on their way to the cemeteries.

One day Willie met a wealthy acquaintance on the cobbled incline to the river, his baggage piled high on a handcart, his passage booked on a steamer to New York. "Don't look at me like that, Willie Gordon," the rich man cried. "You're crazy to stay here!"

"We need more hospitals," Gordon said. "Since you're leaving, how about giving me the key to your house?"

"No," cried the rich man shrilly, "no." And was gone.

The nights were the worst for Willie. Alone in the big house, often too exhausted to eat, it was all too easy to hear the mocking echoes of the rich man's voice: *"You're crazy to stay here . . . crazy. . . ."* If he let it, the voice would go on and on: *"You're still young. You have everything to live for. You've already done your share. Nobody will criticize you if you leave now. . . ."*

But there was also another voice that spoke to him like a whisper from his childhood, his father's voice: *"Being afraid is nothing to be ashamed of, Willie. It's acting on the basis of fear that makes a man a coward. . . ."*

So the dual struggle went on: the external battle with the sickening enemy; the internal battle with fear.

September was a month of horrors. October was no better. The frost came late, that year.

One sultry night, alone in the empty house in Savannah, Willie Gordon's head began to hurt. He ached, and he felt feverish. He knew that he should call in the doctor, or go and see him, but he had reached the point where he had little faith in medicine.

He picked up Nellie's Bible from the desk and opened it to the Ninety-first Psalm. *Thou shalt not be afraid for the terror by night . . . nor for the pestilence that walketh in darkness. . . .* A mighty promise, surely. And yet, he *was* afraid.

Slowly he pulled a sheet of paper toward him and began a letter to his wife. He gave her the best advice he could about finances and the future. He mentioned specific personal items that he wished each of the children to have.

The pen scratched on in the quiet room: "My dear, dear Mother and you, my darling wife, will need no mementoes of me. I trust your hearts.

"Educate our children as well as your means will allow. Teach them never to go into debt and that labor is honorable. Impress upon the girls that an honest man who has learned to work is preferable to a man born rich, and that a wife to be a helpmate must conform to the means of her husband.

"God bless you, Sweetheart, and guard and guide and protect you. You have been a loving and devoted wife. No one

could have made me happier than you have done. I pray
God we may meet in Heaven to be parted nevermore; for
Christ's sake, Amen."

He folded the paper, tucked it into an envelope that held
a copy of his will. Then wearily he climbed the stairs and
flung himself onto his bed. . . .

In the morning, to his surprise, he felt no worse. He gulped
down his quinine, and walked over to see his friend, Dr. War-
ing. Haggard and hollow-eyed, the doctor listened to his
symptoms, smiled a wan smile, and shook his head. "Sounds
to me as if you're coming down with a bad summer cold,
Willie. It's not yellow fever. Better go home, now, and get
some rest."

"No," said his patient, "if it's only a cold, I'll just forget
about it."

The frosts came, the whine of the mosquitoes was stilled.
Gradually the terror subsided, the fugitives returned.

One of the last to come, so the story goes, was the rich man
who had refused to let his house be used as a hospital. When
he finally returned to the locked and shuttered place, he ordered the servants to open the windows. "It's stuffy in here,"
he grumbled. "And there are mosquitoes, too."

So there were, and so he died, the last ironic victim of the
terror by night, the pestilence that walked in darkness.

Willie Gordon lived on, with his wife Nellie, for many
years. The letter that he wrote that sultry night when he
thought his life was ending was found after his death. No
doubt he had forgotten it.

But his children never forgot it, nor his children's children.

No, we remember it still.

A Russian author dared to write a book which expressed the inviolability of an individual's spirit. "Traitor! . . . Leave Russia!" came the demand. Here a Guideposts' Roving Editor retraces part of the path of courage that a great writer once trod.

The Courage of Boris Pasternak

by VAN VARNER

ONCE more my friend glanced at the rear-view mirror.
"For a change, I think I'm not being followed," he said. And then he grinned as though he'd won a point in a game.

He turned the car into another of those enormously broad boulevards of which Moscow has so many and we headed for the suburbs. My friend, an American stationed in the Soviet capital, was making this pilgrimage as a favor to me.

"No," he confessed, "this outing is for me, too. Whenever I can, I come out here. I'm refreshed by it somehow."

Some 20 miles out we reached a road darkened by the profusion of birch and fir trees which crowded close. Sometimes through the trees I could glimpse rustic cottages; we had arrived at Peredelkino, the Soviet writers' colony. A turn to the left and down a lane, and then the car stopped.

"There," my friend whispered.

I peered to the left and saw the house where Boris Pasternak had lived—and died. There was a tangle of growth, not manicured as our lawns are, but tall and thick in naturalness, in accord with the Russian sense of garden beauty, then a frame house, weathered and brown and two-storied.

We just sat and looked until, as though the time had come to intrude upon the spell, my friend said the obvious:

"He was a great writer."

"Yes," I agreed.

"A man of great courage."

"Yes."

I looked back to the house. There, in that tranquil place, a battle had raged. Why is it, I thought, that we automatically consider courage as being raw and physical, a daring performed in noise? Surely the more common valor, and the more highly valued, is mental.

On our right, a vista Pasternak could have seen from the upper windows, was a wide, green meadow, rolling down to a dip and rolling up again, hundreds of yards, until it reached a church. White, red, and blue, with an onion-curl dome, the Orthodox church seemed a fitting symbol in this landscape, for early in his life, Pasternak had become a Christian.

"And now," my friend said, pointing, "beneath the church and to the right, do you see the three tall pine trees?" I did. "He is buried beneath those trees."

Back home, in the States, I had read about the funeral. What with the few hidden lines in the Soviet papers (if mention were made at all), few people read of Pasternak's death. But more than a thousand people had come here for his burial.

We tried to drive the car to the church but it became too muddy, so we set out on foot. As we walked I mentioned a recent conversation with my interpreter-guide, from the government travel agency, Intourist. She had wanted to know how many Russian writers I'd read, especially the modern ones, and I was hard-put for an answer, except for Pasternak.

"Pasternak!" she had laughed, and with a mocking twinkle said, "Oh, you've read *that* book."

She had scoffed as though, even if she had been permitted to read *Doctor Zhivago,** she would not have wanted to do so.

"Odd, isn't it," my companion reflected, "if it hadn't been for '*that* book,' Pasternak would scarcely have been known outside Russia."

* Pantheon Books, Inc., New York

Born in 1890, even before the first World War Pasternak had been an important poet. Always he thought of himself primarily as a poet, and yet his poetry was strangely intractable to translation. This was ironic because he himself was a brilliant translator who brought to the Russian language a host of Western classics. Yet, the world knows him for *Doctor Zhivago*, the novel which embodies his art and philosophy, and his courage.

This courage had been displayed long before *Zhivago*. How many authors could dismiss more than 30 years of work, as Pasternak did, by saying simply, "I do not like my style up to 1940"? Sometimes his bravery could be stark: there was the time during the purge trials of the 1930's when the poet was told to sign a propaganda document about the execution of Red Army generals. Pasternak knew that if he refused, his arrest was all but certain. His wife, pregnant, wept and pleaded with him to sign, but he would not.

Later he was told that it was his colleagues who had saved him—no one had dared to report him. And some people felt that Stalin himself, gratified by the translations of poets from his native Georgia, had been lenient. In any event, Pasternak had held fast to the belief that he once expressed: "What has for centuries raised man above the beast is not the cudgel, but the irresistible power of unarmed truth."

Some geese scurried away with much honking as my friend and I came to the church. An old woman in black, with a black *platok* covering her head, sat stolidly on a stoop.

"Closed for cleaning," she said firmly. And that was that. I looked at her expressionless face, its roughness, its strength. In an afternoon frankly given over to Boris Pasternak I saw even this peasant woman in terms of him. Did she know that *Doctor Zhivago* was written about her? Probably not, yet *Zhivago* was a rich paean to the Russian people, a panorama which Pasternak had filled with love for them and for life. For years he had dreamt, as he said once, "of a novel in which, as in an explosion, I would erupt with all the wonderful things

I saw and understood in this world." He wanted to write about "the forces that make life beautiful—love, victory, success, to show the colors of the world."

But some of those colors were ugly. They were the colors of the Revolution, of the Soviet experiment which had robbed man of his individuality. And to rob man of that was to violate his spirit. To Pasternak, the spirit of man was sacred; it belonged to God and no man had the right to give his individual spirit to a collective state.

His novel was not meant to be a political work, but it had to contain life as he saw it and truth as he knew it. Pasternak was not unmindful of other writers who had disparaged the System—Pilniak, for instance, whose book had been published abroad. He had faced a firing squad.

Pasternak finished his book and offered it to *Goslitizdat,* the state publishing house. After Stalin's death, official policy was in flux. Briefly it looked as though his book actually would be published in Russia.

It was then, in 1956, that Giangiacomo Feltrinelli came to Moscow. When he left, a copy of Pasternak's manuscript was in this young Italian publisher's luggage.

Immediately, efforts were made to get the manuscript returned. Letters, wires cajoled the publisher in Italy. Pressure was felt from strange sources. Even Soviet "cultural" delegations appeared in Rome—but Feltrinelli held fast and in November, 1956, *Doctor Zhivago* was published.

"Traitor!" came the cries. Pasternak was denounced as a "low-grade hack," his book called a "squalid, malicious work." A lesser man might have been removed, but Pasternak was a world figure now. His friends could only hope that the controversy would quiet.

Then, on October 23, 1958, word came from Sweden that he had won the Nobel Prize for Literature. Pasternak, overjoyed, sent back a wire: "Immensely thankful, touched, proud, astonished, abashed."

The Red government moved in. "Leave Russia!" came the

demand. Pasternak was expelled from the Soviet Writers' Union.

For six days Pasternak sat in the brown, two-storied house among the fir trees and felt the violence of official hatred. One can only surmise the fervor of his prayers as he realized that if he accepted the Prize, he would be forced to leave Russia. For his own safety it might be well—and in the West he would be welcomed and cherished.

On the sixth day, Pasternak wrote a letter to Premier Khrushchev.

"Leaving the motherland," he wrote, "will equal death for me. I am tied to Russia by birth, by life and work." Thereby, he declined the great Prize, choosing to spend the last of his days in public disgrace, here in the countryside where I, an American tourist, was now wandering.

Pasternak continued at his desk. In early May, 1960, he became too ill to work. On May 30th, he died.

Pasternak's coffin, with its lining of Christian brown instead of the non-believer's red, was borne from the house and a multitude of mourners, many weeping, many clutching wild flowers, followed. There were no representatives from the government. The workers, peasants, writers, actors, all the people who came knew the official attitude towards Boris Pasternak. They came nonetheless.

At the grave there was a recitation from Pasternak's poetry and the emotion it created spread through the vast crowd, bringing forth an uninhibited shock of applause. Then, as bouquets were tenderly offered, someone shouted:

"Make no mistake. He was one of us!"

And now I myself stood at Pasternak's grave. Hundreds of people had been here before me. Thousands and thousands would come after me. He had held firm until the end; his spirit was like unarmed truth. It was inviolable.

Some words came to mind. They were, of course, his words, the last line of a poem called "Hamlet."

"To live life to the end is not a childish task."

Immortality

D EATH is certainly the greatest challenge to faith. For whether or not you feel that death is an end, or a beginning, is a matter of what you believe and how strongly you believe it. So, if you are trying to strengthen your faith, yet find it almost impossible to believe in a life after death, you are in great mental conflict.

All the world's great religions attest to a life after death, although their definitions of it vary. Yet doubts spring up in many minds because they seek irrefutable proof, which man has not yet uncovered.

But there is much evidence of immortality. It is contained in the promises of both the Old and New Testaments. And there are the experiences of people who have been on the threshold of the next world and returned to this one.

Who are some of the people who have experienced adventures in immortality? Meet some of them in the pages that follow: a doctor who saw himself being pronounced dead, yet returned to his body; a clergyman who, with his wife, encountered a heavenly host; a woman who looked through the window of heaven.

What do these stories offer you?—they offer the reassurance that others have overcome their doubts and uncertainties. My personal prayer is that those who fear death will lose their fears by learning from the experiences of others what death really is: a going home to God.

NORMAN VINCENT PEALE

To fear death is normal for we all tend to be apprehensive about the unknown that lies ahead. Yet it is a fact that doctors, nurses and clergymen who have watched many people die report that when death comes it is almost always welcomed as a friend.

The Blessed Assurance

by NORMAN VINCENT PEALE

ALL members of the human race have two things in common: each of us was born, and each of us must die. Most of us are not too concerned with the circumstances of our birth; we don't remember it; it lies far behind us. But the thought of dying is another matter. The knowledge that our days on this earth will come to an end is an inescapable part of our existence—somber, mysterious and sometimes frightening.

Quite often people come to me and confess that they are haunted by a fear of death which they try to conceal from other people, and even from themselves. These people are not necessarily old or ill. Often they are in the prime of life, with many useful years ahead of them. But sometimes, it seems, the more they love life, the more they dread death.

What I usually do with such people is admit that I, too, have moments when I flinch from the thought of dying. I suggest that this is perfectly natural, that in my opinion the good Lord planted a certain amount of this fear in all of us so that we would not be tempted to relinquish the trials and responsibilities of this life too easily. But, I add, I'm sure the Lord didn't intend us to be panicky about it. Finally, I try to reassure these troubled souls by outlining the thoughts that have helped me rise above the fear of death, or at least keep it under control.

Take, for example, the inevitability of dying. This seems

to appall some people, but it always has struck me as a merciful thing. Suppose there were loopholes in this universal law; suppose that somehow there was a one percent chance of avoiding death. Consider how frantically we'd search for that loophole, how wretched we'd be not to find it.

But consider how wretched we'd be if we did find it! No one would be happy trying to live forever. It's a little like being at a wonderful play. During the performance, one hopes that it will go on and on, but one wouldn't really like to stay in the theater all night, or until boredom set in.

Another thing I tell the worried ones is this: you may be frightened in advance, but it is almost certain that when the time comes you will not fear death at all. I have talked to doctors and nurses who have seen hundreds of people die, and they all tell me that at the end, unless tormented by a guilty conscience, people go peacefully and thankfully. The truth is, death has been miscast as a grim reaper. To almost everyone, when it finally comes, it comes as a friend.

"That may be true," say some of the fearful ones. "The moment of death may be less terrifying than we thought. But then what? Is there a life after death? Is there any proof?"

To these I reply, "It depends on what you mean by proof. To me the evidence is overwhelming, whether you consult your reason or your instincts. Look at the vast universe that surrounds us, the laws that govern the spinning solar systems and the whirling electrons, the balance and economy of a stupendous Reality that uses everything and wastes nothing. Does it seem reasonable that the Intelligence behind such a Reality would create a being as complex and sensitive as man just to snuff him out forever like the flame of a candle? Of course it doesn't!"

What is death, then? Obviously, it is a change into some new form of existence. We are not permitted to know exactly what this new existence is like, but I believe that sometimes we are given glimpses. Time and again it has been reported of people on the brink of death that they seem to become aware of a great radiance, or hear beautiful music, or see the faces of departed loved ones who are apparently waiting for them across the line. Are these just hallucinations? I don't think so. Several of them have happened within my own family.

My father, who died at 85 after a distinguished career as both physician and minister, struggled against a very real fear of death. But not long after he died, my step-mother dreamed that he came to her and told her that his fears had been groundless.

"Don't ever worry about dying," he said to her. "There's nothing to it!" The dream was so vivid that she woke up, astounded. And I believe that my father did come to reassure her, because that is precisely the phrase I have heard him use a thousand times to dismiss something as unimportant or trivial.

In 1939 when news reached me that my mother had died unexpectedly in another town, I was alone in my office, numb with grief and loss. There was a Bible on my desk, and I put my hand on it, staring blindly out of the window. As I did so, I felt a pair of hands touch my head, gently, lovingly, unmistakably. The pressure lasted only an instant; then it was gone. An illusion? An hallucination caused by grief? I don't think so. I think my mother was permitted to reach across the gulf of death to touch and reassure me.

Three years ago, when I was preaching at a Methodist gathering in Georgia, I had the most startling experience of all. At the end of the final session, the presiding Bishop asked all the ministers in the audience to come forward, form a choir and sing an old, familiar hymn.

I was sitting on the speakers' platform, watching them come down the aisles. And suddenly, among them, I saw my father. I saw him as plainly as I ever saw him when he was alive. He seemed about forty, vital and handsome. He was singing with the others. When he smiled at me, and put up his hand in the old familiar gesture, for several unforgettable seconds it was as if my father and I were alone in that big auditorium. Then he was gone, but in my heart the certainty of his presence was indisputable. He was *there,* and I know that some day, somewhere, I'll meet him again.

We don't try to prove immortality so that we can believe in it; we try to prove it because we cannot help believing in it. Instinct whispers to us that death is not the end; reason supports it; psychic phenomena uphold it. Even science, in its own way, now insists that the universe is more spiritual than material. Einstein's great equation indicates that matter and energy are interchangeable. Where does that leave us, if not in an immaterial universe? The great psychologist, William James, said, "Apparently there is one great universal mind, and since man enters into this universal mind, he is a fragment of it."

This intangible in all of us, this fragment of the universal mind, is what religion calls the soul, and it is indestructible because—as James said—it is at one with God. The Founder of Christianity said specifically that there is a life beyond the grave. Not only that, Jesus proved it by rising from the dead Himself. If you believe that it happened, death should hold little terror for you. If you don't believe it, you are not a completely fulfilled Christian.

The Easter message is one of such hope and joy that even unbelievers are thrilled by it. Recently, a reporter I know covered the sunrise service that is held each Easter on the rim of the Grand Canyon. It was cold—below freezing, actually—and he had not worn an overcoat. Not a particularly religious man, he stood there shivering dolefully and wishing himself back in bed.

"But then," he told me, "when the sun cleared the canyon rim, and light poured into that stupendous chasm, I forgot all about being cold. One moment everything was gray, formless. Then came torrents of light plunging down the canyon walls, making them blaze with color, dissolving the blackness into purple shadows that eddied like smoke. Standing there,

I had a most indescribable feeling, a conviction that the darkness that had filled the great gorge was an illusion, that only the light was real, and that we silent watchers on the canyon rim were somehow a part of the light. . . ."

Strange words, coming from a hard-boiled reporter, but close to a profound truth. Darkness *is* powerless before the onslaught of light. And so it is with death. We have allowed ourselves to think of it as a dark door, when actually it is a rainbow bridge spanning the gulf between two worlds.

That is the Easter message. Yet there are people, even good Christians, who accept it with their minds but really never feel it in their hearts. I know this from personal experience: the message never got through fully to me until I went to the Holy Land and saw with my own eyes the hills and fields and roads where Jesus actually walked. One day we visited the beautiful little village of Bethany.

This was the home of Mary and Martha and Lazarus. And there is still a tomb there, said to be the tomb of Lazarus. We went into that tomb, down 22 steps, and saw the place where the body of Lazarus is presumed to have lain until the voice of Jesus wakened him from the dead. I was so deeply moved that when we came up out of the tomb I turned to my wife and said, "We are standing where the greatest statement ever uttered was made, 'I am the resurrection and the life: he that believeth in Me, though he were dead, yet shall he live.'" *

At that moment, for the first time in my life, Easter really happened to me, and I shall never be the same again. For the rest of my days I shall preach, out of a conviction so deep that it can never be shaken, that if people will accept Jesus Christ they will have eternal life.

Recently, I was at Mount Holyoke College in New England, visiting my daughter Elizabeth, a student there. Walking around the campus, we came upon a sundial. On it was an

* John 11:25

inscription: *To larger sight, the rim of shadow is the line of sight.*

There you have it in just 12 words. Believe me, death is only a momentary rim of shadow. Beyond it, waiting for all of us who deserve it, is the radiance of eternal life.

"I feel that when my body dies that will be the end of me." The man who said those words sensed that death was near and was desolate over what he felt was the meaninglessness of life. Was there anything about this immortality talk that his intellectual mind could accept?

The Skeptical Mr. Worth

by STELLA TERRILL MANN

IT'S hard for those of us who believe in a life after death to conceive of living without such belief. Yet many people do. Some—ostrich-like—try to put the whole subject out of their minds. Others grope painfully and hesitantly for an answer. I knew such a man once. Let me call him Thomas Worth.

Thomas Worth came to see me because he had read one of my books and because he felt I might help him with a problem. He arrived one spring day when I was in the garden setting a dripper hose under our Rangpur lime tree. I apologized for not shaking hands, because I am an amateur, bare-handed gardener, and my hands were a mess.

Tall, thin and slightly stooped as if he carried many burdens, Mr. Worth was about 65. His tired eyes had a look of hurt and disappointment.

New to California, he was immediately fascinated by the Rangpur limes. The fruit of this tree is a bright orange color when ripe, and varies in size from an English walnut to a normal-size orange. It is sour enough to cut your throat. At that moment the tree was covered by a blanket of white, heavily scented blossoms, the sweetest fragrance of all the citrus trees. It was alive with bees.

"I could smell these blossoms from the street," said Mr. Worth. "What do you do with the fruit?"

We sat down on the low brick retaining wall, and I told him about the life in that wonderful tree—how it bore blossoms and fruits in various stages the year round. I told him I never could see it without thinking about God's goodness and about eternal life.

"I tried many times to make marmalade of the limes," I said. "But it always was too strong. So one day I asked the Lord, 'Please tell me what to do with this heavenly fruit You have created so that the marmalade will be as delicious as it is beautiful.' And the answer came to me, 'Peel half of the fruit; the bitterness comes from the skins.' I tried it and now have a recipe that is perfect."

"The Lord talked to you?" Mr. Worth smiled, as an adult to a child, shook his head and gave a hesitant half-laugh. I came to associate 'that apologetic little laugh with him as we grew to know each other. "Well," he sighed, "if only you could prove to me that there *is* a God."

He went on to tell me about himself, slowly at first, then more and more freely. As he talked, it became evident to me that Mr. Worth was a good, honest, moral man. But his life had been joyless. And now, feeling cheated in life, he dreaded death.

"The sunset of my life is approaching," he said. "I feel that when my body dies that will be the end of me. That's why I came to see you."

"Why, Mr. Worth," I said, "your life is in God's keeping. You, the individual self, the spirit God created, will last forever. When your body becomes unfit as a dwelling place for your spirit, then it, or you will leave the unfit body. But *you* will be more alive than ever before."

Mr. Worth sat motionless and silent. "Well," he said at last, "you are lucky. You have faith. But I have a demanding, restless mind. It wants rational answers. And where this business of life after death is concerned, I don't find any."

Now it was my turn to be silent. Mr. Worth was right: the simplest approach is through faith. But if faith is blocked by skepticism, then another approach must be found. I decided to appeal to his sense of history.

"The great scholars tell us," I said, "that there is no reason to doubt that the Person known as Jesus Christ really lived. He really was crucified, dead and buried, but *He rose from the dead.* There were plenty of authentic witnesses. There were the Jewish and the Roman authorities of the day, soldiers, apostles, and women who were early at the tomb. After the Resurrection, Jesus appeared at least ten times and in one instance to more than 500 persons."

Mr. Worth shrugged. "People make mistakes," he said.

"Yes, but the Resurrection *had* to be true! A mere myth of such victory over death could not have kept the young church alive. It would not be alive today."

"If I just could get this faith inside of my own mind or heart, as you have it," said Mr. Worth. "If I just could believe that the universe is more than a random collection of atoms, that there really is a Plan, and that I have a place and a part in it, I'd be the happiest man in the world and ready to die."

"I'd like you to meet my husband," I told him. "He's an architect and an engineer—and *he* believes. Will you come again soon?" He agreed.

So Mr. Worth began coming several mornings a week and the three of us talked a great deal.

It soon became apparent that Mr. Worth really did believe that he was part of a universe where everything happened by chance, with no purpose or design. In an effort to change this attitude, we persuaded him to study and discuss with us several books, including "Human Destiny," by the great philosopher-scientist, Lecomte du Noüy. The book sets out to prove—and does prove—that evolution could not possibly have happened by chance, that there had to be some tremendous Guiding Force behind it.

"Will you concede," we asked Mr. Worth, "that according to careful studies of radioactive materials, the earth is about two billion years old, and that probably life has existed on it for about one billion?"

Yes, he would concede that.

"In about a billion years, then, life has evolved from the first primitive, mindless organism to infinite complexity represented by the human brain—yours and ours?"

"Evidently," said Mr. Worth.

· "But du Noüy shows—he proves mathematically—that the creation *by chance* of even one of the complex molecules necessary to sustain life would have taken, not just one billion years, but billions represented by the figure one followed by 243 zeros!"

"Go on," he said, "I'm listening."

We did go on, and gradually a concept grew in Mr. Worth's mind, the concept of a Creator with a grand design, of a spiritual as well as a physical evolution in which man can and does co-operate—when he chooses to do so—with the Creative Force, which is God.

But one stumbling block remained. "I can see now," said Mr. Worth finally, "that there must be a Creator, and that He must have a plan. But how do I know that He has any future plans for me?"

I remember how my husband smiled. "Mr. Worth," he said, "I am an engineer, and I had to find an answer to that very question. The answer is this. We engineers know that in the world of nature, nothing is lost. You can't destroy energy. We burn coal, for example, and it changes form to heat and light. But not one particle of energy is lost in the changing. This to me is most impressive. If mere energy is indestructible, then why not mind and spirit?"

Mr. Worth leaned back in his chair, a new glow on his face. "Yes," he said. "Yes, this is so right."

But over and over he came back to the lime tree story. "Tell me again about how the Lord talked to you," he would say. Then he would shake his head and laugh. "You're like a child who believes in Santa Claus."

The summer blazed and blossomed itself through the garden and our hearts and lives. I saw Mr. Worth less and less as he read and prayed and meditated more and more on his own account.

Fall came, filling the air with the fragrance of the ripening pineapple guavas, big as turkey eggs. Mr. Worth visited us one October day and we gave him a bag of guavas which he so greatly enjoyed. "You are much happier," I said.

"Yes," he replied. "I just wish I had learned all this before."

In December Mr. Worth came to bring me a Christmas present. His happiness had increased but his body seemed more tired than in October.

We sat before a fire of oakwood. "I am looking forward to my trip," he remarked, just as he was leaving.

I almost muffed it. I almost said, "Are you going somewhere?" but caught it in time. "Good," I said. "Remember, you will not travel alone."

He nodded in appreciation.

Then it was spring again over the earth and in my garden. One sunny morning I felt a terrible and sudden loneliness and left the house to go down to the garden. I paused beneath the lime tree. As I stood there in the warm sun a breeze ruffled the white blossoms, sending a shower of petals down to the brown damp earth. And then it came—that little half-laugh of Thomas Worth.

Oh, it was as clearly his strange little laugh as ever I had heard it before. Then silence. A dreadful, heartbreaking feeling caught me up and burst through me in sobs and drove me into the house and onto my knees in prayer. *Had it been my imagination?*

About an hour later the phone rang, bringing me the message that Mr. Worth had passed away about an hour before. "He was happy and fully conscious to the end," I was told. "He said to tell you that everything was just fine."

The report was official: "George Ritchie, died Decem-
ber 20, 1943, double lobar pneumonia." Dr. Ritchie
was dead for nine minutes—which is more than suffi-
cient time to cause ruinous brain damage, yet Dr.
Ritchie returned to life without ill effects. Even more
amazing is what happened to him while he was dead.

Return from Tomorrow

by DR. GEORGE C. RITCHIE, JR.

WHEN I was sent to the base hospital at Camp Barkeley, Texas, early in December, 1943, I had no idea I was seriously ill. I'd just completed basic training, and my only thought was to get on the train to Richmond, Virginia, to enter medical school as part of the Army's doctor-training program. It was an unheard-of break for a private, and I wasn't going to let a chest cold cheat me out of it.

But days passed and I didn't get better. It was December 19 before I was moved to the recuperation wing, where a jeep was to pick me up at four a.m. the following morning to drive me to the railroad station.

A few more hours and I'd make it! Then about nine p.m. I began to run a fever. I went to the ward boy and begged some aspirin.

Despite the aspirin, my head throbbed, and I'd cough into the pillow to smother the sounds. Three a.m.—I decided to get up and dress.

The next half-hour is a blur for me. I remember being too weak to finish dressing. I remember a nurse coming to the room, and then a doctor, and then a bell-clanging ambulance ride to the x-ray building. Could I stand, the captain was asking, long enough to get one picture? I struggled unsteadily to my feet.

The whir of the machine is the last thing I remember.

When I opened my eyes, I was lying in a little room I had never seen before. A tiny light burned in a nearby lamp. For a while I lay there, trying to recall where I was. All of a sudden I sat bolt upright. The train! I'd miss the train!

Now I know that what I am about to describe will sound incredible. I do not understand it any more than I ask you to; all that I can do is relate the events of that night as they occurred. I sprang out of bed and looked around the room for my uniform. Not on the bedrail: I stopped, staring. Someone was lying in the bed I had just left.

I stepped closer in the dim light, then drew back. He was dead. The slack jaw, the gray skin were awful. Then I saw the ring. On his left hand was the Phi Gamma Delta fraternity ring I had worn for two years.

I ran into the hall, eager to escape the mystery of that room. Richmond, that was the all-important thing—getting to Richmond. I started down the hall for the outside door.

"Look out!" I shouted to an orderly bearing down on me. He seemed not to hear, and a second later he had passed the very spot where I stood as though I had not been there.

It was too strange to think about. I reached the door, went through and found myself in the darkness outside, speeding toward Richmond. Running? Flying? I only know that the dark earth was slipping past while other thoughts occupied my mind, terrifying and unaccountable ones. The orderly had not seen me. What if the people at medical school could not see me either?

In utter confusion I stopped by a telephone pole in a town by a large river and put my hand against the guy wire. At least the wire seemed to be there, but my hand could not make contact with it. One thing was clear: in some unimaginable way I had lost my firmness of flesh, the hand that could grip that wire, the body that other people saw.

I was beginning to know too that the body on that bed was mine, unaccountably separated from me, and that my job was to get back and rejoin it as fast as I could.

Finding the base and the hospital again was no problem. Indeed I seemed to be back there almost as soon as I thought of it. But where was the little room I had left? So began what must have been one of the strangest searches ever to take place: the search for myself. As I ran from one ward to the next, past room after room of sleeping soldiers, all about my age, I realized how unfamiliar we are with our own faces. Several times I stopped by a sleeping figure that was exactly as I imagined myself. But the fraternity ring, the Phi Gam ring, was lacking, and I would speed on.

At last I entered a little room with a single dim light. A sheet had been drawn over the figure on the bed, but the arms lay along the blanket. On the left hand was the ring.

I tried to draw back the sheet, but I could not seize it. And now that I had found myself, how could one join two people who were so completely separate? And there, standing before this problem, I thought suddenly:

"This is death. This is what we human beings call 'death,' this splitting up of one's self." It was the first time I had connected death with what had happened to me.

In that most despairing moment, the little room began to fill with light. I say "light," but there is no word in our language to describe brilliance that intense. I must try to find words, however, because incomprehensible as the experience was to my intellect, it has affected every moment of my life since then.

The light which entered that room was Christ: I knew because a thought was put deep within me, "You are in the presence of the Son of God." I have called Him "light," but I could also have said "love," for that room was flooded, pierced, illuminated, by the most total compassion I have ever felt. It was a presence so comforting, so joyous and all-satisfying, that I wanted to lose myself forever in the wonder of It.

But something else was present in that room. With the presence of Christ (simultaneously, though I must tell it one by one) also had entered every single episode of my entire life. There they were, every event and thought and conversation, as palpable as a series of pictures. There was no first or last, each one was contemporary, each one asked a single question, "What did you do with your time on earth?"

I looked anxiously among the scenes before me: school, home, scouting and the cross-country track team—a fairly typical boyhood, yet in the light of that presence it seemed a trivial and irrelevant existence.

I searched my mind for good deeds.

"Did you tell anyone about Me?" came the question.

"I didn't have time to do much," I answered. "I was planning to, then this happened. I'm too young to die!"

"No one," the thought was inexpressibly gentle, "is too young to die."

And now a new wave of light spread through the room already so incredibly bright and suddenly we were in another world. Or rather, I suddenly perceived all around us a very different world occupying the same space. I followed Christ through ordinary streets and countrysides and everywhere I saw this other existence strangely superimposed on our familiar world.

It was thronged with people. People with the unhappiest faces I ever have seen. Each grief seemed different. I saw businessmen walking the corridors of the places where they had worked, trying vainly to get someone to listen to them. I saw a mother following a 60-year-old man, her son I guessed, cautioning him, instructing him. He did not seem to be listening.

Suddenly I was remembering myself, that very night, caring about nothing but getting to Richmond. Was it the same for all these people; had their hearts and minds been all concerned with earthly things, and now, having lost earth, were they still fixed hopelessly here? I wondered if this was hell. To care most when you are most powerless; this would be hell indeed.

I was permitted to look at two more worlds that night—I cannot say "spirit worlds" for they were too real, too solid. Both were introduced the same way; a new quality of light, a new openness of vision, and suddenly it was apparent what had been there all along. The second world, like the first, occupied this very surface of the earth, but it was a vastly different realm. Here was no absorption with earthly things, but—for want of a better word to sum it up—with truth.

I saw sculptors and philosophers here, composers and inventors. There were universities and great libraries and scientific laboratories that surpass the wildest inventions of science fiction.

Of the final world I had only a glimpse. Now we no longer seemed to be on earth, but immensely far away, out of all relation to it. And there, still at a great distance, I saw a city— but a city, if such a thing is conceivable, constructed out of light. At that time I had not read the Book of Revelation. nor, incidentally, anything on the subject of life after death. But here was a city in which the walls, houses, streets, seemed to give off light, while moving among them were beings as blindingly bright as the One who stood beside me. This was only a moment's vision, for the next instant the walls of the little room closed around me, the dazzling light faded, and a strange sleep stole over me. . . .

To this day, I cannot fully fathom why I was chosen to return to life. All I know is that when I woke up in the hospital bed in that little room, in the familiar world where I'd spent all my life, it was not a homecoming. The cry in my heart that moment has been the cry of my life ever since: Christ, show me Yourself again.

It was weeks before I was well enough to leave the hospital and all that time one thought obsessed me: to get a look at my chart. At last the room was left unattended: there it was in terse medical shorthand: Pvt. George Ritchie, died December 20, 1943, double lobar pneumonia.

Later, I talked to the doctor who had signed the report.

He told me there was no doubt in his mind that I had been dead when he examined me, but that nine minutes later the soldier who had been assigned to prepare me for the morgue had come running to him to ask him to give me a shot of adrenalin. The doctor gave me a hypo of adrenalin directly into the heart muscle, all the while disbelieving what his own eyes were seeing. My return to life, he told me, without brain damage or other lasting effect, was the most baffling circumstance of his career.

Today over 22 years later, I feel that I know why I had the chance to return to this life. It was to become a physician so that I could learn about man and then serve God. And every time I have been able to serve our God by helping some brokenhearted adult, treating some injured child or counseling some teenager, then deep within I have felt that He was there beside me again.

*Her husband's one great prayer was to face the mo-
ment of death with dignity and in full consciousness.
His wish was fulfilled in a way too unusual to be coin-
cidental. Here is a poignant story about an end and a
beginning.*

The Supreme Moment

by ANN MORETON

HOW many times I've nodded gratefully when I heard the
statement "He died quietly in his sleep." Then four
years ago my husband passed away. He died awake. Alert.
Participating in the momentous event with his whole mind.
And in doing so he left me a legacy of faith that I want to
pass on to all who fear to trust God in life's greatest moment.

I wish I could relate some stirring event of my husband's
54 years on earth to make you understand how he was able
to accept the challenge of death. But his simply was not a
dramatic life. Fred seemed happiest working in his nursery
which he called Chinquapin Farm. It was here on a Mississippi Bayou beneath ancient streamers of Spanish moss
that he grew his surpassingly lovely camellias.

I used to get secret pleasure from watching this modest,
deeply honest man struggling to write truthful advertising for
his plants. He debated a long time before he settled on the
slogan "Root Strength."

"All growth," he wrote, "comes from a good root stock."

I believe now that in these years on Chinquapin Farm he
was sending down his own spiritual roots. He learned the
farmer's respect for God's timing, the gardener's reverence
for the power that can transform a little brown seed into a
blossoming bush. Somehow the beauty of nature enabled him
to see deep into the wonder of creation.

But it was only after a pain in his left arm was diagnosed as an inoperable malignancy that he was able to talk aloud about these things. All our married life he'd read the Bible each evening as his last act of the day. But now Fred was able for the first time to speak to me about his personal faith: a faith that extended to all life's processes, even to its pain and death.

Because he believed that even these things are part of a whole, acceptable to God, he was able to ease my anguish and come swiftly to terms with the physical ordeal of the illness. As a result, Fred rarely resorted to strong, pain-killing drugs through nearly two years of the disease.

As news of his illness spread, letters of concern poured in from people I had never heard of, and I learned something else: that he had been as much a giver-away of plants as a seller. Other people's pleasure meant a lot to him; I had never known how much. During a period of treatment in Texas we sat by a fire one night opening letters from people who were enjoying his flowers, and I looked up suddenly to see tears of sheer joy streaming down his face.

It was not until he entered the hospital for the last time, however, that he spoke of the wish closest to his heart. Paralysis had come overnight and unexpectedly. Then, as we waited for the ambulance needed to move him, he said suddenly, "Do you believe that if I ask God for something personal for myself He will grant it?"

"I know He will," I said.

"Then I'll ask Him." He closed his eyes and was silent so long that the words when they came startled me, "I want to die in dignity."

One of the supreme moments of life was approaching, he said. He wanted to go into it with his mind clear, and his one fear was that someone would dope him and rob him of the experience. "Don't you let them give me any high-powered drugs at the last to drag me back!"

I promised, not knowing exactly how I was going to influence a hospital staff. And in the end I did nothing at all. No one else knew of this last wish of his: a Power stronger than any human one worked to grant it to him.

The weeks passed. Fred gradually weakened. Late one afternoon he told me he thought I should go back to the motel and get a nap. "But be sure you come back before midnight," he concluded.

A little puzzled at these specific directions, I went back to the motel. After spending 18 hours a day at the hospital for two weeks, I was exhausted. I bathed, slept and had a quiet dinner. At 9:15 I wondered if I should write a letter, read, or go straight to the hospital. Suddenly I felt two strong hands on my shoulders turning me toward the door, compelling me to get to the hospital.

Soon I was tiptoeing down the quiet hall. The door stood ajar and I peeped in, expecting Fred to be asleep. The nurse was standing with her back to the bed. Fred was wide awake, his eyes bright and alert.

In a perfectly normal voice he said, "I'm dying." The nurse seemed not to hear him. I walked in as if I hadn't heard either and said in a cheery voice, "Hello, Freddie, I've come to stay with you."

"That's fine, Sweetie, for I'm dying." And with that he closed his eyes, took four or five deep breaths and began talking in a low voice. I leaned closer to hear.

This is what he was saying, "I love God. I love my family. God, I'm coming." Over and over he said, "God, I'm coming . . . ," his breathing getting shallower and shallower but always easy. Then his voice trailed off until he didn't breathe any more. I stood transfixed, my hand on his head.

Now the room was full of nurses, while an intern frantically slapped his hand. I remember hearing the hall nurse say, "We don't have anything on his chart to give him. He wasn't expected to die now." They were trying to get in touch with his doctors. "I don't understand how they could both be out," the intern kept saying.

But I understood, and kept a silent chorus of praise rising to God.

Now the intern was speaking to me, but he seemed to be on the other side of a cloud. I couldn't see any of them clearly; everything was soft focus. I knew something beyond sense was happening in that room. I didn't try to understand it. I just let the impressions come into my being, believing I would be given the meanings later.

The intern took me to a small room to wait for the doctors. The room was utterly still. This was the first moment of inactivity in nearly two years of Fred's illness. I just laid my head down on the table and rested.

At last the two doctors came in together. They spoke the kindly phrases of sympathy and kept using words like "unusual" and "remarkable" and "unexpected." In effect, they were saying, "We've never known anyone to go in such an open, clear-eyed way."

Our grown son and daughter hurried home, the funeral was held, and still I was haunted by the feeling that the most significant part of Fred's death lay just beneath the surface of my consciousness. Something immense and wonderful had happened in that hospital room—something I had known— and yet not quite known.

It was summertime before the answer was given to me. I was lying in the hammock one day, gazing up at a white oak tree when I noticed an empty cicada shell clinging to the bark. The yard was full of them at this time of year, yet I'd never seen an insect actually shedding its case. Perhaps, I thought, it happens in the very early morning.

The following morning I was outdoors before sunrise, waiting before the same tree. Sure enough, a fat gray cicada larva soon began to climb the trunk. A more purposeful act I'd never seen; the cicada moved slowly up the tree, feeling with his claws for a suitable place.

At last about seven feet up the trunk he found the right spot. I ran for a stepladder, my heart beating with a strange excitement. Now the shell was firmly anchored to the solid tree, and a thin, barely perceptible line appeared down its back. Inside, the winged creature was struggling to be free. It would push forward, rest, push backward, rest. Then it twisted from side to side. At last it broke loose and the new insect lay beside its old house, exhausted, new wings still folded.

I scarcely moved, for I had the uncanny feeling that I had watched it all before. The wings slowly expanded and grew as they moved back and forth gently in the breeze. When the wings dried in the sunlight, I caught my breath: they were all irridescent color and light. The glorious thing then soared off above me, and I was left staring at the tree trunk and the gray, earth-bound body which had housed that unimaginable splendor.

And still the feeling of familiarity persisted, the conviction that I had watched this miracle before. Several weeks later I remembered. It had taken place in the hospital room and what I had watched was the eager, willful thrust of the soul toward a new beginning.

What I actually saw in that room, I have never recaptured except in terms of the cicada. I only know that Fred's spirit struggled to be free from a body grown suddenly too small, that there was no break in his consciousness as the tremendous transition took place, that he was there in that room even after the shell was laid aside, but in form too marvelous for me to grasp. I know that he stepped with God to the very door of death and found Him utterly trustworthy for that supreme moment and beyond.

*Within hours, this Senior Editor of Guideposts would
be in surgery, undergoing an operation for cancer. He
did not know how he should pray. There wasn't time
for his customary "objective" reasoning about faith—
nor did his understanding of Christ allow for anything
else.*

Eternity Can Begin Now

by JOHN L. SHERRILL

I STILL remember that I whistled as I strode up New
York's Park Avenue that spring morning five years ago.
I stepped through the door of my doctor's office and nodded
to his receptionist—an old friend by now. I'd been coming
here every month since a cancer operation four years previous,
and it was always the same: the doctor's skilled fingers running down my neck, a pat on the back, "See you in a month."

But not that day. This time the fingers prodded and worked
a long time. When I left I had an appointment at Memorial
Hospital for surgery two days later. What a difference in a
spring morning!

I walked back down the same street in the same sunshine,
but now a cold fear walked with me. All cancer patients know
this fear. We try to stay on top of it in various ways. Now I
could no longer hold the fear down. It rose up, scattering
reason before it: this was the Fear of Death.

I dove into the first church I came to, looking for darkness
and privacy. It was St. Thomas Episcopal, on Fifth Avenue.
Mechanically, I sat down. A few minutes later a young minister mounted the pulpit to give a noonday meditation. I didn't
know it then, but this brief address was to provide the key
which would rid me of this most basic of all fears.

At the time it seemed wretchedly irrelevant to my problem.

His text was: . . . *Whosoever believeth in Him should not perish, but have everlasting life.** I wasn't ready for everlasting life; it was life here and now I wanted!

The next morning, however, I was to hear these words again. My wife, Tib, and I were having coffee after a sleepless night when the phone rang. It was a neighbor, Catherine Marshall LeSourd.

"John," she said, "could you come over for a few minutes? I've heard the news and there's something I've got to say to you."

Catherine met us at the door wearing neither make-up nor a smile, which said more than words about the concern she felt. She led us into the family room and plunged in without polite talk.

"I know this is presumptuous of me. I'm going to talk to you about your religious life, and I have no right to assume that it lacks anything. After all, you've been writing for Guideposts for ten years. But often the people who are busiest with religion are farthest from the real, life-changing heart of it."

I looked at Tib. She sat still as a rock.

"John," said Catherine, "do you believe Jesus was God?"

It was the last question in the world I expected. I thought she would say something about God being able to heal—or prayer being effective—something to do with my crisis. But since she had put the question to me, I considered it. Tib and I were Christians in the sense that we wrote "Protestant" on application blanks, attended church with some regularity, sent our children to Sunday school. Still, I knew that these were habits. I never really had come to grips with the question, was Jesus of Nazareth, in fact, God?

"You might ask what difference it makes," said Catherine. "It spells the difference between life and death, John. The Bible tells us that when we believe in Christ we no longer have to die, but are given everlasting life."

* John 3:16

There it was again. But it was precisely at this point of belief that I always had my difficulty. I knew what the Bible promised, and I admired and envied people who accepted it unquestioningly. For myself, there were roadblocks of logic which invariably halted me. I started to list them for Catherine, but she stopped me.

"You're trying to approach Christ through your mind, John," she said. "But it's one of the peculiarities of Christianity that you have to experience it *before* you can understand it. And that's just what I'm hoping for you today—that without understanding, without even knowing why, you make the leap of faith—right over all your doubts—to Christ."

There was silence in the room. I had an eternity of reservations and, at the same time, a sudden desire to do exactly what she was suggesting. The biggest reservation, I admitted frankly: it didn't seem right to shy away all these years and then come running when I had cancer and was scared. "I'd feel like a hypocrite," I said.

"John," said Catherine, almost in a whisper, "That's pride. You want to come to God in *your* way. When you will. Where you will. Healthy. Maybe God wants you now, without a shred to recommend you."

When we left, I still had not brought myself to take that step. But halfway home, passing a certain telephone pole on Millwood Road in Chappaqua, a pole which I can point out today, I turned suddenly to Tib and said:

"I'm taking that leap, Tib. I believe in Christ."

That's all I said. Yet I believe now that in some mysterious way, in that instant, I died.

I didn't think of it in those terms at the time—but certainly it wrenched like death. It was a cold-blooded laying down of my sense of what was logical, quite without emotional conviction. And with it went something that was essentially "me." All the bundle of self-consciousness that we call our ego, somehow seemed involved in this decision. I was amazed at how much it hurt, how desperately this thing fought for life, so that there was a real slaying required. But when it was dead and quiet finally, and I blurted out my simple statement, there was room in me for something new and altogether mysterious.

The first hint that there was something different about me came rather amusingly at the hospital. Shortly before the operation a snappy young nurse came in to give me an injection. Since Army days I have had a morbid horror of needles. Yet this time it was different.

"All right, over we go," said my nurse efficiently. But when she had finished, her tone changed. "My, you're a relaxed one! You act like you're taking your vacation here."

It wasn't until after she had left that I realized how true and how remarkable this was. I *was* relaxed. Before the operation, during it, and afterwards. As we waited out the report, my attitude was one of a man who had nothing to fear. How was it possible?

Then I had a strange thought: a man who already had died would certainly not be afraid of death. And that was just how I felt—as though death was behind me.

I wondered if there was any Biblical backing for this idea. Back home and still in doubt on the doctor's verdict, I got out a Bible and a concordance. And there it was in Christ's own words:

"In very truth," Christ told His Disciples, "anyone who gives heed to what I say, and puts his trust in Him who sent Me, has hold of eternal life and does not come up for judgment, but already has passed from death to life." *

How can I describe the excitement that leapt to me from that page? Was it possible that when I took that leap of faith a new life began for me, existing parallel to my earthly life but strangely independent of it? A life that was born of the Spirit and which would use my perishable body only temporarily?

If so, then I should see evidence of something new inside

* John 5:24

me that owed nothing to my earth-bound existence.

And I did.

The first evidence came when the doctor's report arrived. It was a hopeful one: but I found that this had ceased to be of primary importance to me. Something else seemed far more pressing: to discover what this new life was, where it came from, what it meant.

I had a strange new hunger to explore the New Testament, which I read with a sense of excitement and of recognition. Wasn't it likely that this was the new life, recognizing its natural environment of spirit, feeding on a new kind of food which it needed as my body needed food?

The same was true of church. Suddenly, I *wanted* to attend church: it was no longer a habit, but an experience which quenched a deep thirst.

And—perhaps the most important evidence of all—Christ whom I had approached as a problem in logic, became for me a living Person. I feel now that it was Christ I sought and found in the Bible, in the sacraments, and in the company of Christians.

Five years have passed since the day Tib and I drove past that telephone pole on Millwood Road. They have been fabulous years, filled with meaning and excitement and wonder. I found, as the months passed and I came down from my mountain top, and slipped into old patterns I'd hoped I'd left behind, that the door always was open for my return. I always was drawn back. It was as if the new life which began that day was not dependent on my faithfulness, but on Christ's.

And it is this which gives me conviction that it is an undying life, a part of the eternity of God.

What does science have to say about the immortality of man? Here's a report from the director of the parapsychology laboratory at Duke University.

The Reality of the Spirit

by Dr. J. B. Rhine

FORTY-TWO years ago my wife and I began to look into a question that has intrigued and troubled mankind since the dawn of history, the question of life after death. Having been educated as biologists, we approached it as scientists, respectful of religious teachings and beliefs, but primarily concerned with studying and testing scientifically claims that communication with the spirit world was possible.

This search took us to Duke University where, under Professor William McDougall, we established the Parapsychology Laboratory and continued our investigations. Our studies led us into intensive research on extrasensory perception, or ESP, for which the Duke Laboratory has become known. Eventually our experimental demonstrations of ESP were confirmed by scientists working in other laboratories in this and other countries.

What we learned, and proved experimentally, is that a part of the human personality is not wholly explainable by physical principles. It can receive knowledge without using sensory means. It can transcend the laws of time and space. Parapsychologists call this mysterious ability of the personality *psi*, a noncommittal term that we use for the time being, while its full explanation and characteristics are still unknown.

It now is known that *psi* ability includes different types of ESP—telepathy, clairvoyance, and precognition (knowledge of things that are going to happen). Under these names, it has now been firmly proved that the human mind can transcend both space and time; and independent of material barriers, it can make contact with other minds.

Since this power is apparently non-physical, it may very well be called spiritual. And if it is non-physical, the question at once arises: does it belong to a part of man that can survive the physical process known as death?

This is a very difficult question, because many phenomena in this *psi* area that might seem to indicate survival after death also can be explained by one form or another of extrasensory perception.

Some years ago we were visited by a general and his wife whose son, a young officer, had died. Very soon after his death, his mother felt a hand on her shoulder. Looking up through her tears she saw—or thought she saw—her son. He looked splendid, immaculate as always in his uniform. "Cheer up, Mother," he said. "I'm all right. It's not like you to give way like this!"

And so this mother put her poignant question to me. "Doctor, was this really our son I saw?"

For one who works in science, there is only the known truth to tell. Even when one wishes it were otherwise, one can give only established knowledge. So my answer had to be, "I cannot give you a definite answer. Perhaps that experience of yours was projected by your own mind, as hallucinatory relief for your grief. I will add that I think it *possible* for such an experience to be the result of an outside agency, of your son's surviving personality. But it was so much what you wanted to hear, and it left no trace beyond that. And so as scientific evidence of anything beyond your own unconscious needs, I am afraid it does not qualify."

Occasionally people have experiences that *do* qualify as scientific evidence—of something. During World War II a man and wife were sleeping when suddenly the man sat up, wakening his wife. He said:

"I just dreamed that my brother Joe was killed in action. He wants me to break the news to Father."

"Oh, Honey, it's just a nightmare. Go back to sleep!" the wife replied.

This was July 26, 1945. A week later the telegram came. Joe was killed in action July 26, 1945.

Did Joe come to his brother after his own death with that message? The question is the same one the general's wife asked, but in this case the agony of grief was lacking, for the brother had not received the news until the experience itself brought it. As an example of extrasensory perception, at least, the case is valid. As evidence for the survival of the spirit, it is not enough for a scientific decision. But here too one can say, "It could have been"—and for those most intimately concerned, a "could be" is better than nothing, and surely much better than a "can't be."

Much of the evidence that has seemed most convincing toward an affirmative answer on this question of survival after death has come from mediums, persons who act (so they believe) as links of communication between the spiritual world and ours. Messages seeming to come from deceased persons giving information not normally available to the medium often have been taken as evidence of the continuing existence of those persons.

For instance, some years ago the friend of a non-professional medium said to her, "I wish you could help my brother's wife, for my brother's death has left her overwhelmed."

When the young widow went to the medium, a message came for her. She was convinced that it was from her husband because it gave the answer to her last whispered hope, as he was dying, "I hope your suffering is ended." The message was, "Tell her I did not suffer."

A few days later one of the children broke her leg. A month later the medium got a message, "Write to my dear love and tell her to have it set perfectly. There seems to be a little vein between the break—like a thread."

An extra X-ray was taken. Despite the warning, all seemed satisfactory. But a little later paralysis of two of the child's toes set in. Examination showed that a scar had formed where the bone had pierced the flesh. The scar was pressing on a nerve, the "thread," which even the X-ray had not revealed.

To many persons, messages like this have appeared to offer proof of survival after death. But the same ESP ability that would be necessary for the medium to get the message from the discarnate spirit might also enable her to get the information more directly. Her clairvoyance could be used for medical diagnosis, presumably, just as in tests it has revealed the symbols on cards when no one was looking at them.

The further research on this question progresses, the more man's mind and body appear to be one highly complex unity. But even if we cannot see at present any complete separability, still we know now that the spiritual side is no less real than the physical, and incomparably more important. It is the knowledge of its reach and independence that still is incomplete.

To the student of ESP, the most significant type of case history where this question of survival is concerned is one in which the information transmitted to the living person was known only to the deceased, or one in which the *method* of transmission is beyond the capabilities of the person through whom the information comes.

A professor at Northwestern University received the following case from one of his students which is noteworthy on both counts:

"One evening when I was a boy of four, before I knew anything of school or the alphabet, my mother was working at her desk in our hotel, and I got hold of a note pad and began scribbling on it. Mother, noticing what I was doing, told me to stop and play with something else.

"The next morning my mother saw the papers with my scribblings and was about to throw them away when the day clerk, who had taken shorthand at night school, told her they looked like shorthand. He insisted on taking the papers to a teacher for examination. They *were* shorthand, the old-fashioned square-type shorthand.

"On these papers was a message to my mother from my father who had died two weeks before in New York, while my mother and I were in Oregon. It started 'Dearest Beloved,' and spoke of a letter that had not been posted. It was an urgent letter containing information about Father's safety-deposit box in the East. His death had been sudden, and mother had not known the location of that box.

"My father always had called my mother 'Dearest Beloved,' and as a young man had learned the old-fashioned method of shorthand. Mother still has those pieces of paper, and the message has been verified by other people too."

To a scientist, does such a story offer acceptable proof of life after death? No, but it is in line with scientific research that has proven that there is something in man that has a wholly different set of properties from those of his physical body—and it is this finding that makes survival a logical possibility.

We know now that man is, as he has long intuitively believed, a spiritual being. That much seems definite. Is this spiritual side of his nature sufficiently strong and independent to survive the death of the physical body? This we cannot demonstrate—at least, not so far.

The fact is, then, that it is the *living* human spirit about which we know most and it is that about which we most need to know. For it has been on the assumption of a spiritual aspect of man that religion, morality, free will and true democracy have been founded.

So let us get on with the discovery of this side of man's nature, both in its potential for human life and its destiny beyond the grave. We need this larger understanding.

"Doctor, her pulse is going!" At that moment Julia Ruopp began slowly to slip away to another reality which she found she desired to be a part of with all her being.

The Window of Heaven

by JULIA PHILLIPS RUOPP

THIRTY-TWO years have passed since the experience I am about to describe; 32 years of active life as a minister's wife and as a mother. But it remains, to this day, the most vivid and extraordinary happening in my whole existence.

When our first son, "Phipsy," was four years old I became ill with a glandular condition and was told that I must have a thyroid operation to save my life. Accustomed to trusting all my cares to God, I did not fear the operation. It was far harder to come to terms with the future of our child, should I not be there. After a heart-wrenching night, peace came when I knew that his Creator loved Phipsy more than I possibly could, and would guide his future. I knew also that he would be happy with his earthly father, so I could let go of him and pack my bag for the hospital.

My husband, Harold, took me to Crile's Clinic. Dr. Crile himself was to operate. As only a local anesthetic was used during the surgery, the doctors kept me talking and singing in order to more readily locate the vocal cords.

I was feeling rather pleased about my ability to think of things to say and sing in spite of the unpleasantness when suddenly, to my amazement, I seemed to be looking down at myself and the group around the operating table from a short distance just over their heads. The nurse was saying with a startled expression, "Doctor, her pulse is going." Then I started through what seemed to be a long, dark passageway,

316

and as I went along I thought calmly, "This must be what they call dying."

This journey continued uneventfully for some time and I was beginning to wonder how long it would last when I emerged into an overwhelmingly wide space of light—a pulsing, living light which cannot be described in words. Here my body felt light and free and for a little while I drifted about with no apparent destination. Finally, it was with great relief and pleasure that I found myself sitting on what seemed to be a cloud, or some kind of heavenly island, looking into an enormous convex window which resembled one-half of a huge crystal ball. I knew that it was not glass, for I could easily have stepped through to the other side; at the same time the thought came to me that I must be looking through a window into one bright spot of heaven.

What I saw there made all earthly joys pale into insignificance. I longed to join the merry throng of children singing and frolicking in an apple orchard. The air had a brilliant clarity that made small details stand out in a new light: the orchard in translucent white and pinks, startling shades of greens, reds, yellows and russets—for there were both fragrant blossoms and ripe red fruits on the trees.

As I sat there drinking in the beauty, gradually I became aware of a Presence: a Presence of joy, harmony and compassion. My heart yearned to become a part of this beauty.

But somehow, I could not bring myself to go through the window. An invisible, tenacious restraint pulled me back each time I leaned forward with that intention. I remember thinking that I had lost consciousness of my identity, and that my name no longer mattered. All I needed to do was to keep my eyes wide open and step through the window to be a part of what I saw. I frowned at my inability to move, and gradually, unable to bear the light and vibrant life of this small corner of heaven, my eyes closed tight. As I squeezed them tighter I seemed to recede farther and farther away from that convex window.

After another long journey through the passageway, I returned to the bed upon which a body was lying, motionless and limp, while nurses and doctors were working over it. Reluctantly I entered it through what seemed to be the natural door, the former soft spot at the top of my head, at the same time asking myself, "Why must I return? Do I have to come back? Could I ever get that weak frame back into action again?" Experimentally, I moved one finger, wondering at the same time who "I" was.

One of the nurses exclaimed, "Glory be; she's coming to. It's been 15 minutes." I tried again to remember my name with no success, but another name did come to me—"Harold," and then "Phipsy." They were the ties that had pulled me back, and I needed them now if I was to stay. With great effort I whispered my husband's name.

Then suddenly I knew—I was Julia.

"Am I Julia? Can *this* be Julia? This flattened out figure with the bandaged neck?" I did not want it to be Julia, and yet I did—if there were a Harold and a Phipsy waiting. But to have left all that glory, for this painful return, was almost unacceptable. Then a dearly loved voice spoke—a hand held mine—I *did* want to stay.

The rest of that day and the next, that other world was far more real to me than the one to which I had returned. I insisted that my husband hold my hand day and night; when he had to leave from sheer exhaustion, my sister came. I sensed that there was some mysterious link between my soul and the palm of my hand, and felt that my staying in this life depended upon the pressure of love through the hand of another holding mine. The lure of that heavenly place that I had glimpsed was very strong. But their firm grasp, even though they did not entirely understand, kept me from escaping again to its freedom.

During the next 24 hours, while I was hovering between two dimensions of life, all the meanings of life and death seemed to pass before my inner eyes. Awareness came strong that the dying of the earthly body was not a calamity. Death was a natural transformation into another phase of living, where one could go right on joyfully progressing, if ready. One graduated from this room of learning into another, just as real and important.

I believe there is a comparison to be drawn between birth of the spirit and childbirth. We know that if the infant has ready the equipment for breathing—nostrils, lungs and air-passages, then he is able to live in a world of air. However, if the fetal development is incomplete or faulty, he is unprepared for a world where breathing is a necessity.

In like manner, in this life, if one's soul or spirit remains undernourished, underdeveloped and unrelated, then it cannot enter into or function freely in the highest form of life to which it is capable of attaining. It came to me with certainty, then, that one *began there* in the next world, where he *leaves off here* in this life. And if one is unprepared, or unable to "breathe" the atmosphere of that state, or bear the light of a more intense or luminous quality, then one would have to go through a period of waiting or adjustment.

This seemed to give a deeper meaning to suffering, to all experience and to one's everyday relationships. Not to grow spiritually, seemed to me then, and still does, the *real* death of the individual.

Thus, I believe that my brief glimpse through the window of heaven was a flash of revelation about the meaning of life itself.

Now I watch eagerly as each new day brings its lessons and its blessings, and I am at peace in the belief—no, the conviction—that in the sight of God the world we live in and the world of my vision are really one.

It started with an English assignment. Fifteen-year-old Billie Kay wrote a paper on the subject, "The Last Week of My Life." Then she told her mother, "I'm not afraid of death anymore." Here is a story you won't soon forget.

To Live Each Day

by BETTY BOTHWELL

PARENTS never are prepared for the day that their children become young men and women. But inevitably, faces that once wore smiles of egg yolk and jam come to us washed and serious, bearing news that is startlingly mature.

With our son Bob it was his decision to pay his own way through college. He said his schooling would mean more if he earned his own money. When he told me this, I suddenly realized I wasn't talking to a boy in knee pants any longer. And through a scholarship and a summer job, he already has made it on his own through three years of college.

A similar awareness occurred this spring when my only daughter, Billie Kay, a 15-year-old sophomore at Mississinewa High School, surprised my husband and me with her spiritual perceptiveness. This first came through some themes she prepared as English assignments. One was entitled "The Last Week of My Life." Billie Kay wrote:

"Today I live; a week from today I die. If a situation came to me such as this, I would probably weep. As soon as I realized that there were many things to be done, though, I would try to regain my composure.

"The first day of my suddenly shortened life, I would see all my loved ones and assure them that I loved them. I wouldn't hint that anything was wrong because I wouldn't want to remember them sorrowing but as being happy. I would ask God to give me strength to bear the rest of my precious few days and give me His hand to walk with Him.

"On the second day I would awake to see the rising sun in all its beauty that I had so often cast aside for a few extra moments of coveted sleep. I would gather all my possessions and give them to the needy, trying to console them as much as possible and urge them to consult God for courage.

"The third day, I would spend alone in a woods with the presence of God's creation and goodness around me. In the sweetness of nature I would sit and reminisce of my fondest memories.

"On the fourth day I would prepare my will. The small sentimental things I would leave to my family and friends. This being done, I would go to my mother and spend the day with her. We have always been close and I would want to reassure my love to her especially.

"Friday would be spent with my minister; I would speak to him of my spiritual life. I would like to go with him to see those who were ill and silently be thankful that I knew no pain.

"Saturday I would spend seeing the shut-ins I had so often put off until another day. On this night before my death, I would probably remain awake fearing my impending death, yet also preparing for it knowing that God was by my side.

"Upon awakening Sunday I would make all of my last preparations. Taking my Bible, I would go to my church to spend my last hours in prayer. I would ask Him for the courage to face the remaining hours that I might die gracefully. I would hope that my life had bearing on someone and had glorified His holy name. My last hours would be spent in perfect harmony with my God. . . ."

This is the end of Billie Kay's theme, "The Last Week of My Life," but it is not the end of the story. Billie Kay's English paper which was dated Friday, March 15, 1963, was finished just seven days before her life was snuffed out in an automobile accident.

While returning from a movie with three teen-age friends
March 22, about 11 o'clock, the car in which Billie Kay was
a passenger was struck from the rear and rolled over two or
three times. Then it caught fire.

My daughter's three friends were pulled out of the wreckage with injuries from which they have since recovered. Billie
Kay, who died instantly, was pinned inside.

The last time I saw Billie Kay was earlier that evening
when my husband and I dropped her off at a church meeting.
She joined friends, laughing and talking.

The events which followed in the next few hours still bring
on a vertigo. My husband, Joe, was at work. I was lying down
reading when I heard the doorbell ring. When I opened the
door, I looked into the face of a police officer.

I don't remember much of anything for the next few hours.
I never had known a pain so piercing. Over and over we asked
ourselves the question which accompanies all tragedy: why?
Why?

At the moment we could not understand how her death
could figure in God's plan. Such a waste it seemed: taking a
life in its bud. A life which promised to be as productive as
Billie Kay's. She was an excellent student, planning to go to
college like her brother; a wonderful Christian, active in our
church. How could a loving God permit such a thing to happen?

If I told you that now I accept this tragedy with complete
resignation, I would not be telling the whole truth. It is so
difficult to accept. Yet, now, a few months after our loss I
am able to praise God for His abiding love; praise Him for
understanding when we were ready to desert Him for "fail-
ing" us; thank Him for loaning us an angel for the short time
He did.

You see, I now know that our children are not ours, but
God's. He sends them for us to shepherd, but they do not belong to us.

Too often, I think, we count up our material accumulations

and boast about what is ours when really not even the next breath we take is ours without God's grace. Since Billie Kay has gone, I have had time to think a great deal. I have come to realize the importance of listening for God's calling and responding immediately. Time is so precious. None of us know exactly when our personal judgment day will come. Each fleeting moment wasted is one less minute we have to do Christ's bidding.

Joe and I know that Billie Kay's life was not a waste, but a great inspiration—to us and to many others. It was a life which fulfilled His purpose. By our standards 15 years does not connote completeness, but our finite minds can't understand God's yardstick. He does not measure life by length alone, I am sure.

Though I doubt that Billie Kay had any premonition of her death as some have suggested, I feel—without reservation —that she was prepared for it. This belief sustained me in the period of torment following her death.

For Billie Kay also wrote another essay in January, entitled "A Visitation," which also reassures me that Billie Kay was in the center of God's will. Here, in part, is what she wrote:

"I am walking in a forest to escape the noise of the city when suddenly the path all about me grows dim, until at last a heavy fog surrounds me. And finally nothing but deep, lasting darkness fills my entire being; yet it is strangely peaceful and I feel as though I am in the presence of someone powerful and great. . . .

"Peace, wonderful peace is now flooding my entire person and I feel no want or pain. . . . Then approaching me on the path are two glowing yet very gentle eyes, drawing closer and closer. . . .

"Within these gentle eyes I find peace beyond understanding. I am no longer driven with wants and duties. I feel content, secure. I fall on my knees and pray—for what I do not know. The eyes tell me to rise. Though he did not speak, suddenly I realized this was death. He seemed to tell me not to be afraid for it was an eternal, lasting place, a part of everything. . . .

"As I walked home I thought of that one phrase over and over in my mind: 'It is a part of everything,' and when one thinks about it, death really is a part of everything. I fear death no longer and I feel I have a purpose in life. The great power I felt and saw must have been the Almighty Himself. I shall not speak of this until the right time, as it was much too wonderful. Yes, I will keep it in my heart until the right time, maybe even until death."

As I re-read Billie Kay's essays, I find a guide for my life. I see clearly that I must live each day, not as if I had seven days remaining, but as if today I die. Whatever comes, I take great solace in Jesus' promise: *Let not your heart be troubled: ye believe in God, believe also in Me. In my Father's house are many mansions: if it were not so, I would have told you. I go to prepare a place for you, and if I go and prepare a place for you, I will come again, and receive you unto Myself; that where I am, there ye may be also.**

I rest assured that Billie Kay has already taken residence in my Father's house.

* John 14:1-3

A startling and incredible story, you will say. Truly hard to believe. But the event was verified by two people who were walking together one beautiful spring day in the woods near Ballardvale, Massachusetts.

The Host of Heaven

by Dr. S. Ralph Harlow

IT was not Christmas, it was not even wintertime, when the event occurred that for me threw sudden new light on the ancient angel tale. It was a glorious spring morning and we were walking, my wife and I, through the newly budded birches and maples near Ballardvale, Massachusetts.

Now I realize that this, like any account of personal experience, is only as valid as the good sense and honesty of the person relating it. What can I say about myself? That I am a scholar who shuns guesswork and admires scientific investigation? That I have an A.B. from Harvard, an M.A. from Columbia, a Ph.D. from Hartford Theological Seminary? That I have never been subject to hallucinations? That attorneys have solicited my testimony, and I have testified in the courts, regarded by judge and jury as a faithful, reliable witness? All this is true and yet I doubt that any amount of such credentials can influence the belief or disbelief of another.

In the long run, each of us must sift what comes to us from others through his own life experience, his view of the universe, his understanding. And so I will simply tell my story.

The little path on which Marion and I walked that morning was spongy to our steps and we held hands with the sheer delight of life as we strolled near a lovely brook. It was May, and because it was the examination reading period for students at Smith College where I was a professor, we were able to get away for a few days to visit Marion's parents.

We frequently took walks in the country, and we especially loved the spring after a hard New England winter, for it is then that the fields and the woods are radiant and calm yet show new life bursting from the earth. This day we were especially happy and peaceful; we chatted sporadically, with great gaps of satisfying silence between our sentences.

Then from behind us we heard the murmur of muted voices in the distance, and I said to Marion, "We have company in the woods this morning."

Marion nodded and turned to look. We saw nothing, but the voices were coming nearer—at a faster pace than we were walking, and we knew that the strangers would soon overtake us. Then we perceived that the sounds were not only behind us but above us, and we looked up.

How can I describe what we felt? Is it possible to tell of the surge of exaltation that ran through us? Is it possible to record this phenomenon in objective accuracy and yet be credible?

For about 10 feet above us, and slightly to our left, was a floating group of glorious, beautiful creatures that glowed with spiritual beauty. We stopped and stared as they passed above us.

There were six of them, young beautiful women dressed in flowing white garments and engaged in earnest conversation. If they were aware of our existence they gave no indication of it. Their faces were perfectly clear to us, and one woman, slightly older than the rest, was especially beautiful. Her dark hair was pulled back in what today we would call a ponytail, and although I cannot say it was bound at the back of her head, it appeared to be. She was talking intently to a younger spirit whose back was toward us and who looked up into the face of the woman who was talking.

Neither Marion nor I could understand their words although their voices were clearly heard. The sound was somewhat like hearing but being unable to understand a group of people talking outside a house with all the windows and doors shut.

They seemed to float past us, and their graceful motion seemed natural—as gentle and peaceful as the morning itself. As they passed, their conversation grew fainter and fainter until it faded out entirely, and we stood transfixed on the spot, still holding hands and still with the vision before our eyes.

It would be an understatement to say that we were astounded. Then we looked at each other, each wondering if the other also had seen.

There was a fallen birch tree just there beside the path. We sat down on it and I said, "Marion, what did you see? Tell me exactly, in precise detail. And tell me what you heard."

She knew my intent—to test my own eyes and ears; to see if I had been the victim of hallucination or imagination. And her reply was identical in every respect to what my own senses had reported to me.

I have related this story with the same faithfulness and respect for truth and accuracy as I would tell it on the witness stand. But even as I record it I know how incredible it sounds.

Perhaps I can claim no more for it than that it has had a deep effect on our own lives. For this experience of almost 32 years ago greatly altered our thinking. Once both Marion and I were somewhat skeptical about the absolute accuracy of the details at the birth of Christ. The story, as recorded by St. Luke, tells of an angel appearing to *shepherds abiding in the field* and after the shepherds had been told of the Birth, *suddenly there was with the angel a multitude of the heavenly host praising God, and saying, Glory to God in the highest.**

As a child I accepted the multitude seen by the shepherds as literal heavenly personages. Then I went through a period when I felt that they were merely symbols injected into a fantasy or legend. Today, after the experience at Ballardvale, Marion and I are no longer skeptical. We believe that in back

* Luke 2:8-14

of that story recorded by St. Luke lies a genuine objective experience told in wonder by those who had the experience.

Once, too, we puzzled greatly over the Christian insistence that we have "bodies" other than our normal flesh and blood ones. We were like the doubter of whom St. Paul wrote:

*But some man will say, How are the dead raised up? and with what body do they come?**

In the 32 years since that bright May morning, his answer has rung for us with joyous conviction.

*There are also celestial bodies, and bodies terrestrial: but the glory of the celestial is one, and the glory of the terrestrial is another. . . . So also is the resurrection of the dead. . . . It is sown a natural body; it is raised a spiritual body. There is a natural body, and there is a spiritual body. . . . And as we have borne the image of the earthly, we shall also bear the image of the heavenly. . . . For this corruptible must put on incorruption, and this mortal must put on immortality.***

All of us, I think, hear the angels for a little while at Christmastime. We let the heavenly host come close once in the year. But we reject the very possibility that what the shepherds saw 2,000 years ago was part of the reality that presses close every day of our lives.

And yet there is no reason for us to shrink from this knowledge. Since Marion and I began to be aware of the host of heaven all about us, our lives have been filled with a wonderful hope. Phillips Brooks, the great Episcopal bishop, expressed the cause of this hope more beautifully than I can do:

"This is what you are to hold fast to yourself—*the sympathy and companionship of the unseen worlds*. No doubt it is best for us now that they should be unseen. It cultivates in us that higher perception that we call 'faith.' But who can say that the time will not come when, even to those who live

* I Corinthians 15:35
** I Corinthians 15:40-53

here upon earth, the unseen worlds shall no longer be un-seen?"

The experience at Ballardvale, added to the convictions of my Christian faith, give me not only a feeling of assurance about the future, but a sense of adventure toward it too.

There is much in human experience to reassure us about a life after death. Yet when doubts came to this author after the loss of her husband, she did not find comfort in opinions or personal testimony. She found help in the only real authority on the subject of immortality.

The Final and Greatest Proof

by CATHERINE MARSHALL

RECENTLY, I was deeply moved by a plea from a broken-hearted mother. A short time ago her golden-haired three-year-old daughter was hit by a car in the street and killed instantly.

"Who is God, and where is He that He would allow this thing to happen?" she asked. "How do we know there is anything beyond death? I must *know*, somehow, that Jan is not dead, just gone for awhile, and that I will see her again someday...."

Out of my own experience I understand this need of knowing. It always comes when death invades one's personal world. Prior to my husband Peter Marshall's sudden death in January, 1949, I had never seriously considered the subject of immortality. In fact, for years I had been doing what many do—ducking, pretending that I and the members of my family had a long lease on life. We were still young. Why should we even think about such gloomy matters?

But then came that day when, like the young mother, I needed answers. And I wanted them to be authoritative answers, not just someone's opinions. So I went directly to the most authoritative source I knew—the Scriptures, "the only infallible rule of truth and conduct." Here I found solid help.

My first discovery was that the Scripture writers never

argued about immortality any more than Jesus argued about the existence and the love of His Father in Heaven. The reason for these assumptions is that wise men knew that certain matters can never be proven by logic. They must be experienced. Then we know, and not until then.

During His last talk with the Apostles on the night of His betrayal, Jesus pointed them to the path that they should follow in order that they might know. "Because I live, ye shall live also," was His confident statement (John 14:19). Watch Me, He seemed to be saying. Watch what happens to Me on the third day. Then you will know finally and forever that there is no death.

And they did watch, and they did know. They knew so surely that they became utterly changed men. From timid, fearful creatures who had crept away into hiding following the Crucifixion, after they had seen the risen Christ, suddenly they became courageous men whose flaming declarations of faith nobody could silence. . . .

"That which we have heard with our own ears, seen with our own eyes, handled with our own hands, declare we unto you." *

Then we find Paul picking up the joyous tidings and reiterating the same line of reasoning, that the Resurrection is the only real proof of immortality:

"And if Christ did not rise, then those who have slept the sleep of death . . . have perished after all.

"But it is not so!

"Now is Christ risen from the dead. . . . He was seen at Cephas, then of the twelve.

"And after that, He was seen of about five hundred brethren at once; of whom the greater part remain unto this present. . . .

"After that, He was seen of James; then of all the Apostles.

"And last of all He was seen by me. . . ." **

Yes, but what if He has not been seen by us in this 20th

* I John 1:1-3
** I Corinthians 15

century? How then would Jesus' resurrection be proof of immortality for us?

When I look back over the years of my own seeking, I know that once again the New Testament has not misled us. For I have come full circle in my thinking about immortality. A variety of evidential experiences have been granted me, but I know now that they are just that—evidence, not the final word.

Nevertheless I am grateful for them, and have shared most of them in some detail in my books: like the comfort of the everlasting arms some four hours before Peter Marshall was to step over into the next life. It happened in the midst of churning emotions of fear from the realization that Peter was suffering another massive heart attack. Quite unexpectedly, a strange, all-pervading peace replaced the fear. Love, of a quality that I never had felt before, flowed through and around me. Not love in the abstract, but as from Someone who cared tenderly for Peter, for me, for our small son. Only later did I realize that this was granted me, so that when the blow fell, I would have this proof that God's love had been with us every step of the way, in death as in life.

Then there was to come a dream in which I was allowed to see Peter briefly in his new setting. I spied him at a distance working in a rose garden. He looked as he always had; I would have recognized his characteristic gestures anywhere. As I sped to him, running with a lightness and freedom I had not known since childhood, he held out his arms to me. And yet, my impression was that Peter was preoccupied, bewildered by the swiftness of events that had dropped the curtain on his earth life. He had not expected his own death. And the work in the rose garden had been lovingly provided to give him time to get his bearings, to make a difficult transition. For me there were so many new concepts implicit in this dream that to this day I cannot doubt its relevance.

Years later there was to be my father's death at 76, a gentle shepherding into the next life with every circumstance surrounding his going a series of blessed providences.

I even have had, all unsought, some psychical experiences through a Christ-centered couple who have gifts in this direction. The wife, in particular, has an extraordinary ability to see through the curtain which separates this world from the next.

There was that evening shortly after Easter, 1962, when we were chatting in their living room. Suddenly, apropos of nothing, the wife said, "Catherine, your father is here with us now. There are some things he wants to relay to you."

She spoke in a matter-of-fact voice. The room was fully lighted. There was not a trace of the atmosphere that one associates with seances or the like. In fact, I had come seeking nothing of the sort. . . . "Your father wants you to know that he has had a reunion with his family. It has been a time of rejoicing."

I sat there thinking how typical this was of Dad. He adored family reunions more than anyone I've ever known. But my friend had no way of knowing that. She never had met him in this life.

Then she went on, "He says that he has had many adjustments to make, rigid ideas to shed. . . . He is a part of a little group which gets together frequently to check one another out on spiritual progress. At intervals, they are allowed the great privilege of sitting at Jesus' feet for fellowship with Him.

"He says he is tremendously happy. . . ."

I was moved by this experience, but to those who feel they must have this kind of confirmation of immortality, I point to the Parable of Lazarus and Dives. When Dives pleads that someone return from the dead to warn his five brothers, we have Christ's surprising statement that this kind of evidence would not convince or make them repent.[*]

Jesus was making an important point, namely that a psychical experience can be fascinating, even sometimes danger-

[*] Luke 16:31

ously compelling, but it is periphery evidence. It is like seeking out medical advice from a nurse or midwife rather than making direct contact with the physician. Jesus Himself is the door . . . the way, even as He said.*

There is another point that should be mentioned. The most valuable adventures in immortality usually come unexpectedly. Those whom I have known who went out deliberately seeking contact with their beloved dead, or messages from them, or proof, almost always have been disappointed.

Psychical or spiritualistic experiences fall short on another level too. They may convince the mind, but to me they cannot satisfy the deep needs of a bereaved heart. So this is why I have come full circle right back to the path to assurance pointed out in the New Testament.

For if the Resurrection really happened, then Christ is alive today. And if He is alive, then we, free spirits that we are, can choose to become His disciples. Then we, too, can get in touch with Him. When that personal contact is made, then we shall be convinced that He is, in fact, who He said He was. We can then trust what He told us—including His quite definite and clear-cut promises about immortality.

This means that Paul's argument as given in the 15th chapter of I Corinthians is just as valid in our century as it was in his. The alternative is stark. . . . If Jesus did not rise from the dead, then He is dead like any other man, merely an historic figure with a fine ethic. He is a memory, a melody that has haunted succeeding generations—nothing more. The New Testament therefore is false. Christian preaching has been in vain. Generations of men have been deluded; we have no basis for our faith. We are, as Paul said, still in our sins. All who have died, have perished, and we shall perish too. Eternity is a nothingness. All that—if Jesus did not, in fact, rise from the dead.

Then how can I be so sure that He is alive today? Because

---

* John 14:6

I decided to follow those New Testament signposts to see if they did bring proof of immortality. The signposts said, *Make Jesus Christ the center. Turn your life over to Him. He will tell you and show you and teach you what He wants you to know.*

The turning over of my life came in June, 1944. The teaching and the showing have been going on ever since. For since 1944 I have been living out one of the Bible's basic teachings about immortality: that we do not wait for physical death to enter into eternal life; rather it happens the moment we are "born again."

Thus every time I have known God's guidance . . . or an incisive answer to prayer . . . or have watched the miracle of His taking disappointments and frustrations and turning them into joys and blessings, I have had a foretaste of immortality.

Every time I have had depth-dimension fellowship with a friend . . . or have seen even a modicum of love let in to transform a sour human relationship, I have had a preview of immortality. Every time I have had real joy, I have glimpsed eternal life. For all of these are attributes of the life to come. They illustrate one of the chief messages of John's Gospel: that "heaven" is not so much a place as a quality of living.

Therefore eternal life can be partially realized here and now. And in these daily realizations of a personal contact with Jesus Christ lie the real proof of immortality.

Immortality

by WILLIAM JENNINGS BRYAN

TO every created thing, God has given a tongue that proclaims a resurrection. If the Father deigns to touch with Divine power the cold and pulseless heart of the buried acorn and make it burst forth from its prison walls, will He leave neglected in the earth the soul of man, made in the image of his Creator? If He stoops to give the rose bush, whose withered blossoms float upon the autumn breeze, the sweet assurance of another springtime, will He refuse the word of hope to the sons of men when the frost of another winter comes? If matter, mute and inanimate, though changed by the force of nature into a multitude of forms can never die, will the spirit of man suffer annihilation when it has paid a brief visit, like a royal guest, to the tenement of clay? No. I am as sure that there is another life as I am that I live today.

In Cairo, I secured a few grains of wheat that had slumbered for more than three thousand years in an Egyptian tomb. As I looked at them, this thought came into my mind: if one of those grains had been planted upon the banks of the Nile the year after it grew, and all its lineal descendants planted and replanted from that time until now, its progeny would today be sufficiently numerous to feed the seething millions of the world.

A grain of wheat has the power to discard its body and from earth and air fashion a new body so much like the old one that we cannot tell one from the other. If this invisible germ of life in the grain of wheat can thus pass unimpaired through three thousand resurrections, I shall not doubt that my soul has the power to clothe itself with a new body, suited to its new existence, when this earthly frame has crumbled into dust.